THE ST LAWRENCE AND THE SAGUENAY AND OTHER POEMS

HESPERUS AND OTHER POEMS AND LYRICS

Literature of Canada

Poetry and Prose in Reprint

Douglas Lochhead, General Editor

The St Lawrence and the Saguenay

and Other Poems

Hesperus

and Other Poems and Lyrics

CHARLES SANGSTER

Introduction by Gordon Johnston

UNIVERSITY OF TORONTO PRESS

© University of Toronto Press 1972
Toronto and Buffalo
Printed in Canada
Reprinted in 2018
ISBN 0-8020-1935-8 (cloth)
ISBN 978-0-8020-6169-0 (paper)
ISBN Microfiche 0-8020-0276-5

Preface

Yes, there is a Canadian literature. It does exist. Part of the evidence to support these statements is presented in the form of reprints of the poetry and prose of the authors included in this series. Much of this literature has been long out of print. If the country's culture and traditions are to be sampled and measured, both in terms of past and present-day conditions, then the major works of both our well known and our lesser known writers should be available for all to buy and read. The Literature of Canada series aims to meet this need. It shares with its companion series, The Social History of Canada, the purpose of making the documents of the country's heritage accessible to an increasingly large national and international public, a public which is anxious to acquaint itself with Canadian literature – the writing itself – and also to become intimate with the times in which it grew.

DL

Charles Sangster, 1822-93

Gordon Johnston

Introduction

We can imagine, I think, a music lover so discriminating in his taste that he listens to nothing but the last quartets of Beethoven. But what kind of love is that? What kind of discrimination? The range of possible expression in music is as significant as the greatness of any individual works. The same is true of poetry. An understanding and appreciation of poetry depend in part on familiarity with the breadth of poetic concerns, methods, and accomplishments. In his essay 'What is Minor Poetry?' T.S. Eliot does much to justify our reading poets less-than-great, and to explain why we are often attracted to them. There may be, as he says, in the least talented writer something to which we, for special reasons, can respond.

Why specifically should we read the work of Charles Sangster? There are a number of possible reasons. If we are inclined to regard literature as sociological data, then in a sense the least poet is as interesting or important as the greatest. If our point of view is historical, Sangster's poetry is evidence of cultural progress in Canada West of the middle nineteenth century. If the psychology of artists interests us, Sangster is in fact a more rewarding subject than many, because in his poetry he deals explicitly with the reasons for writing poetry and the problems of writing. A self-centred nationalistic feeling might even be sufficient motive for reading him.

What about literary reasons for reading Sangster? Desmond Pacey refers to him as 'a very minor Victorian versifier,'[1] but in reviewing his first volume of poetry, *The St Lawrence and the Saguenay*, the London *National Magazine* said shortly after it was published, 'There is much of the spirit of Wordsworth in this writer, only the tone is religious instead of being philosophical,' and he is called in a number of places 'The Father of Canadian Poetry.' The curious fact about critical reactions to Sangster over the years is that different readers have discovered different poems with passages of 'poetic merit'; different readers have preferred different poems. This suggests that Sangster's poetry is wide enough, various enough to satisfy different tastes and different ages. Readers of his time and in the years after Confederation preferred his patriotic pieces, his martial songs, and his sentimental poems about the Red Man. More recent readers praise the more delicate songs and introspective sonnets. Most readers agree in admiring some of the poems that describe the Canadian landscape — he is the first effectively to regard the Canadian wilderness as a proper subject for poetry — but those readers do not agree on which descriptive poems are the best. In general, in order to understand our proper response to Sangster's poetry, we may pull inside out Horace's advice to writers that they 'delight and instruct' — and see *our* responsibility as that of learning from Sangster and enjoying him.

We may look first at Sangster's background, historical and literary, in order to discover what we may expect from him. He was born 16 July 1822 at the Navy Yard, Port Frederick, across from Kingston, Canada West. Both his grandfathers were Scots; one a United Empire Loyalist who fought with distinction in the American Revolutionary War, the other a farmer who came to Ontario by way of Prince Edward Island. Sangster's father was a joiner and shipbuilder in the Royal Navy; he died when Sangster was two years old. The boy started working at the age of fifteen making cartridges in the laboratory at Fort Henry, at the time of the Rebellion of 1837. His formal education was extremely limited; he said of it: 'All that I possess mentally has been acquired by careful reading of the best authors (chiefly Fiction), properly directed thought, and a tolerable share of industry.'[2] He claimed that the only books available to him when he was young were the Bible and *The Citizen of the World* in two volumes. This situation did not change until the spread of cheap publishing in the nineteenth century. Sangster says in spite of this that he began writing 'snatches of verse' at an early age.

Even if his poetry demonstrates that he did not read with any deep understanding, it is clear that later in his life he read very widely. He mentions by name in the poems, Byron, Moore, Burns, Dante, Alfieri, Chaucer, Shakespeare, Milton, Homer, Locke, Hume, Smollett, Bryant, Whittier, and others. His poetry also shows the influence of James Thomson, Oliver Goldsmith, Wordsworth, Tennyson, Longfellow, and perhaps religious poets such as George Herbert and Edward Taylor. Because his education was not a thorough one, his literary allusions often lack conviction or seem slightly out of context. For example, he knows the Bible well enough to be able to refer to 'Marah' in the first of the 'Orillia Woods Sonnets,' but not well enough to know that the word means 'bitter' — and so he describes Marah as bitter.

In 1839, Sangster became a clerk in Fort Henry and spent ten years in that position hoping for a promotion and failing to receive one. During this period he began to write poems for newspapers and magazines such as *The Literary Garland*, *Barker's Magazine*, and *The Anglo-American Magazine*. He eventually decided to make a career in journalism, beginning with a short term as editor of the Amherstburg *Courier* in 1849. From 1850 to 1864 he was a bookkeeper and proofreader for *The British*

Whig in Kingston, where he again suffered lack of advancement. During this period he brought out his two volumes of poetry, *The St Lawrence and the Saguenay and Other Poems* in June of 1856 and *Hesperus and Other Poems and Lyrics* in 1860. It is interesting to note that he was married to Mary Kilbourne in September of 1856. She died of pneumonia eighteen months later and Sangster was married again in October 1860 to Henrietta Charlotte Meagher. Both books of poetry appeared in years when he married. This may have some significance for the predominance of sentimental and idealistic love poems in his writing.

In 1864, he became a reporter for the Kingston *Daily News;* in 1868 he accepted a position in Ottawa in the post office of the new federal civil service. He remained there until he retired in 1886, once again failing to achieve promotion. W.D. Lighthall suggests in his anthology that in 1875 Sangster was appointed private secretary to the deputy postmaster-general. After his retirement he spent the rest of his life, when his health permitted, revising his two published volumes and preparing the text for two more volumes of poetry. No publication has come out of these revised manuscripts other than two poems, 'Taapookaa' and 'A Northern Rune,' which appear in E.H. Dewart's anthology, *Selections from Canadian Poets* (1864), and a chap-book, *Our Norland* (1896?), published by Copp Clark.

Desmond Pacey quotes from a description of Sangster by Joseph Bawden which speaks of his 'frankness and freshness of expression,' his 'quiet self-possession,' his 'direct not discursive conversation,' and his 'soft though manly voice.'[3] Pacey also quotes from a 'phrenological character' of Sangster done by L.N. Fowler of New York City – in October 1859 – which describes him, not in so many words, as impressionable, sensitive, high-strung, and impractical in worldly affairs.[4] There is a picture of Sangster in middle age in Caswell's *Canadian Singers and Their Songs* and one of him in more advanced age in Garvin's *Canadian Poets*. But since (for our purposes) the most important fact about Sangster, whatever his character and background, is that he wrote poetry, we should now turn to that poetry.

We need not expect that he will tell us a great deal about himself in his poetry — at least, directly or intentionally. He is not a typical Romantic poet revealing a unique and sensitive mind. For Sangster, as later for Archibald Lampman, originality was not an issue of the magnitude it is for us in these days of relativism and frustrated individualism. As he says in the 'Dedicatory Poem' in *Hesperus*:

> I speak not of myself, but stand
> In silence till the Master Hand
>   Each fluttering thought sets free.

In his own humble way, he is concerned not with self but with the Truth. It is both a grander and lesser view of the poet to see him as a mouthpiece for the Muses or, in Sangster's case, for God.

Moreover, poets of Sangster's type are not concerned with cleverness of expression and the convolutions of language; rather, as Carl Klinck explains, they are interested in 'making the ideas come out right in cadences.'[5] Their concern is not with what is eye-catching but with what is effective, not with ingenuity, but with propriety. In Sangster's case, there are a number of possible explanations of this reserve and conventionality — among them, genuine religious humility, shyness because of his lack of formal education, or Canadian self-conscious restraint. In any event, we should remember that it was his very conventionality which endeared him to many of his readers and which will continue to do so.

I suggested that Sangster willingly sacrificed formal concerns to the truth of his content, and of course the matter is not that simple. A brief glance through the poems will show that many of his ideas, although perhaps fashionable then, are now unfashionable — and far from impressing us as undeniably true. His teetotal beliefs, his sentimental patronizing attitude to the Indian, his weakness for small children, his belief in the British connection, his restraint (amounting to asceticism) in love poetry — although each issue still has its fanatics, each will now strike us as quaint or criminal depending on our point of view. Sangster's interest in peace may strike us as more modern in tone; it is curious and touching in light of his military background to hear him say:

> But dearer than a hundred victories,
> With their swift agony, the earnest Calm.
> ['From Queenston Heights']

Still he retains a marked fondness for martial songs and victory celebrations, to the imperial overtones of which we are now deaf.

There is, of course, no requirement that a poet have new ideas or that he be a profound thinker. In a conversation with Eckerman, Goethe said of Byron, 'Lord Byron is only great when he "poetizes," whenever he philosophizes he is a child.' The comment is relevant to a discussion of Sangster because the immediate source for 'The St Lawrence and the Saguenay' was Byron's *Childe Harold's Pilgrimage*, and because Sangster was obviously influenced by Byron's ideas about the ideal and the real.

Moreover, Sangster's attitude towards philosophy and human

perceptions of the truth must be qualified by his religious beliefs. He has a basic distrust of human knowledge, of the potential of scientific rationalism. He accepts as easy Raphael's advice to Adam in Book VIII of *Paradise Lost* that we be content knowing only what we should know. He is much more confident of the intuitions of faith, which he formulates unhesitatingly in the orthodox terms of his age, than of the conclusions of empirical thought. Perhaps, if he sounded less sure of the 'Known Unknown' (as he describes It/Him) we might feel closer to him.

The most interesting aspect of Sangster's content is the relation between that heavenly knowledge and the earthly knowledge based on human experience. Finally, of course, he does not understand the relation – and his constant use of words like 'mystery' and 'veil' is an indication that he knew he could not understand it. But it is the contemplation of this relation that precipitates in his mind most of the questions to which he addresses himself. What is the relation of the ideal to the real? Of art to nature? What are the proper subjects for poetry? What is the significance of sorrow and of death? What is the significance of human love? In religious terms what is the relation of the Creator to his Creation? What is the significance of human life? of nature?

His attitude towards the real and the ideal is not consistent. Sometimes he is struck by the Byronic melancholy caused by the failure of real feelings, people, and places to live up to their ideals. But occasionally in Sangster there are triumphant moments when the real does match the ideal, and in some sense guarantees it – as in the sonnet, 'Dark-eyed one! When I first beheld thy face' where there is a 'faultless likeness' between the form of the ideal and the girl. Occasionally Sangster gives the impression that the ideal essentially is unreal, opposed to the real and destroyed by the real, as in the lines:

> Periling the wild Ideal
> By the presence of the Real.
> ['Mariline,' st. XIII]

These considerations are related in Sangster's mind to those of art and nature. In the sonnet mentioned above he goes on to say that Angelo's and Titian's images will end with time, but his is timeless because it is real — because it appears in nature. In a remarkably good poem, 'Absence,' the image of the woman (in this case a memory) is again seen as distinguishable from art — here it is seen as 'love's true daguerrotype.' Human love is directly implicated for Sangster in the questions of art and reality and nature. Many of his love poems are about a poet's love, and about the ability of love to transform perception. The poet in love can see his natural surroundings as if they were Eden.

The distinction between art and nature is also made explicitly in the 'Proem' to the 'Orillia Woods' sonnets: 'This [art] is the spirit merely; that, the soul.' Sangster goes on in the 'Proem' to say he loves his art because:

> Through it I rev'rence Nature, and improve
> The tone and tenor of the mind He gave.

Art allows him to be able to see through nature to the great artificer, God. The other side of this coin is the feeling on his part that art is dangerous because it draws attention to itself — is essentially vain. This has always been a problem for religious poets. In Sangster this belief necessitates the rejection of the earthly or pagan aspects of poetry, such as mythological figures.

In stanza VII of ' The St Lawrence and the Saguenay' he says:

>   No Nymphic trains appear
> To charm the pale Ideal Worshipper
> of Beauty...

There are numerous poems in which the lady or little girl he is describing is fairer far than any nymph or neriad could be, if they existed.

This does not mean for Sangster that the ideal world is uninhabited, but rather, he sees it peopled either by abstract qualities or entities such as truth and beauty, or by angels. This brings us back to Sangster's central interest, the relation between earth and heaven. He wants to see the abstracts enthroned in heaven but he also wants to see them in human form here on earth. He may not see nymphs but he claims to see beauty. Angels are clearly representatives of 'the other side,' but he also wants to see them in nature (as in 'Hesperus'), and to see the women and children he loves as angels — he says of little Aurelia's conversation, 'every word an angel-lyric/Falling on my ears empiric' ('Aurelia'). There are a number of poems in which people die and turn into angels — death, not surprisingly, is seen as the connection between the two worlds.

For Sangster, it is love that transforms our perceptions of the creation. Love is usually related for him to our perception of the divine, to thought and morality. The awkward phrase 'richly thoughted Mariline' is typical of his praise for his otherwise traditional beautiful ladies. Even 'merry Margery' is capable of a sermon-like speech of unsettling dryness. The love of men and women is passionless in his poetry because its significance is that it points in the direction of divine love. In the same way, poetry aspires upwards, songs become hymns; and in the same way, the earth's natural beauty points towards heaven — unfortunately it does not point any clear way, and so Sangster's poetry, like Lampman's, is full of enigmatic voices, of mysteries and dreams. In general, Sangster is trying to go beyond mortal experience, but trying to get there *in terms of* mortal experience. He wants to hear the music of the spheres, but is not sure he really could.

With these considerations in mind, we may turn to 'The St Lawrence and the Saguenay.' This is, I think, the best place to start reading Sangster because it contains a great deal that is typical of his writing, and provides a basis for understanding the other poems. The incidental beauties of this poem and its general weaknesses have been noted by most of Sangster's critics — a few arresting 'pictures,' some interesting turns of phrase, but for the most part inflated diction, frequent faulty rhythm, and a lack of variety in the scenes described. (As I suggested, there is never a concensus of opinion — the *Toronto Colonist*, for example, in a contemporary review regarded this poem as an invaluable aid to the prospective tourist.) But so far, there has been no fair judgement of the general intention or significance of the poem.

This is admittedly a difficult issue to judge because we are never entirely convinced that Sangster was conscious of his poetic objectives or of alternative poetic methods. Still we may fairly ask what Sangster meant by writing this poem. Since Sangster is imitating Byron's form and style in *Childe Harold*, it is possible that he is imitating Byron's intention as well — to narrate a journey, to record impressions of places and events, in terms of the past and the present. The present for Sangster is in the villages along the shore — the boats, the picnickers, and the fishermen. History is in the references to the Indians and voyageurs, to Wolfe and Montcalm, and to the Stately Maiden with the outlaw father of stanzas IX and X. The problem of history for Sangster is a result of the nature of the past in Canada — most of it is prehistoric.

Another possible intention for the poem is to describe generic Beauty by giving concrete manifestations of her in the Canadian landscape. Again the problem for Sangster is that he is heading into the Laurentian shield, and traditional notions of beauty have to be qualified, or abandoned.

The questions we should be asking about this poem are 'Where is he going? Where does he arrive?' and 'What about that strange shadowy girl who accompanies him?' To find possible answers we may turn to those general concerns of Sangster I mentioned earlier — primarily the relation between earthly and heavenly knowledge. This journey in the poems is a physical one, but it is also a journey of the soul. The girl is his companion because in fact she is his guide; it is his love for her which allows him to perceive 'the other world' and directs him towards it. There is a sense in which the voyage is made outside the body, or through a resurrected body. In the first stanza he says, '...love's mysterious power ... lifts my dead heart up, like Lazarus from the tomb.' The voyage is also made in the earthly sense:

>   if its musings [the spirit's] be
> Oft'ner of earth than heaven, bear awhile
> With what is native to mortality.
> [st. II]

The relationship between the poet and the woman is also qualified by the understanding that they must eventually part — and here, as elsewhere in Sangster, parting implies death, and movement to a new world, Eden or Heaven.

The girl is clearly significant for her relation to the pursuit of truth. In the climactic last stanzas of the poem which describe the divine vision, Sangster sees it as

> Like a calm Student seeking Pearls of Thought
> In some fair Beauty's mind...
> [st. CI]

To understand the nature of the climax we have to go back and ask about the direction of the journey and the poem. Why is it up the Saguenay? Surely a trip westward makes more sense at this point in history — or a trip back to Britain. Because Sangster is looking through Nature to its meaning, we can ask — what is the meaning of their destination? The scenes he describes have some direct relation to concerns of the mind and the soul — for example, the villages on the St Lawrence represent contentment for him. There are some descriptions, such as of the thunderstorm and of the rapids, which he finds exciting but disturbing in terms of their meaning. When the travellers enter the Saguenay River (st. LXXVI), Sangster suffers an initial shock at the newness (really the oldness) of the scene, but recovers (st. LXXXIX) his perspective through love. Then in stanzas XCV to the end, he is forced beyond traditional human experience. The perceptions of the body and of the soul are simultaneous. They move past Cape Eternity into Trinity Bay under Trinity Rock — and the cliff, as he says, is 'like Truth made manifest' (st. CIV). The aesthetic and the religious sublime are viewed simultaneously. In these last stanzas, most of Sangster's themes come tumbling out — man is both great and small; the dreams of love and art are shattered, and true or real love and art are guaranteed by the divine vision and by immortal love.

And then there is the question of silence. It turns out to be another central question in Sangster's thought and poetry. His response to his vision of the divine is, he says, silence:

> My lips are mute. I cannot speak the thought
> That like a bubble on the placid sea,
> Bursts ere it tells the tale with which 'tis fraught.
> Another comes, and so, eternally,
> They rise in hope, to wander spirit-free
> About the earth. 'Twere best they should not break
> The Silence, which itself is ecstacy
> And Godlike Eloquence, or my frail voice shake
> A single echo, the expressive Calm to break.
> [st. CIII]

There are reasons for this response and they include that religious uncertainty about the function of art, and an understandable modesty about his artistic abilities. Throughout his poetry, Sangster is attracted towards communication without speech — the power of music and the speechless messages from the eyes of his beloved. Women's voices do mean a great deal to him (perhaps because they are related to the real rather than to art or the ideal), but usually he hears them as a kind of angelic music. 'Into the Silent Land' is another 'poet's love poem' with the same direction as the voyage up the Saguenay, except that in this case the destination is seen specifically as death and the true vision that death provides. Even more significant than the fact that he is silent, silence is for Sangster an attribute of God (the Godlike eloquence and expressive calm); and it is this revelation of God in the silent northern wilderness that represents for me the true basis of Sangster's claim to be called the Father of Canadian Poetry.

In point of fact, although Sangster does recognize the importance and expressiveness of silence, he chooses to speak up, and so he is faced with all the problems involved in speech and poetry. Even on the basic level of word meanings, Sangster has a certain amount of difficulty. He has a surprisingly wide vocabulary, much of it derived from his reading of romantic writers — he knows interesting words like 'daedal,' 'fane,' and 'simoom'; but he does not always give the impression of being in control of his language. Sometimes his poetic short forms ('ope,' 'eterne') go awry — as in 'scintil' or 'insignific.' Sometimes the word is simply misused: he thinks 'evangel' means 'angel,' in 'The Dreamer' he speaks of 'pursuing a race,' the wife in 'Morning in Summer' cannot be 'expectant' if her husband is already home, he uses 'allure' in 'Let Them Boast as They Will' when he means 'lure.' Occasionally he uses a past tense for a past participle. Sometimes his expressions mean nothing at all — 'man of mind-like amplitude' or 'anatomic form.' Occasionally he is using the correct word even if it sounds wrong. He uses 'redundant' in its Latin sense of 'overflowing'; he uses 'intellectual' in one of its secondary meanings, 'that appeals to or engages the intellect, apprehensible or apprehended only by the intellect.' So the phrase 'intellectual eyes' has to do with that speechless form of communication mentioned earlier. The strange proper nouns he uses are most often from the Bible and can be found in a concordance. But the overall effect on us, the readers, is that we are unwilling to trust him. Where in a greater poet we would say he is recreating the language, in Sangster we feel he is misusing it. The failures in syntax are often even more apparent — 'Clara and I' should most definitely be 'Clara and Me.'

The same problem arises in his imagery. He mixes metaphors

('Let him sip from the cup where perdition is sowing/her tares' in 'Let them boast as they will'); and some of his similes mean nothing – a 'river like a rivulet' for example. But he is also capable of sharp effective images: 'We will be true as Damascus steel' ('Song. – Clara and I'). So the best advice (unfortunately vague) is that we not expect too much of him, and at the same time that we not underestimate him. We should be ready to be delighted.

Our chief poetic interest in Sangster then is not his method but his subjects and his attitude to them. He is the first to look at the Canadian wilderness; and although he sees it as God's creation, he also recognizes its dangers and terrors. This recognition of God's voice in the thunder is partly the result of religious training (the God of love is the God of vengeance), and partly the result of his reading of poetry. He is influenced by James Thomson's view of nature in *The Seasons* and by the romantic melancholy of Byron. But as well, his is a genuine reaction to a distinctive landscape. Later poets will relate the darkness, cold, and destruction to the amorality of nature and the smallness and alienation of man; Sangster relates them to man's limitations and immorality, but nevertheless he recognizes them. 'The Voice of God' is in the thunder, the night, and the sea that buries mariners. 'Pleasant Memories' ends with memories of winter and school and death. 'The Frost King's Revel' is a terrifying account of the 'tyrannous pleasantries' of sub-zero weather. Even in an innocent poem like 'The Wren,' the marsh overflows and the rushes rot, and in 'The Rapid,' perhaps the most continuously popular of Sangster's poems, the rowers rush headlong and unsuspecting to their destruction. If we like, we could see Sangster the way he sees the evening star in 'The St Lawrence and the Saguenay':

> Pale Hesper smiles upon us through the gloom,
> An unassuming Pioneer of Night.
> [st. XXVI]

Sangster does not write only nature poems — a glance at the titles of his poems shows that he has a fairly wide range of subjects. He writes elegies, songs, love poems, and even a dramatic monologue ('Edith to Harold'). 'Uncurbed Passion,' although the idea seems hopelessly out of date, is like George Herbert's 'Prayer,' and contains several very striking images. 'Hesperus' tries too hard to sound like Milton, but still has many rewarding passages. In 'The April Snow-Storm – 1858,' Sangster finds an extremely moving image for an untimely death and his reaction to it. The use of the word 'gently' is particularly effective. His patriotic songs, although they were once highly regarded, now will seem little more than historical curiosities — especially those written for Prince Albert, and those written about the Crimean War. But even in these, he is considerably better than his contemporaries, for example in 'Brock,' which was commissioned for the inauguration of the monument on Queenston Heights. Sangster's interest in peace in 'The Plains of Abraham' and 'From Queenston Heights' is still impressive, allied as it is in the latter poem to the startling detail of the fissure in the rock, caused by the 'angry missile.'

There are many such details in the poetry of Sangster and their effect is in most cases our being convinced of the immediacy of his emotional response to the scene before him. The nature poems perhaps contain proportionately more of these details. An introduction is not the place to list all the examples; in any case, this too is a matter of personal preference; moreover, one of the chief joys of reading Sangster is making all those discoveries that are left to be made. Vivid scenes that remain in my mind are the marsh and its birds in 'Autumn,' and the 'rural sports' in Part IV of 'The Happy Harvesters':

> Up the wide chimney rolls the social fire,
> Warming the hearts of matron, youth, and sire;
> Painting such grotesque shadows on the wall,
> The stripling looms a giant stout and tall,
> While those whose statures reach the common height
> Seem spectres mocking the hilarious night.
> From hand to hand the ripened fruit went round,
> And rural sports a pleased acceptance found;
> The youthful fiddler on his three-legged stool,
> Fancied himself at least an Ole Bull;
> Some easy bumpkin, seated on the floor,
> Hunted the slipper till his ribs were sore...

As much as Sangster is suspicious of empirical knowledge, he is often an acute observer. He is distrustful of the potential of scientific knowledge (as in 'The Comet – October, 1858' where he says 'Pale Science ... Still fails to read the secret of its soul'); but at the same time he is fascinated by it. For an uneducated man, Sangster refers a surprising number of times to details of geology and of astronomy. He is interested in the effects of light and in daguerrotypes; he is even more interested in electricity. Geology and astronomy are the sources for Sangster's favourite images – gems and stars. In fact his favourite gem comes from the sea – it is the pearl: perhaps he is thinking of the biblical pearl of great price or the pearls cast before swine. He is interested in small things, and it is helpful for us to know some earlier meanings of words like 'electric,' 'atom,' and 'germ' when we read his poetry, especially when we will encounter such strange-sounding phrases as 'love's electric germ' in 'Mariline.' These images are central to Sangster in exploring his primary concerns – knowledge and faith. A phrase like 'a vast idea concentrated to a point' in 'The Yellow Curl,' which might otherwise seem simply awkward, makes more sense in terms of these images. In 'The Mystery' he is talking about his mind:

> There germs of contemplation sleep,
>   Like stars beyond the Milky Way, –
> Like pearls within the gloomy deep,
>   That never saw the light of day.

Those tiny compressed images are seen against immense backgrounds – the sky and the sea. They are usually seen as emerging from that immensity – as in the case of the evening and morning star. They are crucial for his understanding of poetry, of human thought and of religion. In 'The Voice of God' he says:

> There's not a living atom but doth sing
> The praise of the Almighty...

The images are crucial for an understanding of him too. He may not have seen himself as 'Hesper ... the unassuming pioneer of night,' but in a letter to E.H. Dewart he did say, 'What little light I have shall not be hidden under a bushel.'

How wide should our interest in poetry be? Wide enough that we read (and even enjoy) the efforts of Charles Sangster.

NOTES

1 Desmond Pacey, *Ten Canadian Poets* (Toronto 1958), 23
2 Charles Sangster, quoted in Pacey, ibid., 4
3 Cf. ibid., 13
4 Ibid.
5 Carl Klinck, 'Canada East and West,' *Literary History of Canada* (Toronto 1965), 142

ND Other Poems
The St Lawrence and the Saguenay

and Other Poems

THE

ST. LAWRENCE AND THE SAGUENAY,

AND

Other Poems.

BY

CHARLES SANGSTER.

KINGSTON, C. W.
JOHN CREIGHTON AND JOHN DUFF.
NEW YORK:
MILLER, ORTON & MULLIGAN.
1856.

Entered according to Act of Congress, in the year one thousand eight hundred and fifty-six,

BY MILLER, ORTON & MULLIGAN,

In the Clerk's Office of the District Court for the Northern District of New-York.

AUBURN:
MILLER, ORTON & MULLIGAN,
STEREOTYPERS AND PRINTERS.

TO

JOHN SINCLAIR,

MY FRIEND AND CORRESPONDENT

OF MANY YEARS,

This Volume is Dedicated,

BY HIS FRIEND,

CHARLES SANGSTER.

KINGSTON, C. W., *June*, 1856.

CONTENTS.

	PAGE.
The St. Lawrence and the Saguenay,	9
Spring,	63
A Poet's Love,	66
Light in Darkness,	77
Rideau Lake,	78
Aurelia,	81
Sonnet,	86
Evening Scene,	87
Gentle Mary Ann,	90
Death of the Old Year,	92
Despondency,	94
The Voice of God,	95
The Fine Old Woods,	98
Elegy in Memory of Rev. Robert D. Cartwright,	101
Morning in Summer,	102
Password—"Truth is Mighty,"	110
The Whirlwind,	112
Elizabeth's Birth,	113
Henry's Grave,	115
Snow Drops,	116
Pretty Faces,	117
Beyond the Grave,	118
Canadian Sleigh Song,	118
Pity's Tear Drop,	119
Annie by my Side a Sitting,	120
The Name of Mary,	122
The Kneeling Heart,	124
Autumn,	125
Remembrances,	129
Little Annie,	130

CONTENTS.

	PAGE.
Sun, Moon and Stars,	133
The Chieftain's Last Sigh,	136
Holy Ground,	137
Pleasant Memories,	139
My Kitten,	145
The Frost King's Revel,	147
England and America,	154
The Wreck,	158
The Lofty and the Lowly,	159
I Dreamed I Met Thee,	161
The Changes of a Night,	162
To Rev. James G. Witted,	166
Edith to Harold,	168
Song of the New Year,	172
Soul, Thou art Lonely,	175
Peace, Fond Soul,	176
Merry Christmas,	178
A Plea for the Woods,	180
Little Libby,	182
The Yellow Curl,	186
Let them Boast as they will,	188
Limerick Cathedral Bells,	190
Love's Guiding Star,	192
The Angel's Gift,	193
Love's Signet Ring,	195
Mary's Twentieth Birthday,	196
Love's Morning Lark,	197
Song—The Banner of Old England,	198
Song—The Heroes of the Alma,	199
The Twofold Victory—An Alma Lyric,	201
Song of the British Mariner,	202
The Indian Summer,	204
The Betrayal,	205
The Impatient Lover,	206
The Grape,	207
A Thousand Faces,	208
The Past,	209
Imagination,	210
The Spirit of the Woods,	212
Love's New Era,	215

CONTENTS.

	PAGE.
Faith,	216
From Queenston Heights,	217
Fanny,	220
Lament of Shingwakonce	222
Absence,	231
Festus,	231
Sonnet,	232
Hope,	233
The Trio,	233
The One Idea,	234
Uncurbed Passion,	235
Peace,	235
Bertram and Lorenzo—A Dramatic Fragment,	237

CORRECTION.

Stanza xxviii "The St. Lawrence and the Saguenay," first, line for "*you* queenly Moon," read "*yon* queenly Moon."

POEMS.

THE ST. LAWRENCE AND THE SAGUENAY.

I.

There is but one to whom my hopes are clinging,
  As clings the bee unto the morning flower,
There is but one to whom my thoughts are winging
  Their dove-like passage through each silent hour:
One who has made my heart her summer bower.
  Feeling and passion there forever bloom
For her, who, by her love's mysterious power,
  Dispels the languor of my spirit's gloom,
And lifts my dead heart up, like Lazarus from the tomb.

II.

Maiden! from whose large, intellectual eyes,
  My soul first drank love's immortality,
Plume my weak spirit for its chosen skies,
  'T would falter in its mission without thee.
Conduct its flight; and if its musings be
  Oft'ner of earth than heaven, bear awhile
With what is native to mortality :

A*

It dare not err exulting in thy smile:
Look on it with thine eyes, and keep it free from guile.

III.

The bark leaps love-fraught from the land; the sea
Lies calm before us. Many an isle is there,
Clad with soft verdure; many a stately tree
Uplifts its leafy branches through the air;
The amorous current bathes the islets fair,
As we skip, youth-like, o'er the limpid waves;
White cloudlets speck the golden atmosphere,
Through which the passionate sun looks down, and graves
His image on the pearls that boil from the deep caves,

IV.

And bathe the vessel's prow. Isle after isle
Is passed, as we glide tortuously through
The opening vistas, that uprise and smile
Upon us from the ever-changing view.
Here nature, lavish of her wealth, did strew
Her flocks of panting islets on the breast
Of the admiring River, where they grew,
Like shapes of Beauty, formed to give a zest
To the charmed mind, like waking Visions of the Blest.

V.

The silver-sinewed arms of the proud Lake,
Love-wild, embrace each islet tenderly,

The zephyrs kiss the flowers when they wake
At morn, flushed with a rare simplicity;
See how they bloom around yon birchen tree,
And smile along the bank, by the sandy shore,
In lovely groups—a fair community!
The embossed rocks glitter like golden ore,
And here, the o'erarching trees form a fantastic bower.

VI.

Red walls of granite rise on either hand,
Rugged and smooth; a proud young eagle soars
Above the stately evergreens, that stand
Like watchful sentinels on these God-built towers;
And near yon beds of many-colored flowers
Browse two majestic deer, and at their side
A spotted fawn all innocently cowers;
In the rank brushwood it attempts to hide,
While the strong-antlered stag steps forth with lordly stride,

VII.

And slakes his thirst, undaunted, at the stream.
Isles of o'erwhelming beauty! surely here
The wild enthusiast might live, and dream
His life away. No Nymphic trains appear,
To charm the pale Ideal Worshipper
Of Beauty; nor Neriads from the deeps below;
Nor hideous Gnomes, to fill the breast with fear:
But crystal streams through endless landscapes flow,
And o'er the clustering Isles the softest breezes blow.

LYRIC TO THE ISLES.

Here the Spirit of Beauty keepeth
    Jubilee for evermore;
Here the Voice of Gladness leapeth,
    Echoing from shore to shore.
O'er the hidden watery valley,
    O'er each buried wood and glade,
Dances our delighted galley,
    Through the sunlight and the shade—
    Dances o'er the granite cells,
    Where the Soul of Beauty dwells:

Here the flowers are ever springing,
    While the summer breezes blow;
Here the Hours are ever clinging,
    Loitering before they go;
Playing round each beauteous islet,
    Loath to leave the sunny shore,
Where, upon her couch of violet,
    Beauty sits for evermore—
    Sits and smiles by day and night,
    Hand in hand with pure Delight.

Here the Spirit of Beauty dwelleth
    In each palpitating tree,
In each amber wave that welleth
    From its home, beneath the sea;
In the moss upon the granite,
    In each calm, secluded bay,

With the zephyr trains that fan it
    With their sweet breaths all the day—
    On the waters, on the shore,
    Beauty dwelleth evermore!

VIII.

Yes, here the Genius of Beauty truly dwells.
I worship Truth and Beauty in my soul.
The pure prismatic globule that upwells
From the blue deep; the psalmy waves that roll
Before the hurricane; the outspread scroll
Of heaven, with its written tomes of stars;
The dew-drop on the leaf: These I extol,
    And all alike—each one a Spirit-Mars,
Guarding my Victor-Soul above Earth's prison bars.

IX.

There was a stately Maiden once, who made
These Isles her home. Oft has her lightsome skiff
Toyed with the waters; and the velvet glade,
The shadowy woodland, and the granite cliff,
Joyed at her footsteps. Here the Brigand Chief,
Her father, lived, an outlaw. Her soul's pride
Was ministering to his wants. In brief,
The wildest midnight she would cross the tide,
Full of a daughter's love, to hasten to his side.

X.

Queen of the Isles! she well deserved the name:
In look, in action, in repose a Queen!

Some Poet-Muse may yet hand down to fame
Her woman's courage, and her classic mien;
Some Painter's skill immortalize the scene,
And blend with it that Maiden's history;
Some Sculptor's hand from the rough marble glean
An eloquent Thought, whose truthfulness shall be
The expounder of her worth and moral dignity.

XI.

On, through the lovely Archipelago,
Glides the swift bark. Soft summer matins ring
From every isle. The wild fowl come and go,
Regardless of our presence. On the wing,
And perched upon the boughs, the gay birds sing
Their loves: This is their summer paradise;
From morn till night their joyous caroling
Delights the ear, and through the lucent skies
Ascends the choral hymn in softest symphonies.

XII.

The Spring is gone—light, genial-hearted Spring!
Whose breath gives odor to the violet,
Crimsons the wild rose, tints the blackbird's wing,
Unfolds the buttercup. Spring that has set
To music the laughter of the rivulet,
Sent warm pulsations through the hearts of hills,
Reclothed the forests, made the valleys wet
With pearly dew, and waked the grave old mills
From their calm sleep, by the loud rippling of the rills.

XIII.

Long years ago the early Voyageurs
Gladdened these wilds with some romantic air;
The moonlight, dancing on their dripping oars,
Showed the slow batteaux passing by with care,
Impelled by rustic crews, as debonnair
As ever struck pale Sorrow dumb with Song:
Many a drooping spirit longed to share
Their pleasant melodies, that swept among
The echo-haunted woods, in accents clear and strong.

XIV.

See, we have left the Islands far behind,
And pass into a calm, pellucid Lake.
Merrily dance the billows! for the wind
Rises all fresh and healthful in our wake,
Up start large flocks of waterfowl, that shake
The spray from their glossed plumage, as they fly
To seek the shelter of some island brake;
Now like dark clouds they seem against the sky,
So vast the numbers are that pass us swiftly by.

XV.

Merrily dance the billows! Cheerily leaps
Our fearless bark!—it loves to skim the sea,
The River and the Lake, when o'er them sweeps
The swift unwearied billow fearlessly.
Stretches its spotless sail!—it tightens—see!
How the wind curves the waters all around,

Ploughing into their bosoms fitfully.
Hark to the tempest's dismal shriek! its bound,
Like to an earthquake, makes the river's depths resound.

XVI.

Through the dense air the terror-stricken clouds
Fly, tortured by the pursuing hurricane.
Fast bound the milky billows—the white shrouds
That wind around the mariner on the main.
Nay, shrink not, dark-eyed one! they weave no chain
For us—we're free! Ha! ha! our gallant bark
Spurns the white wave with eloquent disdain;
She laughs to scorn the waters wild and dark,
She revels in the Storm, the Tempest loves to mark.

XVII.

Hoarsely reverberates the thunder loud
Through the charged air. The fiery lightnings leap
Forth, from their mystic dwelling in the cloud;
Electric shafts through all the heavens sweep,
And penetrate the surface of the deep,
Like flaming arrows from the bow of wrath,
Shot down some dark and cloud-pavillioned steep;
Each red-hot bolt the fearful power hath
To scatter blight and death along its burning path.

XVIII.

A wild joy fills my overburdened brain.
My ears drink music from each thunder peal.

I glory in the lightnings and the rain.
There is no joy like this! With thee to feel
And share each impulse, makes my spirit kneel.
Sing to me, love! my heart is pained with bliss!
Thy voice alone can quicken and unseal
The inner depths of feeling. Grant me this:
Flood me with Song, and loose the founts of Happiness.

HYMN TO THE LIGHTNING.

Oh! mighty, Oh! mysterious One!
Thou willest, and the lightnings fly,
Flame-winged and silent, through the sky,
   Outglowing the exultant sun.

Along the hills reverberates
The eloquent, sonorous bass,
Shaking the earth from place to place,
   Then heavenward to Thy temple gates,

Where every whisper, every tone
Of music, from the earth, rolls in,
Whether from putrid lips of sin,
   Or girdled by a prayerful zone.

Thy Voice is in the thunder cloud,
Thy Presence in the lightning's fire—
Breathings of an Almighty Ire,
   That wraps the heavens in a shroud

Of blinding light, before whose heat
The granite mountains melt away,

And finite Man falls down to pray
  For mercy at his Maker's feet.

    How Vast art Thou! how minute he!—
A human tissue which a breath
Can hurl from quickest life to death—
  An atom to Immensity.

    Oh! wondrous Power! Oh! strength Divine!
Oh! weak and insignific Man!—
Weak here, but in the After-plan
  Not less eterne than Thee and Thine!

XIX.

Mysterious power of Song! the lips of Love
Make mellower music than a thousand strings
Of harps. Thine eyes my grosser thoughts remove,
But thy sweet voice doth give my spirit wings,
As up the air melodious whisperings,
Ethereal harmonies, divinely low,
Float, like the echoes which the morning flings
From the pleased valleys—hymns that upward flow,
Warming the purple hills with praises as they go.

XX.

Hast thou not heard upon a summer's eve
The musical pulsations of the air?
The voices of the mountain pines, that weave
Their low complainings with the atmosphere?
Thus, throughout Nature, floating everywhere,

Eternal symphonies, low, rich and deep,
Pass from her Poet-lips. Her children hear
And treasure up these lyrics, as they sweep
With Zephyrus through the air, or visit them in sleep.

XXI.

First, the sweet Idyls from the shepherd vales,
Where Peace and rural Happiness abide;
Bird-hymns and wild rejoicings in the dales,
Where the swart Peasant cheers his rustic Bride;
Anthems from solitary plains that glide
To where the death-dirge wails along the sea;
Low chantings from the stars, and far and wide
The Minstrel Breezes, meeting playfully,
Rehearse their wanderings in Canzonet and Glee:

XXII.

While the deep forest rolls its Psalmody
Of Voices from its music-haunted aisles;
And the strong Choruses leap joyfully
From hill to hill, or where the sunlight smiles
Upon the mountain summits, tinging miles
Of clouded crag and heaven-tinted air;
Last, the winged Tempest, from the long defiles
Emerging, like a Lyric God, to share
The genial Feast of Sounds that roused him from his lair.

XXIII.

The Spirits of the Storm are all abroad;
Of various natures, good and bad, are they;

Like mortal dwellers on this mundane clod,
Some evil natures, others good, obey.
As through the air they cleave their weird way,
Their separate passions show : Some smite the trees,
The innocent flowers, or the granite gray,
Or in huge heaps uproll the shouting seas;
While others weep, as now, wrecked Nature's obsequies.

XXIV.

In the far distance rolls the Thunder-Car,
Faintly the echo of its wheels is heard;
No more is felt the elemental jar;
The Curtains of the Storm are gently stirred,
And pushed aside; and slowly, at the Word
Of Him who placed it first within the cloud,
A gorgeous rainbow rises. The dark bird
Of night is on the wing; it cries aloud;
And the white sea gull floats where erst the thunder
      ploughed.

XXV.

The storm is lulled; the heaving waves subside;
The lightning's flash grows fainter; and the eye
Can just perceive the silver girdle tied
About the groups of pleasant Isles that lie
Before us. Down the hurrying stream we fly,
Like a white dove unto its nest. The eve
Has closed around us, and the brightening sky

Yearns for the coming stars. Nobly we leave
The Lake, and glide through scenes that Fairy hands
    might weave.

XXVI.

Pale Hesper smiles upon us through the gloom,
An unassuming Pioneer of Night,
Like a chrysalis that had burst its tomb,
And spread its gleaming pinions to the light.
Soft moon-beams fall like love-looks on the sight,
And earth and sky seem blending into one,
Even as our hearts' deep virtues, love, unite,
Like meeting pilgrims at the set of sun
Grasping each other's hands, their joyous labors done.

XXVII.

Mild Evening, like a pensive Vestal Nun,
Sits veiled, lamenting for the truant Hours;
The Day has sprung to heaven to seek the Sun,
And left her weeping on her couch of flowers;
Heaven's Angels, bearing moonlight to the bowers
Where True love dwells, and Virtue sits enthroned,
In golden urns collect the pearly showers,
Singing sweet idyls, low and silver-toned,
Till the enameled tears some cherub brow have zoned.

TWILIGHT HYMN.

God of the early Morning light!
  Whose Hand the Gates of Dawn unbars;
God of the Evening and the Night!

Who guides the chariots of the stars :
We thank Thee for the air we breathe,
  The waves that roll, the winds that rise,
For all Thy wondrous works beneath,
  For all the glories of the skies.

We bless Thee for the soothing Calm
  That broods below the Evening's wings,
We bless Thee for the Spirit-balm
  The gentle-footed Twilight brings.
Promptings of Hope, and Joy, and Love,
  Exalt our minds and set them free,
And Prayer-wreaths white as Aaron's Dove
  Ascend like incense up to Thee.

Gently the shades of Night come down,
  Glooming the Evening's silver gray,
Pale Twilight puts aside her crown,
  And follows the dim Ghost of Day.
So at the threshold of life's close,
  We tread the verge of heaven's goal,
Peace, like a spirit, brings repose
  To the calm Twilight of the Soul.

XXVIII.

There is no Twilight in you queenly Moon.
At least the philosophic vision ne'er,
At midnight's solemn, thought-inducing noon,
Could trace the existence of an atmosphere.
No Twilight and no Song! No blue sky, clear
As Woman's purest and most crystal thought

Rising to heaven on the wings of prayer!
No mountain echoes, like wild music, caught
From Nature's hallowed lips, to waiting Genii taught.

XXIX.

Its valleys know not either day or night;
Like mountain shadows darkening the plain
They slumber on, unconscious of the light
That falls on earth, like sun-thoughts on the brain.
And yet we feel her presence, as the main
Thrills to the diapason of the storm;
When the waves spring to their feet and join the strain,
These mighty wrestlers a strong chorus form,
And sing her praise, in tones deep, passionate and warm.

XXX.

Yon rock, that felt the lightning's burning kiss,
Has melted at the fervor of its breath,
As it leaped, glowing, from the deep abyss,
On wings of fire, to the distant heath,
Shaking the firm foundations underneath.
Yon shattered trunks that strew the watery way,
Yon floating beds of flowers, where many a wreath
Was woven by the storm, have felt the play
Of the hot lightning's wings, whose touch is swift decay.

XXXI.

And now 'tis Night. A myriad stars have come
To cheer the earth, and sentinel the skies.

The full-orbed moon irradiates the gloom,
And fills the air with light. Each Islet lies
Immersed in shadow, soft as thy dark eyes;
Swift through the sinuous path our vessel glides,
Now hidden by the massive promontories,
Anon the bubbling silver from its sides
Spurning, like a wild bird, whose home is on the tides.

XXXII.

Here Nature holds her Carnival of Isles.
Steeped in warm sunlight all the merry day,
Each nodding tree and floating greenwood smiles,
And moss-crowned monsters move in grim array;
All night the Fisher spears his finny prey;
The piney flambeaux reddening the deep,
Past the dim shores, or up some mimic bay:
Like grotesque banditti they boldly sweep
Upon the startled prey, and stab them while they sleep.

XXXIII.

Many a tale of legendary lore
Is told of these romantic Isles. The feet
Of the Red Man have pressed each wave-zoned shore,
And many an eye of beauty oft did greet
The painted warriors and their birchen fleet,
As they returned with trophies of the slain.
That race has passed away; their fair retreat
In its primeval loneness smiles again,
Save where some vessel snaps the isle-enwoven chain:

XXXIV.

Save where the echo of the huntsman's gun
Startles the wild duck from some shallow nook,
Or the swift hounds' deep baying, as they run,
Rouses the lounging student from his book;
Or where, assembled by some sedgy brook,
A pic-nic party, resting in the shade,
Spring pleasedly to their feet, to catch a look
At the strong steamer, through the watery glade
Ploughing, like a huge serpent from its ambuscade.

XXXV.

We have well-nigh outstripped the nimble breeze;
The silken sail incurves the pliant mast;
As flies the comet through the infinities,
So speeds our darling shallop, lightning-fast.
The merry Isles have floated idly past;
And suddenly the waters boil and leap,
On either side the foamy spray is cast,
Hoarse Genii through the shouting Rapid sweep,
And pilot us unharmed adown the hissing steep.

XXXVI.

The startled GALLOPPES shout as we draw nigh,
The SAULT, delighted, hails our reckless bark,
The graceful CEDARS murmur joyously,
The vexed CASCADES threaten our little ark,
That sweeps, love-freighted, to its distant mark.
Again the troubled deep heaps surge on surge,

And howling billows sweep the waters dark,
  Stunning the ear with their stentorian dirge,
That loudens as they strike the rocks' resisting verge.

XXXVII.

And we have passed the terrible LACHINE,
  Have felt a fearless tremor thrill the soul,
As the huge waves upreared their crests of green,
  Holding our feathery bark in their control,
  As a strong eagle holds an oriole.
The brain grows dizzy with the whirl and hiss
  Of the fast-crowding billows, as they roll,
Like struggling Demons, to the vexed abyss,
Lashing the tortured crags with wild, demoniac bliss.

XXXVIII.

MONT ROYALE rises proudly on the view,
  A Royal Mount, indeed, with verdure crowned,
Bedecked with regal dwellings, not a few,
  Which here and there adorn the mighty mound.
ST. HELENS next, a fair, enchanted ground,
  A stately Isle in glowing foliage dressed,
Laved by the dark St. Lawrence all around,
  Giving a grace to its enamored breast,
As pleasing to the eye as Hochelaga's crest.

XXXIX.

I've stood upon yon Mountain when the sun
  Entered his cloud-built palace in the west,
Like a proud, Royal Nimrod, who had won

His home, and doffed his richest-broidered vest.
Beneath me, the vast city lay at rest;
Its great heart throbbing gently, like the close
Of Day. A prayer lay folded in my breast,
And from my lips in silence it uprose,
For heaven's blessing on that city's calm repose.

XL.

For there dwelt one, who, in my Boyhood's days,
I loved with a deep passion. Many years
Have sung around me the wild paraphrase
Of life since then; and I've shed bitter tears,
And smiled heart-smiles; known many hopes and fears;
But my Boy-love has stood the test of time,
And ripened like her beauty. The fool leers
At Love's sun mellowing fair Childhood's clime,
Love, beauteous to the Child, to Man becomes sublime.

XLI.

There was a joyousness within her eyes,
Like the sun's light illumining the blue
Of heaven, making earth a paradise.
Gladness, like a celestial spirit passing through
The gates of morn, rose white-winged on the view,
Whene'er you looked upon her lovely face.
Love sat upon her lips, and love's sweet dew
Fell from them, leaving there a sunny trace,
As 'f touched by angel's wings they caught angelic grace.

XLII.

I could have mellowed in her light of Love,
And breathed my soul out on her lips of Song!
Afar off have I worshipped her, and strove
   With my pure passion day by day. How long
Will my lone spirit wander through the throng
   Of human hearts until it lives in thine ?
Know, Maiden, that my love is deep and strong
   As yonder Rapid, and as serpentine,
Rock after rock it strikes, seeking a joy divine.

CANZONET.

The balmy summer days are here,
   The Robin warbleth in the tree,
But Summer, Spring, nor song-birds bring
   One note of love from thee.

The roses will put forth their buds,
   Green leaves adorn each ardent tree,
But in my heart will never start
   One rose-bud hope for thee.

The sun leans down to kiss the flowers,
   To flush the blossoms of the tree,
But to my love no carrier-dove
   Brings warmth and light from thee.

The happy woodlands throb with song,
   Music is breathed from tree to tree;
With Winter's fleece these songs will cease,
   But not my love for thee.

XLIII.

The dancing current, like a happy child,
Mellifluously laughs, as down the stream
We glide, past many a cot and rural wild,
Like visions mellowed by the moonlight's beam.
We cannot stay for these; a loftier theme
Awaits us. See! our shallop seems to feel
The joyous impulse of our waking dream,
And parts the waters with its anxious keel,
Exulting in the joys that through our bosoms steal.

XLIV.

Yet there are graceful landscapes thickly strewn
Along these banks, to muse on and admire;
Here stands a maiden cottage all alone,
There the low church extends its gleaming spire.—
Scenes, where Arcadian dreamers might retire,
And live in pastoral meditation, free
From every low, inordinate desire.
Yon group of dwellings—what felicity
Speaks from their eloquent repose! where even he

XLV.

Of lonely Vaucluse might have sighed, and ne'er
Been tempted by fair Psyche's winning smile
From his pure love's Penelope. And here,
VARENNES, like a fair Eden purged from guile,
Sits smiling on the night; yon aged pile
With its bright spires reposing on its breast.

Yonder, the Holy Mountain of Rouville,
Like a huge cloud that had come down to rest,
Looms far against the sky, and on its sombre crest

XLVI.

Shineth the Pilgrim's Cross, that long hath cheered
The weary wanderer from distant lands,
Who, as his stately pinnace onward steered,
Bless'd his Faith's symbol with uplifted hands.
Swift through the Richileau! Past the white sands
That spangle fair Batiscan's pleasant shore
We glide, where fairy dwellings dot the strands;
How gracefully yon aged elms brood o'er
The shrubbery that yearneth for their mystic lore,

XLVII.

When the winds commune with the tell-tale limbs,
And many-voicéd leaves. That is St. Pierre,
Where the tall poplars—which the night bedims,
Lift their sharp outlines through the solemn air.
Past these white cottages to L'Avenir,
Another site of beauty. Lovelier yet
The Plateau, slumbering in the foliage there;
And gay Cap Sainte, like a Wild Love, beset
With wooers, bringing gems to deck her coronet.

XLVIII.

The Whippoorwill, among the slumberous trees,
Flingeth her solitary triple cry

Upon the busy lips of every breeze,
That wafts it in wild echoes up the sky,
And through the answering woods, incessantly.
Surely some pale Ophelia's spirit wails
In this remorseless bird's impassioned sigh,
That like a lost soul haunts the lonely dales!
Maiden, sing me one of thy pleasing madrigals.

THE WHIPPOORWILL.

Ere the dawn, one morning early,
 Jeannie tripped the meadows o'er,
Passing by the fields of barley,
 By the cottage at the shore:
"There his faith was pledged and broken,
 'Neath yon tree beside the Mill!"
From the tree, when she had spoken,
 Came a dismal "Whip-poor-will!"
  "Whip-poor-will! Whip-poor-will!"
   From the tree beside the Mill
   Piped the doleful Whippoorwill.

"Truly," Jeannie said, "poor Willie?
 He was false to heaven and me;
He was false, and I was silly,
 Yet the bird sings heartlessly.
Nevermore we'll sit at gloaming,
 'Neath the tree beside the Mill;
Willie's heart has gone a-roaming!"
  Quoth the harsh bird—"Whip-poor-will!"

"Whip-poor-will! Whip-poor-will!"
From the tree beside the Mill
Piped the doleful Whippoorwill.

Jeannie's heart was all compassion,
　Jeannie's lips a pardon sighed;
"Absent loves are all the fashion!"—
"Whip-poor-will!" the rude bird cried,
From the pasture tripped the Maiden,
　With her foamy milking pail,
Every roaming breeze was laden
　With the strange bird's heartless wail:
"Whip-poor-will! Whip-poor-will!'
In the tree beside the Mill
Piped the doleful Whippoorwill.

From the cottage by the river
　Truant Willie, blushing, came,
Jeannie's heart would still misgive her,
　Though he softly spake her name:
"Ever since that evening, Jeannie,
　That we parted at the Mill,
All the night long, bright or rainy,
　Shrieked that noisy Whippoorwill."
"Whip-poor-will! Whip-poor-will!"
From the tree beside the Mill
Piped the saucy Whippoorwill.

On the Maiden's lips paused Willie,
　Jeannie never asked the cause,

But all patience, like a silly
  Little Maiden as she was,
Held her mouth up like a flower,
  That her bee might sip his fill,
While the bird, with startling power,
Shrieked his wildest "Whip-poor-will!"
    "Whip-poor-will! Whip-poor-will!"
    Nevermore beside the Mill
    Piped that noisy Whippoorwill.

XLIX.

Th' inconstant moon has passed behind a cloud,
CAPE DIAMOND shows its sombre-colored bust,
As if the mournful Night had thrown a shroud
Over this pillar to a hero's dust.
Well may she weep; hers is no trivial trust;
His cenotaph may crumble on the plain,
Here stands a pile that dares the rebel's lust
For spoliation: one that will remain—
A granite seal—brave Wolfe! set upon Victory's Fane.

L.

QUEBEC! how regally it crowns the height,
Like a tanned giant on a solid throne!
Unmindful of the sanguinary fight,
The roar of cannon mingling with the moan
Of mutilated soldiers years agone,
That gave the place a glory and a name
Among the nations. France was heard to groan;

England rejoiced, but checked the proud acclaim—
A brave young chief had fall'n to vindicate her fame.

LI.

WOLFE and MONTCALM! two nobler names ne'er graced
The page of history, or the hostile plain;
No braver souls the storm of battle faced,
Regardless of the danger or the pain.
They pass'd unto their rest without a stain
Upon their nature or their generous hearts.
One graceful column to the noble twain
Speaks of a nation's gratitude, and starts
The tear that Valor claims, and Feeling's self imparts.

LII.

Far up the Golden Ladder of the Morn
Had climbed the sun, upon the Autumn day
That led me to these battlements. The corn
Upon the distant fields was ripe. Away
To the far left the swelling highlands lay;
The quiet cove, the river, bright and still;
The gallant ships that made the harbor gay;
And, like a Thought swayed by a potent Will,
POINT LEVI, seated at the foot of the Old Hill:

LIII.

What were the Gardens and the Terraces,
The stately dwellings, and the monuments

Upreared to human fame, compared to these?
Those ancient hills stood proudly ere the tents
Of the first Voyageurs—swart visitants
From the fair, sunny Loire—were pitched upon
Wild Stadacona's* height. The armaments
Whose mighty thunder clove the solid stone,
Defaced yon granite cape, that answered groan for groan.

LIV.

Down the rough slope Montmorenci's torrent pours,
We cannot view it by this feeble ray,
But, hark! its thunders leap along the shores,
Thrilling the cliffs that guard the beauteous bay;
And now the moon shines on our downward way,
Showing fair Orleans' enchanting Isle,
Its fields of grain, and meadows sweet with hay;
Along the fertile shores fresh landscapes smile,
Cheering the watchful eye for many a pleasant mile.

LV.

It seems like passing by some Fairy-realm.
The cottages are whiter than the snow.
Joy at the prow, and true love at the helm,
Both heaven and earth smile on us as we go.
Surely they never feel the breath of woe,
The dwellers on this Isle. Spire after spire
Points to the heav'n whose presence seems to glow

---

* Stadacona—the original name for Quebec.

Within their happy bosoms who aspire
To naught beyond their hearths, their own dear household fire.

LVI.

Peace to their cheerful homes! where bless'd Content
Reigns paramount throughout the circling year.
A courteous, gentle race, as ever blent
Religion with Simplicity. The cheer
That greets the stranger who may wander here
Glows with the zeal of hospitality.
Peace to their quiet homes! where blanching fear
Ne'er enters, nursed by jealous rivalry.
From the world's bitter strife the Habitant is free.

LVII.

The billowy River rolls its proudest wave,
The zephyrs have fled, dancing, o'er the hills,
And the winds tread the waters, wildly-grave,
Like the Storm-Harpists gliding down the rills
Of their own native mountains, 'gainst their wills.
Brighter the moon above us; brighter all
The patient stars, whose pensive beauty thrills
Our yearning souls, like distant tones that fall
On waiting ears hearkening for an Angel's call.

LVIII.

Brighter the night, and whiter every cot
And glancing spire that silvers in the moon;

Intensely glows each little garden plot;
The sparkling villages at random strewn
Along the brooding shore, where Bacchus,* boon
Companion of the merry crowd, once held
His regal court: his prudent subjects soon
Stripped off his purple vestments, and rebelled,
And wisely still disown the Monarch they expelled.

LIX.

Now swiftly down towards the salt-breathed sea
The cool wind wafts us, and we bid farewell
To the lone Isle that slumbers on our lee;
Farewell, perchance, forever. Who can tell?
Years hence, in separate lands, our thoughts may dwell,
But for a little moment, on this night,
And Memory may wake within her cell,
And lead us here by this same starry light,
Our long-divided souls, embracing, reünite.

PARTING SONG.

Part! the word must not be spoken!
Part! our hearts must ne'er be broken!
Rivers meet and mix forever,
Why are we, love, doomed to sever?
Oh! the cruel, cruel anguish!
How the senses droop and languish!

---

* The Island of Orleans—once called the "Isle of Bacchus" from the abundance of its grapes, which have now entirely disappeared.

For the fiat may be spoken,
And our hearts may both be broken!

Comes the Night, the Evening greeting,
Ever thus behold them meeting;
But for us—what hope before us?
Not a star is shining o'er us;
But the heav'n of love is clouded,
Wildly, darkly, blackly shrouded,
For an iron tongue hath spoken,
And our hope in hope is broken!

In my brain a fire is burning,
Backward to my heart returning,
And my nerves, that drooped to sadness,
Are re-strung to desp'rate madness!
Leap, ye burning thoughts that rend me,
Let not Pity's voice befriend me!
Curs'd the lips that lie hath spoken!
For our hearts shall not be broken!

LX.

Cape Tormente lifts itself above the hills
That gird it round about, like sentinels
Guarding some great king's palace, whose grandeur fills
Their hearts with pride and love. Up the steep dells
Crawl the night-vapors, dimming the gray swells
Of mount and hill that in the distance rise,
Cloud-like and faint. Ev'n on those uplands dwells

The faithful Habitant; and when he dies,
His children, jealous of the ancient family ties,

LXI.

Keep the old Homestead sacred. What a night!
It must have borrowed somewhat of the day,
In honor of thine eyes, love. The warm light
That bathes yon church and village, is as gay
And cheering as if the first golden ray
Of morning's sun had pierced it with its beams.
Some Recluse, yonder, keeps his holiday
In that obscure ravine. Peace to his dreams!
Uncursed with lust of gold, or wild, unholy schemes.

LXII.

Still loftily looms the Cape! Still proudly soar
The vassal Hills—innumerable—vast!
And majesty and beauty evermore
Surfeit the sense with a divine repast.
Another group of dwellings—'t is the last;
Another spire flashing above the trees
That screen the little church. Our slender mast
Leans to the gale, and while the glorious breeze
Quickens our speed, look round, for there are charms to please

LXIII.

On either hand. A dream it well might be:
Hills rising here, and mountains looming there;
Islands reposing on a moonlit sea

With which the winds are toying; everywhere
The shores are bold, precipitous and fair.
GROSSE ISLE sits dreamily-languid; all around,
Its subject-islands slumber. In the air
The clouds have melted into light. No sound
Stirs the sweet calm, save where the jovial billows bound.

LXIV.

Press on, courageous bark!—the wind is fair,
As it should ever be when Love sets sail
Beneath such skies as these, whose glowing air
Quickens our souls, as odors scent the gale.
Soon will the stars be dim, the Moon grow pale,
As with Orion down the dreamy west
She wanders, like a Beauty, proud and frail,
To where her lonely couch waits to be press'd,
A fearful secret in her warm, voluptuous breast.

LXV.

This Isle* might guard the entrance to a sphere
Of heavenly tranquillity! The mind
Puts off its weight of cares, for Beauty here
Sits like a wondrous deity enshrined
Among the hills. Oh, God! but Thou art kind!
ST. PAUL'S delightful BAY, fit mirror for
The stars, glows like a vision which the wind
Wafts by some Angel standing on the shore,
As bless'd as if he trod heaven's star-enameled floor.

*Isle Aux Coudres—Filbert Island.

LXVI.

The distant knolls are soft as midnight clouds
Filled with bright memories of departed day.
Like purple glories rolling up the woods,
This rugged wilderness which we survey
Extends in wild, magnificent array,
To regions rarely trod by mortal feet.
Ev'n here, love, though we would, we cannot stay;
We cannot loiter near this calm retreat;
The Morn approaches, and his fiery steeds are fleet.

LXVII.

These two majestic hills* kneel down to kiss
The village at their feet; the cottages,
Pearl-like and glowing, speak of human bliss,
With a low, eloquent tongue. Fit symbols, these,
Of a diviner life—of perfect Ease
Allied to bless'd Repose. The church spire looks
Like a sweet promise smiling through the trees;
While far beyond this loveliest of nooks,
The finely-rounded swells dream of the babbling brooks.

LXVIII.

Eboullemens† sleeps serenely in the arms
Of the Maternal hill, upon whose breast
It lies, like a sweet, infant soul, whose charms

---

* At Little St. Paul's Bay—one of the most delightful pictures on the route.
† A most delightful little village of this name, looking like a vision of Romance or Fairy-tale.

Fill some fond mother's bosom with that rest
Caused by the presence of a heavenly guest.
How coyly—close—it nestles! how retired,
Half conscious of its charms, and half oppress'd,
As with a blushing sense of being admired;
As modest as a gem, with gem-like beauty fired.

LXIX.

The stream reflects these cottages, like swans
Reposing on its surface, or faint dreams
But half remembered when the morning dawns,
And tremulous sleep wakes with the day's first beams.
Past the monotonous "CAPES."* The moonlight gleams
Full on the mossy slopes and banks that lie
Along the silent shores, as well beseems
So fair a region. Why, love, dost thou sigh?
But wherefore ask, loved one? My own heart tells me why:

LXX.

Our spirits are as one. The morning, love,
Will part us. We have lived an age to-night.
Love is immortal. Hope is from above.
Sit nearer to me, for thine eyes are bright
With tears. There is a fairer land in sight.
Our love is sphered with truth. Eternity
Will crown that love, if we but love aright;

*Le Caps.

If Love be Truth, indeed. Soft-eyed one! we
Must seek beyond the veil what here can never be!

LXXI.

Welcome the granite sternness of MALBAIE!*
The last dim light of the declining moon
Falls dimly on its rugged banks. The day
Will shortly waken from its dreamy swoon;
His chariot long hath swept the sullen noon
Of midnight; and beneath our feet, the sun
Rolls, flaming, towards the East. His fierce breath soon
Along the undulating hills will run,
Rousing the piney vales and forests, one by one.

LXXII.

And Darkness, like a Fate, comes stealing down
In her black mantle, step by step, until
The trembling stars have dwindled down to one
Pale, solitary watcher. Lone and chill
Falls its meek glance on river, wood and hill.
See, you can even mark its heart-beats, love!
Each mortal has his mission to fulfil,
Each planet is accountable to Jove,
Both do His high behests, His sovereign Will approve.

LXXIII.

I knew a man whose prayerful soul was set
To a devotional music, like a psalm

*Murray Bay.

Fresh from a Master-Artist's brain ; and yet,
There came a time when his mind's starriest calm
Was quenched in Unbelief. Once, like a palm
He flourished, till deep thinking brought a doubt
Of a Hereafter, and the Great I AM !
Like a new light, Faith slowly came, and out
Of his dark world he strode, believing and devout.

LXXIV.

So rolls the bright Dawn up the Orient,
Out of the pitchy hour that precedes
The flush of Day. Darkness was surely sent
To make the Light more blessed. The heart bleeds
That has been sown with Error—lo ! the seeds
Have brought forth Truth. So Good from Evil springs
And all is mystery. Our noblest deeds
May bring us bitter fruits. Frail man who clings
To Life, is perfected when Death reveals all things.

LXXV.

The Morning Star has gone back into heaven,
The Sun's light-footed Herald, the gray Dawn,
Is passing upwards, and the dusk is riven
By a warm tinge, like to a purple lawn,
O'er which a misty saffron veil is drawn.
But warmer is the rose tint spreading now
Along the dim horizon, erst so wan,
Like Health returning to the pallid brow
And cheek of some young sufferer, with a welcome glow.

PÆAN TO THE DAWN.

In the East the blooming Angel,
    Morning, hov'reth, like a gorgeous rose,
Waking many a fair Evangel
    From her heavenly repose.
From her brow a radiant glory
    Falls, like fire from above,
Telling the impassioned story
    Of God's everlasting love.
Love's Angels ever walk their starry round,
And each new Morn beholds Love newly crowned.

    Love, that at the primal waking
        Of the Dawn in Eden's bowers,
    Wandered through the Garden, slaking
        His warm thirst from Eden's flowers;
    And the same sweet Eden-nectar
        Flows wherever Love is found,
    Even when the midnight's spectre
        Treads upon earth's hallowed ground.
Love's Angels ever walk their starry round,
And with each Morning Love is newly crowned.

    Blessed light of early Morning!
        At whose dawn the stars retire,
    With thy warmth our souls adorning,
        Fill us with love's ardent fire—
    With the love that comes from heaven,
        With the hope that soars on high,
    That our faults may all be shriven,

As thy splendors fill the sky.
Love's Angels ever walk their starry round,
And with each Morning Love is newly crowned.

    Calmly is the River glowing,
      Like a burnished, crystal sea,
    Like pure thoughts forever flowing
      Heavenward eternally.
    Slowly up the distant mountains
      Rolls the changing purple screen,
    While the swift rills, from their fountains
      Leaping, clothe their sides with green.
Love's Angels ever walk their starry round,
And with each Morning Love is newly crowned.

    O'er the earth Love's blooming Angels
      Loiter, hand in hand with Morn,
    Fair-browed, golden-crowned Evangels,
      Twin companions, heaven-born.
    Life, and Light, and Joy attending,
      Hymns and prayers salute their ears,
    Earth's sweet hallelujahs blending
      With the anthems of the spheres.
Love's Angels ever walk their starry round,
And with each Morning Love is newly crowned.

LXXVI.

Like maid-wife waiting for her wedded lord,
The morn waits for the sun with a flushed cheek.
I hear the songs of birds; the breeze has stirred

Their dwellings, as it rustled from the peak
Of yonder mountain with a playful shriek.
Now my fair shallop, leap! the blessed Day
Opens its crystal gates, and up the meek
And wan-faced sky the sun's darts cleave their way,
As our bark cleaves the black and frowning SAGUENAY.

LXXVII.

Mysterious Source of Light, triumphant Sun!
A Royal Witness hast thou been to me
Of th' existence of the Eternal One!
But e'en thy light compared with Deity,
Is as a dew-drop to the boundless sea.
What Angel-plaudits from surrounding spheres
Must have been echoed through infinity,
When first above thy myriads of compeers
Thou rod'st, exulting o'er the starry charioteers.

LXXVIII.

Couldst thou reveal the secret of thy birth,
The pain and travail of thy Parent, Night,
The worlds would glow with wonder, as the earth
Glows with the fervor of thy glorious light.
Roll on in all thy mystery and might!
For thou art worthy of the Hand Divine
That waved thee into being, in the sight
Of His archangels, and the heavenly line
Of saints, who, wondering, praised the Omnipotent
    Design.

LXXIX.

In golden volumes rolls the blessed light
Along the sterile mountains.   Pile on Pile
The granite masses rise to left and right:
Bald, stately bluffs that never wear a smile;
Where vegetation fails to reconcile
The parchéd shrubbery and stunted trees
To the stern mercies of the flinty soil.
And we must pass a thousand bluffs like these,
Within whose breasts are locked a myriad mysteries.

LXXX.

Here is a barren crag, at whose brown feet
Patiently sits the church and gleams the spire.
Commerce has found this a deserved retreat;
Here groan the mills, and there, the household fire
Sends up its smoke above the struggling briar
And dwarfish evergreens that grow between
The stubborn rocks—that grow but to expire.
Not here the thrifty farmer's face serene—
The lumberer alone lends life to the grim scene.

LXXXI.

No further evidence of life, save where
The young whales bask their broad backs in the sun,
Or the gay grampus, sportive as a hare,
Leaps and rejoices, playfully as one
In youth who sees some holiday begun.
Perhaps a crowded steamer, passing by,

Lights up the scene a moment. Trebly dun
The shades of sullen loneliness that lie
On rugged L'Ance l'eau when no living thing is nigh.

LXXXII.

Over the darkening waters! on through scenes
Whose unimaginable wildness fills
The mind with joy insatiate, and weans
The soul from earth, to Him whose Presence thrills
All Beauty as all Truth. These iron Hills!
In what profusion did He pile them here,
Thick as the flowers that blossom where the rills
Chant to the primal woods. Year after year
In solitude eternal, rapt in contemplation drear.

LXXXIII.

Dreaming of the old years before they rose
Triumphant from the deep, whose waters roll'd
Above their solemn and unknown repose;
Dreaming of that bright morning, when, of old,
Beyond the Red Man's memory, they told
The Secrets of the Ages to the sun,
That smiled upon them from his throne of gold;
Dreaming of the bright stars and loving moon,
That first shone on them from the Night's impressive noon:

LXXXIV.

Dreaming of the long ages that have passed
Since then, and with them that diminished race

Whose birchen fleets these inky waters glassed,
As they swept o'er them with the wind's swift pace.
Of their wild legends scarce remains a trace;
Thou hold'st the myriad secrets in thy brain,
Oh! stately bluffs! As well seek to efface
The light of the bless'd stars, as to obtain
From thy sealed, granite lips, tradition or refrain!

LXXXV.

But they are there, though man may never know
Their number or their beauty. Pass the eye
Along the ever-looming scene, where'er we go,
Through these long corridors of rock and sky—
What startling barriers, rising sullenly
From the dark deeps, like giants, seem to place
An adamantine gateway, close and high,
To bar our progress; meet them face to face,
The magic doors fly open, and the rocks recede apace.

LXXXVI.

Hills piled on rugged hills! But see, how drear,
And with what startling solitariness,
The TETE DE BOULE looms yonder! Cold and clear
In isolated grandeur, the huge mass,
Like the stern MAGI of this granite pass,
He stands amid-stream, thoughtfully apart
From his far-off companions. Once, alas!
I knew a stately soul, with lone, sad heart,
And thus to me he sung—that mountain's counterpart:

VANISHED HOPES.

I've supped with depression and feasted with sorrow,
   The hot tears of anguish have withered my heart;
And now, death might strike down my last hope
      to-morrow,
   Not one tear is left me to deaden his dart.

From youth up to manhood a scourge was upon me,
   Few roses of pleasure have bloomed in life's crown;
No rainbow of promise wherein I might sun me,
   The grasp of a fate is still bearing me down.

And thus like a tree in the lone desert—blasted,
   Dry, leafless and withered—dead, sapless and bare,
I long for love's sweet dews, once mine, now untasted,
   And stand like a wretch stricken dumb with despair!

LXXXVII.

Not often these imperishable hills
Are startled by the cheering Voice of Song.
Swift flies our fleet bark onward, ev'n as rills
Leap, crystal-footed, like starbeams, along
Steep mountain sides, that, resolute and strong,
Heed not their graceful steps. There is no sign
Of human habitation seen among
These heaven-reaching bluffs; no beach supine,
Or banks inviting, where the weary might recline.

LXXXVIII.

One solitary sea gull hovering,
Like an adventurous spirit, o'er the deep,

And he, too, glides as silent on the wing
As a child's thoughts of heaven. Parched and steep,
The red-browed mountains slumber, like the sleep
Of a drugged giant—dreamless, deep and wild.
A few dwarfed pines and impish cedars creep
Along the embrowned summits, half-beguiled
By the warm sunbeams, where no foliage ever smiled.

LXXXIX.

But as our restless shallop from her prow
Scatters the liquid pearls in her mad haste,
These naked boulders lag behind, and now
The smiling hills with verdant life are graced.
Like a lone star twinkling above the waste
Of ocean, when the youthful mariner sees
That the portentous storm has safely pass'd,
Is yonder distant dwelling, where the breeze
Frills the calm bay, and flirts with the coquetting trees:

XC.

Slumbering at the base of two high rocks,
It looks like Patience at the feet of Death.
Or, fancy it some grave magician's box,
Which, opened, wafts a pestilential breath
Along the mountains, an invisible wreath
Of subtlest essence, permeating through
Their granite pores, sapping all life beneath,
And robbing their bald summits of the blue
And rich ærial tints, where the tall cedars grew.

XCI.

A green delightful valley, sweetly smiles
Close to those rocks, as if an Angel-path
Led to the shore from the remotest hills,
That lave their heads in an ambrosial bath
Of vapors and warm sunlight, such as hath
Been carried down from heaven in the urns
Of ministering spirits. Free from scathe
Is this sweet vale, where some fair sprite sojourns,
In smiling contrast to the blasted mountain ferns.

XCII.

Here, the dark pines clothe the steep mountain-side,
There, heavy beetling cliffs, rugged and bald,
Lift their gray heads above the sunny tide—
Like the stern phantom of some Prophet-Scald
Of the old time, by magic wiles enthralled:
Full of his Scandinavian fire, and yet
Spell-bound and silent, like a ghost appalled.
A river, winding, like a rivulet,
Through the thick woods and reverential hills, has set

XCIII.

Its seal of freshness on the changeful wild.
A stately ship lies anchored in the bay;
Like an Oasis to the Desert-child,
It speaks of Life. No rocks can bar the way
Where Love and Hope lend wings to human clay:
The granite knots roll from us, like a cloud
Of vapor up the sunny-minded Day,

When Morn looks down from heaven : They have
  bowed
Their stubborn heads, and parted, like a daunted crowd

XCIV.

Of evil spirits who have seen the sun.
These hills lie mingled in a soft embrace,
As if they felt the joy that makes us one
When human hearts unite, and face to face
Love looks on Love, discovering that trace
Of Eden that yet lingers in the heart :
Are they the offspring, love, of some old race
Of mountains, that no Geologic art
Can trace—no whisper of their deep old loves impart ?

SONG.

Oh! give me the love of your woman's heart,
  And the light of your cheerful eye !
    And the earth will change
    From a phantom strange
  To a heaven with stars and sky ;
    And the Sun of Hope
    Up the gleaming cope,
  Like the Genius of Love, will roll,
    And dark Night no more
    Will obscure the shore
  Where beckons Love's mystic Soul !

For your love is as deep as the comet's sweep,
  When it reels from its astral lair,

And your looks as bright
As the lustrous light
The sun shakes from his golden hair.
As pure as the hue
Of the summer blue,
That is warmed by the sunset's glow,
Are the thoughts that rise
In your cheerful eyes
To banish the Demon, Woe.

I'd pillow my head on your snowy breast,
And my heart, like a cymbal fine,
Would throb with a tone
That were Music's own,
When it wakened a chord of thine:
Then the Sun of Hope
Up Life's gleaming cope,
The true Genius of Love would roll,
And dark Night no more
Would obscure the shore
Where beckons Love's mystic Soul.

XCV.

Nature has here put on her royalest dress,
And CAPE ETERNITY looms grandly up,
Like a God reigning in the Wilderness
Holding communion with the distant cope,
Interpreting the stars' dreams, as they ope
Their silver gates, where stand his regal kin.

Oh! for some special gift! to give full scope
To the soul's promptings, so that I might win
To earth some portion of the fire that burns within.

XCVI.

A deep and overpowering solitude
Reigns undisturbed along the varied scene.
A wilderness of Beauty, stern and rude,
In undulating swells of wavy green;
Soft, airy slopes, bold, massive and serene;
Rich in wild beauty and sublimity,
From the far summits in their piney sheen,
Down to the shadows thrown by rock and tree
Along the dark, deep wave, that slumbers placidly.

XCVII.

He, love, who flushed the daisy built the world.
All things come perfect from His Master-hand.
The stars, His Thoughts, through wide creation
    whirled,
Down to the minutest monad of sand
Upon the shore, in equal glory stand
Before His sight. But Man, and man alone,
He holds supremest of the works He planned:
And yet, how like Earth's faintest monotone,
Compared to Heaven's choir, he seems, when thrown

XCVIII.

In puny contrast to a work like this.
Slope after slope, wave after wave of light

And graceful foliage, which the sun's warm kiss
Thrills, from the centre to the farthest height.
The mind soars God-ward with a keen delight,
And proudly beats the undisciplined heart,
Rendering homage to the Infinite,
As from the Cape's embrace the wild shapes start,
Filling the soul with dreams that nevermore depart.

XCIX.

A playful waterfall comes dashing down,
As silvery as the laughter of a child
Dancing upon the greensward, and the sun
Scatters his golden arrows through the wild,
Cleaving the molten-silver stream that smiled
So lovingly upon his earliest beams.
So unsuspecting Innocence, beguiled
By Pleasures, soft as sunlight upon streams,
Flies the swift darts that pierce the enamel of its dreams.

C.

Is there a soul so dead to nature's charms,
That thrills not here in this divine retreat?
Love lures me evermore to Woman's arms,
But here I kneel at Nature's hallowed feet!
Love fills my being with a calm, replete,
But regal Nature sets my spirit free
With grateful praises to God's Mercy seat.
Yet nature binds me closer, love, to thee:
Ev'n as this dreamy Bay,* in sweet felicity;

* Trinity Bay—after passing Cape Eternity.

CI.

Woos both the sun's light, and the cool shade
Of the umbrageous woods to its embrace.
What deep imaginings of Peace pervade
Its heavenly repose, as Nature's face
Peers down, in mild, unutterable grace,
Like a calm Student seeking Pearls of Thought
In some fair Beauty's mind, where he can trace
Through her warm slumber, how her soul is fraught
With pure deep Love, by heavenly inspiration taught.

CII.

Strong, eager thoughts come crowding to my eyes,
Earnest and swift, like Romans in the race,
As in stern grandeur, looming up the skies,
This Monarch of the Bluffs,* with kingly grace,
Stands firmly fixed in his eternal place,
Like the great Samson of the Saguenay,
The stately parent of the giant race
Of mountains, scattered—thick as ocean spray
Sown by the tempest—up this granite-guarded way.

CIII.

My lips are mute. I cannot speak the thought
That, like a bubble on the placid sea,
Bursts ere it tells the tale with which 't is fraught.
Another comes, and so, eternally,
They rise in hope, to wander spirit-free

---

* Trinity Rock—a stupendous mass of granite.

About the earth. 'T were best they should not break
The Silence, which itself is ecstacy
And Godlike Eloquence, or my frail voice shake
A single echo, the expressive Calm to break.

CIV.

Like tears of Gladness o'er a giant's face,
The streams leap perpendicularly down
The polished sides of the steep precipice,
That glooms the waters with its sullen frown,
Until they seem as massive as the brown,
Bold, naked rock, that rears its swarthy crest,
Its anatomic form, and triple crown
Of granite, far above the earth's unrest,
Claiming a lofty seat, like Truth made manifest.

CV.

Let us return, love,* for the goal is won.
Here, by this Rock, 't is doomed that we must part,
And part forever; for the glorious Sun
Of Love, that quickeneth my earnest heart,
Shines not for thee, alone. The Dream of Art
That calms the happy Student's sweet repose,
Is like our Dream of Love—the first swift dart
Shot by young Phœbus from his chamber, goes
Like lightning through his vision's blooming heart of rose.

* Back to Trinity Rock.

CVI.

Already thou art gone, with one last look
Of love from those exalted eyes of thine,
That cheered me as we read from nature's book
Together, and partook of the divine
Ambrosial draught of love's celestial wine.
Another earnest being at my side!—
Not her whose Girlhood's dreamy love was mine;
Not her whose heart Affliction's fire has tried ;
Not her of the Artistic soul, and stately pride,

CVII.

Who shook my being as the autumn winds
Shake down the timid leaves.   Loved-one! I hear
The voice within syllabl'ing words that bind
Our souls, and blend them for a nobler sphere
Of usefulness and action—year by year
Ascending in the scale of being, far
Above the trifling mind's obscure career,
And mounting to Perfection, like a star
For whose triumphant flight heaven's crystalline gates unbar.

CVIII.

My love is strong as yon enduring Rock!
Deep as the thoughtful waters at its feet!—
Oh! could my willing voice find words t' unlock
Its depths, and free the sleeping echoes, fleet
As the swift-footed chamois, they would greet
The far-surrounding hills with such a tale

Of passion as had never left its seat
  Within the heart of man.   The bounding gale,
And the low-whispering breeze, should chant it to the
      vale.

CIX.

And the dread Silence, seated on the brow
Of the exalted Bluff, would start, and find
An hundred tongues to utter vow for vow;
Startling the browsing elk and slumbering hind,
In the resounding woods.   Like Truth enshrined
Within the well, so in my steadfast soul
Love waited for thee, as the patient mind
Waits for the coming thought that will extol
Some lofty purpose struggling skyward to its goal.

CX.

All, all is thine, love, now: Each thought and hope
In the long future must be shared with thee.
Lean on my bosom; let my strong heart ope
Its founts of love, that the wild ecstacy
That quickens every pulse, and makes me free
As a God's wishes, may serenely move
Thy inmost being with the mystery
Of the new life that has just dawned, and prove
How unutterably deep and strong is Human Love.

MISCELLANEOUS POEMS.

SPRING.

The Spring is in the air,
I feel her spirit-kiss upon my lips,
   I lay my forehead bare,
And the blood rushes to my finger-tips,
And back through the full veins of my glad heart:

   Her purple breath is warm
In every pore of my encarmined cheek,
   And through my limbs the storm
Of renewed life, no longer winter-weak,
Gives health and vigor to each vital part.

   I fling my arms abroad,
And clasp the atmosphere unto my breast,
   I feel the grassy sod
Beneath my feet springing from its long rest,
Like buried hopes arising in the soul:

   The erewhile aged hills
With youth reänimate are fresh and green,
   From their old lips the rills
Leap forth, like crystal images serene,
Pearl thoughts of wisdom bounding to their goal.

Close by the gray old stone
Where sat the Boy, where lately paused the Man,
A violet has blown—
The eye of Pallas on the cheek of Pan—
A blue-eyed infant at a giant's feet:

Over the meadows pass
The bronzéd butterflies and the wild bees,
Searching in the young grass
For the fresh daisies; and the lilac trees
Surfeit the odorous air with breathings sweet.

The fields are carpeted
With amethystine hyacinthes; the rose
Peers from its leafy bed
Along the ledge; the purling brooklet flows
Over the white sands to the lilies' side:

Here, in the apple tree,
Where, surely as the spring time comes, is heard
His soft, rich melody,
The happy robin sits—a welcome bird,
Waking the pulse to joy each morning tide.

The music of the bells
Tinkling among the early shepherd flocks,
In silvery pantings, swells
Along the Orient, ere the saffron locks
Of the proud sun have yellowed o'er the sea:

Scarcely a breath of air
Quickens the thrilling silence of the vale;

But the warm Spring is there,
A thousand choirs her rosy presence hail,
Stirring the heart-chords all to minstrelsy—

Rousing the organ-tone
That peals melodiously through the old woods,
Making the forests groan
With music, shaking the deep solitudes
Whose vigorous allelujahs rouse the morn:

The many-voicéd hills
Take up the pæan, bearing it along
Until the wild chant fills
The vocal wilderness with solemn song:
"Shout mighty forests! for to-day is born

" The rosy-featured Spring!
Shout your deep-chested pæans, till the bass,
Upon the lightning wing
Of startled Echo, fills the listening space
With psalmy welcome to our light-robed Queen:

" Her breath is in the air,
It floats upon the distant mountain peak,
The strolling zephyrs bear
Her loving kisses to each human cheek,
And Spring reigns blandly o'er the wide demesne."

C*

A POET'S LOVE.

Oh! solitary heart!
Companionless as the unresting sea;
And yet, how skilled thou art
In Love's impenetrable mystery!

Like a coy maid,
Whose love and virtue are her only dower,
Thou seemest half afraid
Of thy exhaustless and well-governed power.

Thy love is too serene,
Exalted, and immortal, to be felt,
Even by thy chosen queen,
In whose cold arms thou couldst have ever dwelt,

Like a warm pearl
Imprisoned in the granite's rayless breast.
Oh! heart, thou art no churl!
But in Love's Golden Palace formed to rest.

Yes, love for love,
Love like thine own, 't is all thou'st ever sought,
But vainly hast thou strove,
Like flushed youth after fame, and found it not.

Love watcheth evermore
Within thee, from his cruel prison bars,
Like Eleanor in her tower,
Night-blooming Cereus longing for the stars.

A POET'S LOVE.

I knew a noble youth,
He was as timid as a Bengalee,
But in his heart sat Truth,
And Love sat at her feet, all modestly,

As blooms the violet
Beneath the perfume of the queenly rose;
His being's tide was set
Love-ward, like a flushed summer sunset's close.

And there was one he deemed
All worthy of the worship of his soul;
One, who, in all things, seemed
Born but to guide him to his vision's goal.

Hemmed in with Love,
Like a fair island with a coral reef,
His spirit soared above
The world, like Joy exalted above Grief.

Love was his atmosphere,
He breathed it as men breathe the southern balm;
His young mind, year by year,
Grew upright as a Coromandel palm.

Her presence was his shield,
Like the white plume of Henry of Navarre
Upon the battle field,
Where'er he look'd, there loomed his guiding star

She was as fair
And beautiful as the anemone,

Pure as the morning air
Fresh from the mountain summits or the sea.

They loved their rural homes,
And while she helped the aged cottage dame,
He labored at huge tomes,
And on his fane of love built spires of fame.

His were great visions now,
Hers, the sweet joy to elevate his dreams;
Thought sat upon his brow,
Upon her face a glory, such as beams

Upon an angel's face
When a ripe Truth falls from some human brain,
And wins the usurped place
Where Error long had held its iron reign.

There came a gallant youth,
All scent, and curls, and foppery and pride,
Who knew no more of Truth
Than the young infant of the year that died.

And he, too, spake of love,
He spake of gold, and rank, of power and place,
Of courts, where she might move,
Like Love's fair Queen, amongst a Royal race.

Her simple ear was gained,
Loud Flattery triumphed over modest Worth,
And one great heart was pained
To know that Perfidy still walked the Earth.

But 't is the Poet's doom,
To nurse, unknowingly, some ripening pain,
And as he paced his room,
Lonely as Tycho on its herbless plain,

He did not curse the hand
That plucked the lily from his mountain crags,
Cursed not the human brand
Flung loose to scourge him like Pandora's Plagues.

But in his mind still burned
The embers of his love's funereal pyre;
The lesson he had learned,
Bequeathed he to the world in words of fire:

"Well I knew a stately Maiden, flushed with Health's divinest glow,
With a hand as warm as sunlight, and a heart as cold as snow.

"Many a softly-moulded accent floated from her perfect mouth,
Syllabl'ing words as mellow as the fruitage of the South.

"Words that made my heart awaken, and my pulsing spirit bound,
Every stricken chord of Feeling trembling with melodious sound.

"Oriental odors floated in her warm Sabean breath,
And I knew not they were filtered through an atmosphere of Death.

"Sweetly did my dreams deceive me, like the babe's
    upon the sea,
When the noble ship's endangered with a typhoon on
    the lee.

" And a glorious Hope reigned proudly, like a giant, in
    my heart,
Falsely swearing by the Future, Love and he should
    never part.

" Oh! with what a saintly glory the strong eye of man-
    hood beams,
When the youthful soul is flooded with the languor of
    its dreams.

" How the world becomes Ideal, Nature's beauties all
    laid bare,
And a harmonizing fragrance fills the universal air.

" Morning wears a tenfold beauty, evening comes se-
    renely down,
And at night each star is praying for the sin-endangered
    town.

" In the midnight, when the moonbeams warm the bosom
    of the earth,
How divine the swift emotions springing into Godlike
    birth.

" Every drop of dew that trembles, glistening, on the
    pleaséd sight,
Has an eye of sparkling beauty, looking upward through
    the night.

"Every zephyr, like a spirit, breathes a more delicious balm,
Every gust of wind that passes sings its animated psalm.

"To each memory-haunted nook a more exalted beauty clings,
And the summer flies make music with the motions of their wings.

"The anthem of the thunder falls in organ peals upon the brain,
And the passionate clouds smile lightnings through the weepings of the rain.

"To the perfect sense there seems a fuller rolling of the floods,
A more dulcet tone is whispering in the bursting of the buds.

"A more silvery cadence ringeth in the laughter of the rills,
A warmer purple blendeth with the vapours on the hills.

"Angels stepping down from heaven fill the chambers of the mind,
Chanting there their hymns of triumph, waking love for all mankind.

"Every tree, and bud, and flower, has a hue it never wore,
When the soul was love-deserted, in the callous days of yore.

"Birds are warbling from the thickets orisons of wondrous note,
And the wooing dove pairs nestle closer in their blessed cote.

"Where was deadly hatred rankling in the sinful human breast,
Sits Forgiveness, blest and blessing, with a glory for its crest.

"Love, Lord Paramount of all, dispenses, from his thousand thrones,
Sunshine for all clouded sorrows, boundless joy for passion groans.

"Earth, and air, and sky, and ocean, every living, breathing thing,
Sits in peace beneath the shelter of Love's universal wing.

"So sat I beneath it, dreaming of a world of bliss to come,
In a universe of fancies, for my joy had struck me dumb.

"And my quiet heart had yielded every pulsing hope and beat
To that cold and stately Maiden, who had charmed me to her feet.

"Day by day my love grew stronger, and my soul, exultant, trod
Through my mind's illumined palace, with the bearing of a God.

"Every tender word she spake rode to me in a silver car,
Every look she gave at parting rounded to a perfect star.

"Could that voice be all it promised? might that firmament grow dark
Where those star-looks had been treasured?—each a covenanting ark!

"Once my heart the question whispered, lowly, for I scarce could hear,
But I hurled the slander from me, though my spirit crouched for fear.

"Was it not some jealous demon that had crept into my mind?
Dare it crush so pure a passion? or was Love, indeed, so blind?

"Blind, alas! a frantic devil in my heart did stamp and rave,
Like a sightless Cyclop groping madly round his granite cave.

"Oh! from what a height of promise did my stricken spirit fall!
Crushed, and bleeding, and despairing, covered with a raven pall.

"For my heart's pure love was wasted, and my dreams a semblance bore,
To the disappointed moonlight, that convoys each wave ashore;

"Smiling on it in its worship, with a look divinely bland,
And while dreaming on its beauty sees it melt into the
sand.

"Love and Hope went forth together from the Eden of
my Heart,
At the gate they lingered, weeping, all unwilling to depart·

" But I drove them forth in sorrow, on their broken
faith to brood,
And I made my home with nature, for a time in solitude.

"I had sought the love of Woman, that pure joy that
heaven distils,
Better searched for Truth and found it, in the centenarian
hills.

" Better rent the solid granite for a heart of flesh and
blood,
Looked for passion in the iceberg's pulseless and con-
gealéd flood:

" Better these than hoped for love within that faithless
maiden's breast—
'Twas like driving out an Angel when my heart's dove
left its nest.

" Every radiant winged To-morrow hidden in the dis-
tant years,
Has its poise of joy and sorrow, has its freight of hopes
and fears.

"Every hour upon the dial, every sand-grain dropped by
            Time,
Quickens man, by useful trial, for his march to the
            sublime.

"Friendship's hands forever grasping, glad to meet and
            grieved to part;
Love, accursed, or blessed, clasping Woe or Gladness to
            its heart:

"Friendship hath a Jura-presence, thronéd like an Alp
            on high,
Love hath a diviner essence, for, like Truth, it cannot die!

"Thrice since then the Spring has parted from the Win-
            ter's cold embrace.
Thrice the birds in songs were thankful for the light of
            nature's face.

"Thrice the Summer flowers have blossomed on the
            summits of the hills,
Thrice the vales have leaped for gladness to the piping
            of the rills.

"Thrice the red-browed, sheavéd Autumn has lain down
            its golden store,
Like a blessed crop of bounty, on the thankful farmer's
            floor.

"And the passing of the seasons, with their yearly tide
            of wealth,
Braced my mind and flushed my features with a treble
            glow of health.

"Here among these hills eternal, Love and Hope have
    both returned,
Higher aims and wider feelings than of yore my bosom
    burned,

"Ever up my soul are rolling, with a hot Etnæan glow.
As the Eagle from his eyrie views the wide champaign
    below,

"So from this, my lofty station, 'mongst the mountains
    of my youth,
I look round and study Nature, God, and Man, and
    endless Truth."

———

  Blest is the heart whose love
Is fed from the deep fountains of the soul!
  It never can grow old—above
The highest heaven it wins its final goal.

  His mind grew royally,
His visions all were dowered with large hopes;
  Like to some fruitful tree,
His thoughts came crowned all regally; as opes

  The amber gates of Morn,
When through them pours from young Day's
    ardent soul,
  The Light of Love, sun-born:
So loomed his thoughts toward Fame's far-distant
    goal.

His heart was purified
By suffering, but desolate as the moon,
    That wanders far and wide,
By myriads of stars attended, yet alone.

    Some day the tongue of Fame
May bring the old world down upon its knees
    At mention of his name,
And he, be one of earth's divinities,

    With wise men at his feet
Sitting, and worshipping his wondrous speech!—
    Oh! human Love! replete
With Suffering and Truth, what heights through
    thee we reach!

LIGHT IN DARKNESS.

Oh! for the faintest glimmering of hope,
To gild the pinions of Uncertainty
Wherewith I mount to heaven's topmost cope,
To learn th' Eternal Will regarding thee!
No light! no light! a double darkness dread
Englooms my spiritual sense, as when
The midnight wraps her mantle o'er her head,
Shrouding her glories from the gaze of men.
Faith meets me midway up the starry slope,
And lo! the intense Darkness disappears,
And Charity comes smiling down the spheres
On whitest wing to meet us; and my ears
Drink in the heavenly words: "Give Reason scope,
Upheld by Faith, behold! how vast the Hope!"

RIDEAU LAKE.

A warm light permeates the sky,
A silvery mist is lingering nigh,
And floating up the trees near by.

A slumberous silence fills the air,
Silence upon the Lake, and where
The pines drop pearls from out their hair.

The birdlings have no voice to sing,
There's not a bird upon the wing,
Nature, herself, is slumbering.

Morning half opes her drowsy lid,
Her blue eyes 'neath the lashes hid
The Dawn's first kiss have gently chid.

And, Goddess-like, her couch she leaves,
Her golden hair about her weaves—
A Ruth among her autumn sheaves!

Up glides she through the welcoming skies,
A heaven of beauty in her eyes;
Gladness like light before her flies,

Cleaving the Twilight with a smile.
Fast speeds she many a golden mile,
Flinging around each purple isle

Of floating cloud a zone of light,
That widens in swift circles bright,
As the moon silvers o'er the night.

Until in the far-distant heaven
Her milk-white steeds are swiftly driven,
And darkness everywhere is riven

By the white-bosomed Maid of Day.
Morn puts aside her locks of gray,
On every hand the woods are gay.

Up leaps the sun's broad chest of fire,
Up swell the bird hymns—higher—higher,
Phœbus has loosed his forest choir.

A massive mirror seems the Lake,
A mirror that no force could break,
But which the tricksy zephyrs shake.

Shy teal of a quadruple hue,
The golden, green, the gray and blue,
Rise like bright fancies on the view.

The trees are green on either side,
Whole forests standing in their pride,
Steeping their shadows in the tide.

Islets are floating here and there,
Dreamy and languid, passing fair,
Tinted and limned with Artist-care.

Reposing like the Thoughts that lie
Within the meditative eye
Of youth—bright thoughts that never die.

Narcissus-like they stand, and seem
To watch their features in the stream,
Half indistinct, as in a dream.

Like forms Ideal, lo! they stand,
Huge mounds of airy-seeming land,
Fashioned by the Great Artist-hand.

Smiling, like children fresh from sleep
Bathing their soft limbs in the deep,
As from their early couch they leap.

Young, stately cedars, breathing love,
Pines, pointing to the far-above,
Flowers at their feet white as the dove.

Rocks, red-flushed in the ruddy morn—
Young Athlétes, browed with manly scorn,
White birches from their bosoms born.

O'er all, the broad Sun looking down,
O'er all the truant winds have blown,
The wavelets kiss the granite stone.

Visions of Beauty! Isles of light!
Your sunny verdure glads the sight,
Each living fir-tree seems a sprite.

The leaves like woodland pulses shake,
The plover whistles in the brake,
Wide Day sits crowned on Rideau Lake.

AURELIA.

Beautiful, and spirit-like,
  She stands before me now,
An infantine intelligence,
  With sweetness on her brow.
Her bright-blue eyes Elysian
Sparkle with some gentle vision
Of earliest human sinlessness,
Such as spirit forms might press,
With a soft and sweet caress,
To their souls of light and love,
In the heaven of heavens above.
Now these flashing orbs are swimming
  In a calmy sea of Thought,
  With a mystic glory fraught,
Silently but sweetly hymning
Many an anthem mild and holy,
Many a song, divine and lowly—
Hymns and anthems deeply teaching
  How immortal is the soul;
Thoughts, that are intently preaching
  Truths, as vast as those that roll
  Ceaselessly from pole to pole,
On the meteoric pinions
That spread light through night's dominions.

Here and there golden ringlets shadow
  Her fair brow with witching grace,

D

Like the sunlight on the meadow
   Beautifying nature's face,
When the fleecy clouds are sporting
   With the sunbeams as they fall,
Now athwart, now downward glancing,
   'Mongst the rich grain, ripe and tall.
I love the silken ringlets
   That kiss her snowy neck,
Like sun-flecks on a lily's leaf,
   A moral in each speck!
And her teeth of milky whiteness
   Peeping out between her lips,
Where they lie in playful ambush,
   Ever ready to reveal
Their intense and pearly brightness,
   Which the budding lips conceal,
   Lest their beauty should eclipse
The dimples on her cheeks that linger,
Pressed by nature's rosy finger.

Say not that the Fairy race
   Has disappearéd from earth;
Many a truly Fairy face
   Gladdens the domestic hearth.—
Household Fairies, gentle creatures,
Fairies both in mind and features:
Good and lovely Fairies they,
Leading us from day to day
Along earth's dazzling milky way—

The blushing, rose-strew'n path of Love,
  Which Fairies are forever treading,
  Step by step our fancies leading
To the milky way above:
Up and on above the stars—
Charming Venus—stately Mars,
To the realms that stretch eternal,
To the Throne of the Supernal!

  Such a Fairy is Amelia,
Such the gifted, fair Aurelia,
Fair and intellectual
As one on whom is set the seal
Of the Power Omnipotent,
On some useful mission sent:
  Such is Libby, in whose eye
Dwells the spirit of Ideality,
Sitting lost in deepest thought,
As if her young mind had caught
The spirit of a Guardian-angel
Claiming her for an Evangel,
Passing her pearly fingers fair
Through each tress of golden hair:
  Such is Hetty, midnight-eyed,
Nestling closely to my side,
Knowing that my heart must bless her,
Smiling if I once caress her;
Gazing on my studious face,
As I mark each separate grace,
From the boy-curls on her head,

To her lips, and all they said,
Every word an angel-lyric
Falling on my ears empiric:
   Such the pleasing, fond Louisa,
With her God-like memory,
And her gentle words and ways,
And her voice attuned to praise,
Setting the pulses of the heart
Throbbing, like a star at eve,
As its silver glances cleave
The dreamy quiet of the air;
And her soft cheeks' health tinge fair:
   Such the thoughtful Annie, too,
With her laughing eye of blue,
Dimpled cheek of healthy hue,
And her forehead, sculptor-like,
An eternal Truth, deep-set,
On a Thought-browed statuette,
Which its lips will never speak:
   Such is darling Caroline,
Through whose cheeks life's richest wine
Spreads like sunset's rosy glow
O'er some Alpine brow of snow;
One than whom no fairer—purer,
   Ever had a mortal birth,
Whose death would enrich heaven,
   And beggar earth:

These among the household train,
   Neriads from the deeps of love,

Guests from starry realms above,
Are so many Fairies sent,
Filled with love, and innocent,
Down to earth, to bless and gladden
Homes that sin and strife would sadden
With a more than earthly pain.

Fair Aurelia! bright Aurelia!
Favorite of the sunny brow,
An infantine Intelligence,
A child of light, art thou.
A spirit of the ærial Morn,
Or of Evening, bland with glory,
Like some Fairy Queen of story,
For whom Nature's hand had shorn
The bright locks from the glowing sun,
And stol'n the softness of the moon,
As their skyward course they run
At dewy midnight and at golden noon,
Giving to each an extra grace
For thy tresses and thy face.
Ha! a tear-drop in thine eye!
Like a star upon the sky,
Like a clear stalactité
Pendent o'er a summer sea,
Like a trembling dew-drop set
In an opening violet!
Not the Naiads of the Rivers,
Not the Fairies of the Hills,

SONNET.

Not the Nymph, whose sharp glance quivers
    From the leaflets and the rills,
Where the golden-manéd Rhine
Winds along its length supine,
Have a livelier glance than thine.
Come, then, to my heart's embrace,
Infant of the smiling face,
Come, with thy accents soft and winning,
That keep the human mind from sinning,
Give me back the love you stole,
And let me clasp thee to my soul!

SONNET.

Oh! let me gaze upon thy lustrous eyes,
As on the arbiters of my soul's destiny.
My Reason sways—without thee all is dark;
And my poor mind, like to a periled bark,
Looks toward thee as the mariner to the skies;
And looking on those orbs of light, I see
Two guiding stars that draw my soul to thee.
Save my endangered hopes—my shipwrecked fears,
As on the boundless ocean of suspense
They toss and tremble upon Danger's brink,
Above a gulf in which I seem to sink,
No arm outstretched to bear my spirit thence.
'T is the remembrance of thine eyes that cheers
My drooping spirit through the tedious years.

EVENING SCENE,

FROM THE BANKS OF THE DETROIT RIVER.

I stood upon a bank that faced the West,
   Beyond me lay Lake Erie, softly calm,
Calm as the thoughts that soothe the dying breast,
   As the Soul passes to the great I AM.

One solitary bird melodiously
   Trilled its sweet vesper from a grove of elm,
One solitary sail upon the sea
   Rested, unmindful of its potent helm.

There lay the Island with its sanded shore
   The snow-white Lighthouse, like an Angel-friend
Dressed in his fairest robes, and evermore
   Guiding the mariner to some promised end.

And down behind the forest trees, the sun,
   Arrayed in burning splendors, slowly rolled,
Like to some sacrificial urn, o'errun
   With flaming hues of crimson, blue and gold.

And round about him, fold on fold, the clouds,
   Steeped in some rainbow essence, lightly fell,
Draped in the living glory that enshrouds
   His nightly entrance to his ocean shell.

The woods were flashing back his gorgeous light,
   The waters glowed beneath the varied green,

Ev'n to the softened shadows, all was bright,
    Heaven's smile was blending with the view terrene.

The lofty woods, in summer sheen arrayed,
    The trembling poplar with its silver leaf,
The stately walnut rising o'er the glade,
    The willow bending with its load of grief:

The graceful elm, the energetic oak,
    The red-leaved maple, and the slender pine,
The grove of firs, half hidden by the smoke
    From the white cottage clothed with jessamine:

The thirsty cattle drinking from the spring,
    Or standing mid-deep in the sunny stream,
The stream itself, like Joy, meandering,—
    A silver shaft shot down a golden beam:

The ruddy orchard with its tempting fruit,
    The juicy apple, and the mellow pear,
The downy peach, and near the garden, mute
    With eager visions of a fruitful share,

Lolled the young urchin on his bed of grass,
    Thinking of Autumn, with her red-ripe store—
So Boyhood smiles to mark the seasons pass,
    And Manhood sighs that they return no more:

On these the parting Day poured down a flood
    Of radiant, unimaginable light,
Like as in some celestial spirit-dream
    A thousand rainbows melt upon the sight,

Setting the calm horizon all ablaze
  With splendors stolen from the crypts of heaven,
Dissolving with their magic heat the maze
  Of clouds that nestle to the breast of even.

The Fisher ceased his song, hung on his oars,
  Pausing to look, a pulse in every breath,
And, in imagination, saw the shores
  Elysian rising o'er the realms of Death.

And as he dreamed, the sunlight passed away,
  The stream gave back no deep cerulean hue,
Eve's purple finger closed the lips of Day,
  And a dim glory clothed the upper blue.

And down on tip-toe came the gradual Night,
  A gentle Twilight first, with silver wings,
And still from out the darkening infinite
  Came shadowy forms, like deep imaginings.

There was no light in all the brooding air,
  There was no darkness yet to blind the eyes,
But through the space interminable, there
  Nature and Silence passed in solemn guise.

GENTLE MARY ANN.

The artless and the beautiful,
  The fairest of the fair,
Around her shoulders clustering
  Her sunny, light-brown hair,
Her meek blue eye intelligent,
  God's wondrous works would scan,
And a smile would animate the face
  Of our Gentle Mary Ann.

The parted lip, betokening
  The peaceful soul within,
That soul as yet unsullied,
  Unendangered by a sin;
The brow where earnest thoughtfulness
  Some goodly work would plan,
Combined to make us idolize
  Our Gentle Mary Ann.

And thus for sixteen summers
  She grew upon our sight,
A patient girl of tenderness,
  A sinless child of light;
As free from worldly wilfulness
  As when her life began,
Was this, our lovely charge from heaven,
  Our Gentle Mary Ann.

The angels from their starry homes,
  Looked on her smiling face,

And beckoned our darling child
  Unto their resting-place;
When, lo! from out the graceful throng
  An infant cherub ran,
And nestled in the guileless breast
  Of our Gentle Mary Ann.

"Sister," she said, "we wait for thee,
  Yon angel host and I,
To bear thee in thy innocence
  To our dwelling in the sky."
The heavens, slowly opening,
  A psalm of love began,
And the cherub, pointing upwards,
  Said, "come, Gentle Mary Ann."

Calmly she faded from our sight,
  In that infant soul's embrace,
And we watched her passing upwards
  With a smile upon her face,—
Passing upward towards heaven,
  Upward to the Son of Man,
In whose bosom rests the spirit
  Of our Gentle Mary Ann.

DEATH OF THE OLD YEAR.

Old Year! Old Year! my pulsing heart
    Is struggling like a wretch in chains,
    I would fly with thee o'er the plains,
Old Year.—Old Year, we must not part.
      Cold blows the night wind on the wold,
      The starbeams, too, are falsely cold,
      The pale moon's boasted love is sold—
      Old Year, why hast thou grown so old!

Thou broughtest joy, thou broughtest woe,
    And there are hopes alive and dead,
    Thou broughtest faults of heart and head,
And yearnings purer than the snow.
      The plains are wide where thou would'st lead
      Me, barren as a lying creed,
      I cannot go, my heart would bleed—
      Old Year, why is thy fate decreed!

Thou hast struck down the bosom friend,
    That would have soothed our after years,
    And thou hast brought both smiles and tears,
And woes and blessings without end.
      Down come the snows, the night winds play,
      Like elves, through all thy locks of gray,
      Midnight is prone to bar thy way—
      Old Year, thou must not leave to-day!

Oh! motley life! Oh! checkered scene!
    A riddle-world of dreams and doubts,

DEATH OF THE OLD YEAR.

    We dare not trust our latest thoughts,
We nothing know but what has been!
      Moaneth the skies, like stricken souls,
      My practiced sense can hear the ghouls,
      Of centuries rushing from the poles—
      Old Year, what mean these spectral shoals!

And knowing nothing, we would cling
    Like beggars to thy garment's hem,
    Loose leaves upon a withered stem,
We fear what the next breath may bring.
    Old Year, thou'rt passing from my side,
    There is a bark upon the tide
    O'er which thy ghost prepar'st to ride—
    Old Year, put on thy ancient pride!

Oh! cold and heartless is the wind,
    And colder are the heartless stars,
    White Death within their icy cars,
And Darkness clambering up behind.
    The cold moon smiles more coldly still,
    Colder each frozen mount and hill,
    Bleak rolls the storm, the snow flakes chill—
    Old Year, why standest thou so still?

Why tremblest thou? Is Death so nigh?
    Where are the souls which thou hast made
    So happy? Are there none to aid?
Is there no help in all the sky!
    Gather thy garments close, Old Year,
    There is an end to all thy cheer,

A deep voice calls—dost thou not hear?
Farewell! for we must part, Old Year!

Gather thy robes about thy limbs,
    Remember thy ancestral fame,
    Pass bravely on to whence you came,
While shouts the storm its passion-hymns.
    So! thou hast vanished like a King,
    Thou hast found Death a living thing,
    To which brave souls most bravely cling—
    See! where he sits—a Spirit-King.

DESPONDENCY.

There is a sadness o'er my spirit stealing,
A flash of fire up-darting to my brain,
Sowing the seeds—and still the seeds concealing—
That are to ripen into future pain.
I feel the germs of madness in me springing,
Slowly, and certain, as the serpent's bound,
And my poor hopes, like dying tendrils clinging
To the green oak, tend surely to the ground;
And Reason's grasp grows feebler day by day,
As the slow poison up my nerves is creeping,
Ever and anon through my crushed heart leaping,
Like a swift panther darting on its prey;
And the bright taper Hope once fed within,
Hath waned and perished in the rueful din.

THE VOICE OF GOD.

When o'er the cloud-veiled face of heaven
    The far-resounding thunders roll,
When the impending cloud is riven,
    And the lightning leaps from its fiery goal,
The strong earth totters, and the mountains nod,
And nature trembles at the Voice of God.

    That Voice at whose command
Chaos recoiled; and Night, that long had kept
Her gloomy wings outspread, arose and crept—
Like to a guilty thing—into the deep;
    That caused the earth to leap
From its firm anchorage, where it lay
In hidden embryo—a confuséd heap—
And fashioned it with an invisible hand
Into a lovely world; that called the Day,
To banish thence the blackest shades of Night,
And flood the world with heaven-borrowed light;
That Voice which, from the top of Sinai,
In thunder spake the sacred law divine;
At whose presence the mount—the sky—
Glowed bright, illumined by the lightning's fire,
Almighty Love revealed—Almighty Ire!

    The birds that wing their flight
Through the blue skies, or in the sacred groves
Assemble, to rehearse their songs of love,
Or chirp their mellow notes with sweet delight;

They sing His praise,—
And as their thrilling lays
Float through the summer skies,
Attending spirits bear the strains to heaven.
What songs more worthy to be sung above
Than those which God hath given
To the blythe choristers! 'Tis but the Voice
Of God that breathes in theirs;
And their sweet minstrelsies are but the prayers,
The orisons, of sinless breasts, that rise
In music-whispers from the stately trees,
Like worship-incense borne upon the morning breeze.

Look forth into the Night!
Then, most, His Voice in regal silence speaks
To the observant man.
The wondrous heavens scan—
The infinitude of worlds that gleam
Like God-Thoughts flung athwart the gloom, and beam
Effulgent glory on the slumberous earth.
Is there a wish within thy soul that seeks
To know whence they derived their mystic birth?
From what vast source divine,
Like jewels from the mine,
They sprang, ablaze with their redundant light,
While angels sped from orb to orb, and viewed
The gleaming worlds, where all was solitude;
And awed to silence, gazed with wonder on
Each blazing planet and impassioned sun;

Saw the swift meteor urge its burning car
Adown the breathless silences afar,
And watched the advent of each new-born star,
Bursting the blue enamel of the sky,
As it came clothed with splendor from on high,
Launched on its errand of infinity!
Oh! with what aching rapture throbs the sight!
What saith my questioning soul! A Voice Supreme
Strikes like swift sunlight through my ether-dream,
Whispering that these innumerous worlds of light,
Before the foot of man this earth had trod,
Were called from Chaos by the Voice of God!

   But stay not here.
Hark to the psalmy voices of the winds
   That sweep the pathless ocean!
   Look around!—
How the waves moan above the mariner's bier!
Ere this the monsters of the deep have found
His stiffened corse; but the wild wave finds
Another, still another, victim for its rage.
There is a Voice speaks from the chainless winds,
That ceaseless warfare with the billows wage,
Making more terrible their wild commotion.
   There is a voice in every wave;
Whether it swells in anger o'er the grave
Of some poor, shipwrecked mariner, or swims
In gentle ripples on the ocean's breast;
   Or in deep thunder hymns
Its praise tempestuous ere it sinks to rest,

Glutted and surfeited, though not oppressed.
There is a Voice in everything;
There's not a living atom but doth sing
The praise of the Almighty, and rejoice
Beneath His Smile, or tremble at His Voice.

THE FINE OLD WOODS.

Oh! come, come away to the grave Old Woods,
    Ere the skies are tinged with light,
Ere the slumbering leaves of the gloomy trees,
    Have shook off the mists of Night;
        Ere the birds are up,
        Or the floweret's cup
    Is drained of its freshening dew,
        Or the bubbling rill,
        Kissing the hill,
Breaks on the distant view;
        Oh! such is the hour
        To feel the power
Of the quiet, grave Old Woods.
    Then, while sluggards dream,
    Of some dismal theme,
        Let us stroll,
        With prayerful soul,
Through the depths of the grave Old Woods.

Oh! come, come away to the bright Old Woods,
    As the sun ascends the skies,

THE FINE OLD WOODS.

While the birdlings sing their morning hymns,
    And each leaf in the grove replies;
        When the golden-zoned bee,
        Flies from flower to tree,
    Seeking sweets for its honied cell,
        And the Voice of Praise
        Sounds its varied lays,
    From the depths of each quiet dell:
        Oh! such is the hour
        To feel the power
    Of the magic, bright Old Woods!
        Then, while sluggards dream,
        Of some trifling theme,
           Let us stroll,
           With studious soul,
Through the depths of the bright Old Woods.

Oh! come, come away to the mild Old Woods,
    At the Evening's stilly hour,
Ere the maiden lists for her lover's steps,
    By the verge of the vine-clad bower;
        When all nature feels
        The change that steals
    So calmly o'er hill and dale,
        And the breezes range
        Weirdly strange,
    With a low, delicious wail:—
        This, too, is the hour
        To feel the power

Of the silent, mild Old Woods!
Then, while dullards dream
Of some fruitless theme,
We will stroll
With thankful soul,
Through the depths of the mild Old Woods.

Oh! come, come away to the calm Old Woods,
When the skies with stars are bright,
And the mild Moon moves in serenity,
The eye of the solemn night.
Not a sound is heard,
Save the leaflet stirred
By the zephyr that passes by,
And thought roams free
In its majesty,
And the soul seeks its kindred sky:
This, this is the hour
To test the power
Of the eloquent, calm Old Woods!
While the thoughtless dream
Of some baseless theme,
Here we can stroll,
With exalted soul,
Through the eloquent, calm Old Woods.

ELEGY,

IN MEMORY OF THE REV. ROBERT D. CARTWRIGHT.

As sinks the sun at evening in the west,
    A flood of God-like glory o'er his head,
So sank that pious christian to his rest,
    While unseen Watchers triumphed round his bed.

Gently as bursts the new-born moth to light,
    So pass'd that dove-like spirit from its clay,
Pass'd like an infant sleeping, on that night
    When his loved Master summoned it away.

And there was silence through the deep midnight,
    A joyful silence 'mongst the stars, that shone
Serenely on that passing spirit's flight,
    As through their myriad hosts it journeyed on.

And there was silence round the Throne of God,
    Such Silence as can only be in Heaven,
When that meek, evangelic spirit, trod
    The pathway closed against the unforgiven.

And Grief sat pale on many a face that day,
    Both rich and poor bewailed his early death;
Those whom that earnest Pastor taught to pray
    Sobbed forth their heavy loss with broken breath.

And round the city passed from tongue to tongue,
    The mournful loss the people had sustained,

But on each lip, in contradiction, hung
    The blessed change his deathless spirit gained.

Never again throughout St. George's aisle
    Will that clear voice the Gospel thunders hurl,
Never again will he, with christian smile,
    The Gospel Banner of the Cross unfurl.

Never again the dying sinner's ear
    Will drink the words of promise from his lips,
That burned with earnestness to light and cheer
    The soul departing from the mind's eclipse.

But in our hearts each word is treasured up,
    The mild reproof, the invitation strong
To drink salvation from the proffered cup,
    The soul's exultant being to prolong.

And as the germs of Hope in every heart
    Pulsate and quicken with our latest breath,
So will the memory of his words impart
    A blest assurance to our minds in death.

MORNING IN SUMMER.

Darkness has disappeared, and all the stars,
Save one, have ceased to twinkle in the heavens.
Like some lone sentinel, whose comrades all
Have sunk into luxurious repose,
This solitary orb remains behind
    To greet the Morn, a silent, truthful witness,

Ordained by the Creator to attest
To the first dawning of another day,
Of every day throughout the lengthened year.
The silver Dawn flies up the dusky slope,
Like a white dove emerging from a cloud;
Morning imprints its first impassioned kiss
Upon the Orient's lips, her rose-hued cheeks
Blushing with love, and all her being moved
With heart-beats mighty as the throes of Jove.

With what a Queen-like dignity the Morn
Emerges, smiling, from her perfumed bath,
Like a young Goddess from a Marriage-feast,
Or Angel, pregnant with some mighty Truth,
Whose promulgation will illume the world.
How like a universal glory, crowned
With radiance from the primal fount of light,
She comes, a native, heaven-born dignity
Stamped with a hand divine upon her brow.
The lingering shades of sable-featured night,
Like phantoms startled at their parting dance,
Careering round the brightening horizon,
Slowly retire, abashed. Upward they glance,
Feebly at first, those beams of Day-drawn light,
But gathering strength from Morning's glad approach,
Like Beauty ripening in the smile of Love.

Oh! blessed Morn! sweet hour of many prayers,
Of the deep worship of a million souls!
The fair Child lisping at its mother's knee

Its infant thankfulness; the Maiden's vows
Of meek devotion to a Godly life;
Religion from the breast of Womanhood
Welling in silver accents to her lips,
Like the rich purlings of a bubbling spring;
The voice of sober Manhood, calling down
The love of heaven on a fallen world;
The rapt Enthusiast with panting heart,
And lips that move not for his solemn thoughts,
Worshipping in the temple of his love,
And stretching out his soul's arms unto God!
Oh! blessed Morn! we love thee for thy Prayers!

Behold the God-like Sun! all life and light
Awaking with him in the gorgeous East.
How victor-like his chariot mounts the skies!
How many million hearts he fills with joy.
How wakens Nature at his solemn tread.
How the groves throb with music of the birds.
How musical the pine trees on the hill.
How glad the bright-eyed flowerets of the vale.
How lightly bound the zephyrs o'er the seas,
Like Nymphs awakened by his magic glow
In their cool grottoes underneath the wave.
How like a mighty God, in whose great heart
Burns the strong incense of Eternal Love.
How like a fearless conqueror, whose steps
All nature strews with flowers, and glory gleams,
And passion hymns, and protestations deep

Of due submission to his regal will.
Oh! what a march of triumph, Sun! is thine!
How full of hidden mystery to us
Thy everlasting round of burning toil,
Thy rising and thy setting; and the light
Wherewith thou startlest the rejoicing stars!
What triumph and what passion, Sun! are thine.

Who filled the measure of thy beams, Oh! Sun?
Who took thee from the flaming womb of night,
To be a wonder to all coming time?
Who opened up the fountains of thy light?
Who fashioned thee with splendor and with strength,
And sent thee forth on thy victorious way?
What star first paled to thy superior light?
What human eye first drooped beneath thy gaze?
What human voice first broke upon thine ear?
What spot of Earth first felt thy warming rays?
Who held thee o'er the Vale of Ajalon,
And made thee crown the victor's brow with smiles?
For every beat of thy strong pulse, Oh! Sun!
A human prayer ascends from earth to God.

If through the ocean wave he rolls his disc,
The gloomy deep awakens from its dream,
Puts all its golden decorations on,
And robes itself in costliest attire;
Like an old veteran with honored scars,
Obtained in many a hard-contested fight,
Placing his golden honors on his breast,

Ere going forth with pride to meet his king.
The hardy mariner, whose home is on
The perilous wave, o'erjoyed at his return,
Reflects on those for whom his prayerful thoughts,
Rude and unshaped, were hourly offered up,
During the midnight watch, to Him who holds
The reins of every billow in His hand,
And guides the watery mountains at His will.
Or if upon the lofty promontory
Falls his resplendent lustre, the rough crags
Sparkle like coronets inlaid with gems
Of priceless value and of beauty rare.
The glowing trees their gold-green tints assume,
As from their boughs extended drops the dew
In showers refreshing on the moistened grass;
While the young peasant, by some winding path,
Follows his flocks to rich, green pasture lands
Upon the plain beneath. The sportive lambs
Frisk round the glad old ewe, delighted with
The kindly Morn that crowns their liberty,
And bids the shepherd open wide the fold,
That they may sport upon the dewy fields;
In balmy valleys; or on healthy hills,
Where the delicious breeze, in cooling draughts,
Fresh from the lake below, in silence floats
Upon the morning air, reviving all
O'er which its animating breath is borne.

  The rosy peasant girl, with joyous heart,
And health's warm sunshine crimsoning her cheek,

Diligently performs her morning task,
Tending the flocks that answer to her call,
And crowd around her anxious to receive
The dainty morsel from her willing hands.
Some little yeanling nearer than the rest
Approaches, and with cunning look receives
The chosen mite, its mistress' daily gift.
The husbandman, whose sunburned countenance
Proves that his daily labor's well performed,
Repairs with manly bearing to the fields,
And enters on his task with cheerfulness.
The noble steed that drags the blessed plough,
Refreshed, and full of vigor and new life,
Shews no reluctance to begin again
The toil of yesterday; the night has eased
His stiffened joints, and given him new strength,
To aid the Farmer in his arduous work.
Thus they, like two industrious friends, pursue
Their early labor, ev'n before the sun
Has waked the purple hills. The woods long since
Have echoed back the minstrelsy of birds;
The challenge of some proud young chanticleer;
His stately rival's answer, loudly tongued;
The watchful mastiff's bark; or tremblingly
Shook from their leaves the dew, as the strong youth
Discharged his rifle at some passing deer.

Hark to the footsteps of the Iron Horse!
The valley vibrates to his sounding hoofs,

The sombre forests thunder back his tread,
And startled Echo, from the stubborn rock
And grassy hill-sides, rushes forth to greet
The mighty traveller on his early round.
Shrieks the wild whistle in yon forest glen!
Its shrill reverberations leaping through
The answering uplands, and the playful woods,
Pleased, flinging back the scream.—With sudden start,
The puzzled cattle, grazing on the slope,
Or drinking at the spring, erect their ears
In mute astonishment; and at the doors
Of the log cottages, that here and there
Indent the landscape, the coy maiden stands,
With the pleased matron and swart husbandman,
Attracted by the sound. Anon he comes,
The massive giant, his o'erheated sides
Reeking with sweat, and from his nostrils wide
His heavy breathings issuing, in a cloud
Of boiling vapor. Swiftly he glides past,
Shuffling with half-majestic carelessness,
With haughty ease, and time-defying pace,
Until his race is run. Behold him now,
Pawing the ground, impetuous in his haste
To end his swift career. The glowing sun
Glints on his polished sides, and strikes the earth,
In vain attempts to pierce his iron mail,
Or gild his solid mane. Before him flies
The haggard creature Want, and stores of Wealth
Come tackled to his heels. Through every town

And village where he speeds his noisy way,
Gladness appears; the primal wilderness
Awakes to active life; the yeomen smile;
And woodmen-heroes who have battled with
The stubborn forests cheer him on his way.
For to the toiling husbandman he brings
A mine of wealth; his path is strewn with gold;
His whole career is onward, like the march
Of a great conqueror; and by his strength
He rushes boldly through the serried ranks
Of the deep forest; ignorance disappears;
Barrenness flies, screaming, to the ridgy steep,
And Civilization triumphs in his wake.

Stand on the quiet margin of the lake,
And listen to the homely melody
Of the rough Fisherman, as he impels
His deeply-laden craft toward the shore.
Many a sleepless, toilsome night he spends,
Watching his crafty nets, or wielding well
The bearded spear, as his long-practiced eye
Sees by the flaming torch-light, far beneath
The bosom of the water his sure prey,
Which soon leaps, struggling in its agony,
Into the leaky bark. Exposed to storms,
The pestilential vapors of the night,
Dripping with spray, and bending 'neath fatigue,
The uncomplaining fisherman endures
With patience all the ills of his hard life,

Too happy if each morning's sunlight smiles
Upon his homeward way, to cheer him on
To the embrace of his expectant wife,
And the sweet kisses of his infant flock.

And now, 'tis past the meditative hour,
When first the sun above the highest hills
Uprears his crest, whence the warm golden floods
Of heavenly light their diff'rent stations take,
To spread the joyful tidings round the world.
The holy silence of the earlier morn
Is broken by the sounds of active life
That everywhere attract the attentive ear.
Morn's rosy hues, such as are seen upon
The cheek of Beauty, or the happy face
Of Childhood, dimpled with unnumbered smiles
Séraphic, now no longer please the eye,
But the broad light of Day extends o'er all,
And Morning's softest loveliness is lost,
As the day gradually travels on
To the oppressive hour of scorching Noon.

PASSWORD—"TRUTH IS MIGHTY."

Stand not on the Alps of Error,
  Brother, though the tempting height
Lure thee to the grassy hill-top,
  Though the view enchant the sight;

But if sorely tempted thither,
  In some hour of gilded woe,
Stand, and gaze around thee, Brother,
  On the Vale of Truth below.

Watch th' Enchantress from the summit,
  See her wave her golden wand,
Till the far-illumined valley
  Seems a heaven-enchanted land.
Mark the crowds of glowing faces,
  That compose her endless train,
'Till that white-robed, shining army,
  Fills the undulating plain.

Mark their gorgeous banners waving,
  Listen to the peaceful hymn
Pealing from the countless millions,
  Like the song of Seraphim.
Gently toward the blackened summit,
  Where seductive Error stands,
March that Sin-invading army,
  From the pleasant valley lands.

"Truth is Mighty!" shout the foremost,
  "Truth is Mighty!" rends the plain,
Echoes through the mountain-gorges,
  Vibrates over land and main.
And the hill-tops melt before them,
  One by one they disappear,
As their watchword—"Truth is Mighty!"
  Strikes the universal ear.

"Truth is Mighty!" and the valley
  "O'er the hills is seen to rise,
Higher through the sun-lit heavens,
  Till it seems to reach the skies.
"Truth is Godlike!" "Truth is Mighty!"
  Now resound through all the air,
As the mountain-peaks of Error
  Shrink away and disappear.

Not an arm is raised in anger,
  Smiles on every face are seen,
They but breathe upon the mountain,
  On its blackened sides and green :
It has vanished, like a cloudlet
  Penetrated by the sun,
Vanished to the dark abysses
  Of the greatest Evil One.

THE WHIRLWIND.

It comes with its swift, destructive tread,
  It tosses the waves on high,
And it hurries away where the lightnings play,
  Through the black and frowning sky ;
And the weeping clouds are madly driven
By its violent breath, o'er the face of heaven.

It leaps through the woods in its fearless flight,
  Uprooting the firm-set trees ;

And it shivers the trunk of the kingly oak,
  That had long defied the breeze;
Hurling down, in its furious mirth,
  These tough and sturdy limbs to earth.

Away it flies, with a maniac howl,
  To the mountains' dismal height,
And it lifts the rocks from their granite beds,
  By the force of its giant might;
Waking the birds from their brief repose,
And spreading dismay where'er it goes!

ELIZABETH'S BIRTH.

At Elizabeth's birth Love's fair Goddess presided
  O'er a quorum of dames in her high court above;
On the child's future gifts all were strangely divided,
  And contentions ran high through that Chamber of Love.

"I claim her," said Beauty, "her cheeks are as roses,
  Her brow as the Parian marble is fair;
And see these sweet dimples! in each one reposes
  A sting for intrusion, a balm for despair."

"She is mine! she is mine!" said the Goddess of Pleasure,
  "What heart-thrilling looks are concealed in her eyes!
She shall revel in joys and delights without measure,
  Such as seldom are felt in our own sunny skies."

E *

The Goddess of Mirth, her gay voice loudly ringing
  Through the golden-roofed arches of that solemn court,
Laid claim to the sleeper, now laughing, now singing,
  Uniting with Pleasure to furnish her sport.

Like the first purple flush of the warm light of Morning,
  That tinges the east with its mellowy hue,
The Goddess of Smiles, that rich chamber adorning,
  In ravishing sweetness arose on the view.

And pointing with joy to the innocent sleeper,
  Her eyes filled with radiance, her looks all divine,
Said, in musical accents, "She's mine! I will keep her
  'Neath my sheltering wing—She is mine! she is mine!"

As Venus, her wand in the air gently waving,
  Approvingly tendered the gift to the child,
A shower of sunlight came down, gently laving
  The innocent's face, and Elizabeth smiled.

The Angel of Goodness her watch had been keeping,
  Unperceived by the lovely disputants till now,
And softly approaching the infant while sleeping,
  Gently placed her fair seal on the slumberer's brow.

But Cupid, who'd witnessed the scene from his bower,
  Now tendered his claim, with so artful a grace,
That his mother, embracing him, gave him the power
  To mix Love with the Smiles on Elizabeth's face.

HENRY'S GRAVE.

Standing beside the consecrated mound,
   That marked the narrow grave wherein he lay,
I thought upon the Trumpet's welcome sound,
   That would arouse him in the latter day.

I thought of the young spirit, that had fled
   Beyond the keenest search of human eye—
Beyond the limits of a world of dread—
   Beyond the reach of man's philosophy.

And as I strove to lift the distant veil—
   To track the spirit in its upward flight—
My mind was awed—my vision seemed to fail,
   And all became confused as blackest night!

I was an atom of mere mortal mould,
   Too weak to pierce the depths that soul had trod;
Backward to earth my wandering senses rolled,
   And my eye rested on the crumbling sod—

Part of myself—poor perishable clay!
   The child whose corse beneath my feet did lie,
Was, like myself, but mortal, yesterday,
   And now, a dweller with the blest on high!

Oh! Mystery of Mysteries! Oh, Death!
   I sit and muse in deep solemnity,
And wonder how the dust that perisheth
   Must pass to life eternal but through thee!

SNOW DROPS.

Gently fall the snow flakes
  From the clouds above,
Noiselessly and joyously
  As the breath of love,
Noiseless in their gaiety,
  Gentle in their mirth,
As they spread their robes of purity
  Softly o'er the earth.

Beauteous types of Innocence!
  Delicately fair
As the thoughts of Angels
  Hov'ring in the air:
Not less pure and innocent
  Is each little dove,—
Each joyous, sparkling snow-drop
  In the cot of Love.

Yes, prattling little Children!
  Germs of Love are ye,
Spotless as the snow-drops,
  Hearts as pure and free,
Oh! guard them in their innocence,
  Ye to whom are given
These fairy human snow-drops,
  Gifts from Love's own Heaven.

PRETTY FACES.

I could gaze on pretty faces,
  Mark their sweetness all day long;
Though they vied not with the Graces,
  They should mingle with my song.
  Where the lips are slightly pouting,
    Where the full, dark eye, is bright—
Bright and soft as morn and even—
    Bright and dark as noon and night:
    Pretty faces! pretty faces
      Having such delights as these,
    Though they be not perfect Graces,
      Often conquer, often please.

I have gazed on pretty faces,
  Marked their sweetness by the hour,
Searching out the hidden traces
  Of their deep, mysterious power.
  Where the brow is that of Woman,
    Whereon Thought is throned serene,
  Where the eyes deep truths are speaking,
    And the lips in smiles are seen:
    Pretty faces! pretty faces
      Having such fair gifts as these,
    Though they be not perfect Graces
      Always conquer, always please.

BEYOND THE GRAVE.

Shall we not meet in heaven, love,
  And know each other there?
Endearing thought! joy cheaply bought!
  Why should we then despair?
Why grieve to bid farewell to those
  Whom Death removes away!
When we shall meet in brighter worlds,
  Where love has no decay.

But shall we know each other there,
  In that elysian clime?
Consoling thought—to live—to love—
  Through never-ending time!
Hope points to such a God-like gift,
  Within the All-wise decree;
Then let me break my earthly bonds,
  And fly, my love, to thee.

CANADIAN SLEIGH SONG.

Tinkle, tinkle, tinkle,
  Merrily, merrily, O,
Chime the tuneful sleigh bells,
  Singing to the snow;
Tinkle, tinkle, tinkle,
  Merrily, merrily, O,
Laughs the dimpled Maiden,
  Chatting to her beau.

Tinkle, tinkle, tinkle,
  Merrily, merrily, O,
What is glorious Winter
  Without frost and snow?
Time may cast a shadow
  O'er us as we go,
But let us, like the sleigh bells,
  Sing, Merrily, Merrily, O.

Tinkle, tinkle, tinkle,
  Merrily, Merrily, O,
Life is but a sleigh-drive
  Through the frost and snow;
Ever are we learning
  This one truth as we go:
All sadness without sunlight
  Is like Winter without snow.

PITY'S TEAR DROP.

As Pity looked down from on high,
  So smilingly, sweetly, and meek,
A tear-drop that stood in her eye
  Fell on a Drunkard's cheek.

Astonished, he looked above,
  Not a star overhead could he see;
He said: "'T is a tear-drop of love
  Shed by Ella for me."

For he thought of the wife of his youth,
  Of the heart he had broken when won;
And that tear-drop conveyed a reproof
  For the spirit his crimes had undone.

His feelings were seared by the thought,
  Heaven's sunlight had entered his soul,
One of Pity's bright tear-drops had wrought
  A deep-seated hate of the bowl.

Oh! deal not unjustly severe
  With the Drunkard you meet in your path,
For Pity does more by a Tear,
  Than the strong can accomplish in wrath.

ANNIE BY MY SIDE A SITTING.

Annie by my side a sitting,
  Looks intently on my face,
Does she watch the shadows flitting
  From their secret lurking place?
  Where they hide and sit apart
  In the dim depths of my heart,
  Where Hope's sunlight never cometh,
  Where Love's red Rose never bloometh!

Does she deem me cold—unfeeling—
  That I never press her cheek?
From my dull self never stealing
  For a moment, week by week!

ANNIE BY MY SIDE A SITTING.

Is it wonder? Is it love?
Would she bring me back the dove
That my soul so humbly cherished?—
Had it staid, it must have perished!

Little knows she the devotion
  Of my heart of hearts is hers,
Purest is the calmy ocean,
  Truth has silent worshippers!
  Annie sitting by my side,
  Knows not all the love I hide,
  Though my fond looks never sun her,
  Though I seldom smile upon her.

Her blue eyes are vaguely searching
  For a glance of Love's return,
But my thoughts are closely perching
  On my dead love's funeral urn.
  And I read her patient look,
  As a scholar reads a book,
  Gleaning pearls from all its pages,
  Thought-pearls from the brains of sages.

Annie by my side a sitting,
  Gazing mildly on my face,
Cannot see the shadows flitting
  From their secret lurking-place,
  Where they dimly sit apart
  In the cloud-folds of my heart,
  Weeping over hopes once cherished,
  Moaning for the dove that perished.

THE NAME OF MARY.

Of all the names that ever pass'd
   The lips of woman, child, or fairy,
The gentlest, and most sweetly chaste,
   Is that of MARY.

Yet not too gentle to be loved
   By men whose nerves were nerves of iron;
How deeply—tenderly—it moved
   The haughty Byron!

Tom Moore, Corypheus of Song!
   In verse and love no mean empiric,
How gracefully it floats along!
   His beauteous lyric!

Great Burns, the Ploughman-Bard, whose muse
   Was swayed by a more rustic fancy,
Unlike your parlor-bards, could choose
   The homelier Nancy.

But in his most inspired hour,
   Passing the beauties of the dairy,
He struck that note of solemn power
   To her—his Mary!

MARY! sweet name with virtue clothed,
   By dreamy-minded dilettanti,
A sound that might have charmed and soothed
   The gloomy Dante.

Or held in its divine control,
   Bringing it healing balm when weary,
The wild, impassioned Poet-soul
   Of Alfieri.

'T is true we read of, and despise
   The sighing of a certain varlet,
Werther, who sorrowed for the eyes
   Of queenly Charlotte:

We hear, too, of the Trojan brawl
   That the majestic Paris fell in
With Greece, and famed Achilles, all
   For faithless Helen:

We read, with virtuous amaze,
   Of good Queen Bess and Leicester, or a
Petrarch inditing Canzonas
   To nun-like Laura:

And every day or two, we find
   How foplings drain the poisoned chalice—
Fools! perilling their grain of mind
   For Grace or Alice!

We know that there are names that please
   The varied tastes of man and woman—
Ruth, Annie, Nora, are of these,
   All fair and common:

Most welcome, though, to English ears,
   Fit for throned Queen or graceful Fairy,

Is that sweet household word that bears
    The sound of—MARY!

It mingles with our childhood's games,
    It chastens either birth or bridal;
Mary!—to me the very name's
    A perfect Idyl.

THE KNEELING HEART.

When Evening folds her wings of light,
    And bathes her rosy cheeks in dew,
And one pale star proclaims the night,
    From its exalted throne of blue:
My soul! how eager hast thou leaped,
    Cribbed and imprisoned as thou art,
    To be of these a shining part,
In their ethereal essence steeped!
And on this altar, on this heart of clay,
Hast offered sacrifice, and bore away
An incense sweet of Prayer above that starry ray.

When Night flings wide her ebon gates,
    And Darkness, like a flood, pours in,
Shewing the star-born choir that waits
    Its psalm seraphic to begin:
How hast thou caught their burning words,
    That never fall on worlding ears,
    Hast filched the hymning of the spheres,

As it was swept from nature's chords;
Hast known and felt that every ray of light
Brings to our ears a portion of that bright
And star-lipped anthem that pervades the solemn night.

When o'er the everlasting hills
　　The golden Morning soars sublime,
And Day's triumphant Pæan fills
　　The heavens, as in that primal time
When first the birds rehearsed their songs
　　In groves by Angels' visits blest:
　　　Worshipping Soul! some heavenly guest
To thy diviner moods belongs!
In the old Forest, with the whispering trees,
Morn, Eve and Night, thou learnest melodies,
Extracts sweet music from the warbling breeze,
Thou hast my heart forever on its bended knees!

AUTUMN.

Oh! the bright days of Autumn? how they sink
Like dreams of beauty fanned by heaven's airs,
Deep, deep into the mind. There is a soft
And holy feeling floating through the skies,
The breathings of an Angel-troupe that comes
With noiseless footsteps and on wings of love,
To fill the soul with joy. The bay is calm,
And mellowed with the sunbeams of the morn:
God smiling on the mirror of the skies,

Where the light clouds, the stars, and the mad moon
Gaze at their own strange beauty, and the sun
Flings down his amorous breathings, passionate
As a wild lover with a great fond soul,
Drinking his mistress' smiles 'neath distant skies,
While she, at home, sits thinking of his love—
Absent, but ever present. Here an isle,
With one tall tree to sentinel the place,
Floats languidly upon the sleeping wave,
Tinting the water with innumerous hues,
Each little fretful wave kissing its feet,
And toying with the shrubs that drop their leaves
Like playthings on its pearly lips. The marsh,
Like to an indolent sluggard, has lain down
Beneath its faded covering, to dream
Of a long rest: its putrid breath no more
Poisons the air with a malarian stench,
Inducing fevers that burn up the frame,
As the hot summer burns the parchéd leaf—
The purifying air of Autumn has passed o'er
The feverish waste, and given it new health,
E'en in its swift decay; as the free'd soul
Ascends to heaven when the body dies.
The stately bulrush rears its dark brown head
Above the sedgy waste; the water-hen,
Surrounded by her noisy brood, doles forth
Her inharmonious notes; the piping snipe,
The golden plover, and the slender crane,
With here and there a pair of watchful teal,

Seek nourishment from the decaying sedge;
As the rank soil the putrid mass receives
That gives a quickened impulse to its veins.

   The wind blows fresh upon the distant lake,
But here the breezes whisper; through the air
Ambrosial mists are breathed. Nature's great heart
Beats feebly in her old maternal breast,
And balmy sighs, and moanings, keen but weak,
Are heard far-wandering through the aged woods.
Sadly she grieves for the departed flowers;
Sadly she sings the requiem of the leaves,
As they come fluttering down, like withered hopes
Leaving poor shipwrecked youth all cold and bare,
Exposed to the sharp breath of a hard world,
Shuddering, and sick at heart. The red, round sun,
Shorn of his flaming locks, stands in the east,
Like a proud steed divested of its strength,
Stands like a king who has put off his crown,
And lain aside the duties of the state
For a brief season; and the passing clouds
Sport with his rubicund face, and fling a veil
Of melancholy beauty o'er his brow.
Yon group of trees upon the faded bank,
Spreading their broad deep shadows on the wave,
Gaze in the water at their roots, and watch
The gradual fading of their summer-green,
As Autumn, the rich fancy dyer, comes,
Puts on his motley, Joseph-coat of leaves,

And steeps them all in hues of gold and brown,
And glowing scarlet, yellow, green, and dun—
Bright favorite of the undulating shore.
The village church peers o'er the grove of pines
And stunted hickory, on the barren hill;
In the stripped orchard the old Homestead stands,
Above the hazy bank, like a white tent
Seen through the picturesque openings of the trees,
And in the garden a serene old man,
With silvered locks, but mind yet unimpaired,
Strolls to inhale the renovating air,
That gives a healthy vigor to the morn.
A rural cottage in the distance shrinks,
Like a coy blossom, nursed among the grass,
Blushing and trembling at the intrusive steps
Of the young zephyrs; and two golden fields
Slope to the limestone shore, denuded of
Their wavy tresses, by the reapers shorn.—
The pines are green as in their summer days,
Although the oaks are yellow in the vale—
Their strength avails not, Autumn strips them bare.
As a nation strips a Ruler of his badge,
Which he has worn with honor, to make way
For others who are covetous of place;
But the green pine lives on the highest hills,
And wears a youthful freshness all the year,
As the pure soul whose thoughts are ever green
Lives nearest God. Go, man! into the woods,
And watch the multitudinous mass of leaves

Passing from life to death. These are the fruits
That nature gathers for her sustenance,
As they fall ripe and mellow at her feet,
Fit to be garnered in. Behold them sink
Resistless to the ground, and as thy foot
Crushes their withered stems, think of their fall
As emblematic of thy Autumn days,
And of succeeding years, when other feet
Will tread as recklessly upon thy grave,
As thine upon the melancholy leaves.

REMEMBRANCES.

There are remembrances that sear the brain,
There are sweet thoughts of other times, that wing
Their dove-like passage o'er the mind, and bring
Returning peace, and musings free from pain.
I have distinct remembrances of thee,
That fall upon me with a leaden weight,
Revealing days of past anxiety;
And then, again, calm visions, that recall
Far holier joys than Fancy can create.
Indeed, I deem these bright realities
Ofttimes, for they seem breathing ecstacies
Of present bliss passing before mine eyes.
Painful and calm, Remembrance hoards them all,
Their various teachings I dare not despise.

LITTLE ANNIE.

How mildly passed her second birth,
  How sweet the assurance given:
One Angel less upon the Earth,
  One Spirit more in Heaven!
We knew she was a tender flower,
  Dropped, but not planted here,
And, knowing, feared the coming hour,
  Too bitter for the tear
That Grief itself had not the power
  To shed upon her bier.

We watched her with her pleasing smile,
  The first that kissed her mouth,
Like sunlight on some coral isle
  Within the amorous South;
The blue of heaven in her eye,
  The sun's breath in her hair,
Celestial balm in every sigh,
  That pass'd her rose-lips fair—
A living floweret from the sky,
  The Angels missed her there.

And day by day their voices fell,
  Theirs and the cherubims,
As if through some illumined dell
  Swept echoings of hymns:
Fell like harp-whispers on her ears,
  Like star-beams on her mind,

So faintly did they cleave the spheres;
    And like the evening wind
That wafts down prayers from mountaineers,
    Left melody behind.

Then she would sit apart and muse
    Upon their gentle words,
Gentle as falling summer dews,
    Or carolings of birds,
And wonder how these whispers came
    Unto her ears alone;
Above her playmates' loud acclaim
    She felt each Eden-tone,
As feels the Poet the pure flame
    The crowd can never own.

And when her infant mind was filled
    With melody divine,
Down came the starry Angels mild,
    Like pilgrims to a shrine,
Each, with an offering of love,
    To lure her from the earth,—
They envied us the spotless dove
    So quiet in her mirth—
They claimed her for their home above,
    We, for our homely hearth.

They were forever hovering,
    Like halos, o'er her head,
And one, with wider, whiter wing,

Kept watch above her bed;
Her dreams were of a sunny clime,
   Of skies serenely bright,
Where, in their everlasting prime,
   These messengers of light
Joined in a harmony sublime,
   That thrilled through heaven's height.

Thus was her mind forever turned
   From our poor earth away,
For milder scenes her child-heart yearned,
   And when she knelt to pray,
Her strange companions by her side
   Knelt down in silence, too,
And to her inner voice replied,
   As pass the echoes through
Some balmy valley ere they glide
   Above the distant blue.

The Rose of Health still deeply bloomed
   Upon her dimpled cheek,
When, lo! the yearning angels plumed
   Her spirit pure and meek;
They gave it white wings like their own,
   And crowned her wide young brow
With flowers, gathered where the sun
   Doth kiss them as they grow,
Blanching their petals, one by one,
   Till whiter than the snow.

And there stood two, like Faith and Hope,
    Above the child that died,
With thoughts pure as the stars that ope
    Their wings at eventide;
One, struggling with a weight of pain,
    In silence wild and deep,
The other, tranquil as the main
    In whose breast earthquakes sleep—
On their great hearts Grief falls like rain
    God, only, knows they weep.

Like an Ideal Thought she came,
    A star upon Love's crest,
Then vanished like the sunset flame
    That warms the ardent West;
And like a thought of priceless worth,
    Filled with ambrosial leaven,
She passed up to her second birth,
    Above the Pleiades seven,
One Angel less upon the Earth,
    One Spirit more in Heaven.

SUN, MOON, AND STARS.

Sun, Moon, and Stars attest Thy matchless glory,
    Thou mighty Ruler of the World Unseen;
Devout Astrologers of sacred story
    Have loved to bask beneath their gorgeous sheen;
Have looked from them to Thee, and looking, raised

Their song to where the Godhead's essence lurks,
And with a hymn of deep thanksgiving praised
   The greatness of Thy power and Thy works.

And how shall I, an atom, frail and weak,
   Scan the blue ether with an eye of love,
Or in befitting accents sing or speak
   Of those mysterious worlds that shine above?
But Thou hast planted deep within my breast
   A love for all that's beautiful and bright,
From the red Morning's Sun-emblazoned crest,
   To the pale Stars that celebrate the Night.

I love the storm at deepest midnight sweeping,
   The gentle billow and the raging sea,
The vivid lightning, and the thunder, speaking
   In mighty language, Thou Supreme! of Thee.
I love the plunging cataract, the rill
   That, childlike, sparkles through the sunny plain,
The primal forest depths, convulsed or still,
   'Neath the light zephyr's or dark tempest's reign.

And loving these, I turn my eyes above,
   And there behold the wondrous mysteries
Which blameless men in every age have loved—
   For where is aught exalts the mind like these?
By day and night, alike, behold the scene!
   The King of Light upon his golden throne,
Night's silver-mantled and seductive Queen,
   Encircled by the stars as with a zone!

The lofty Sun in mid-day greatness rolling,
   Calmly pursuing his majestic way,
Is silently but powerfully extolling
   His great Creator's glory day by day.
No clouds can wholly dim his brilliant light,
   No eye can gaze upon his steady flame,
His course, from rosy morn to dewy night,
   Is one unceasing Pæan to Thy name.

But scarcely is his evening anthem ended,
   When lo! the Moon walks blushing up the East,
Her first soft accents with his last have blended,
   And thus their silent song has never ceased,
Since the Creator's Voice first bade them hold
   Their course untiring through eternal space,
And with their voiceless eloquence unfold
   His boundless power, excellence and grace.

Not less the Stars their gentle hymns are blending
   With the impressive silence which the night
Upon her myriad tongues is ever sending
   Throughout creation's trackless realms of light.
There's not a ray that cleaves yon ethery void,
   But has a tongue to sound its Maker's praise,
There's not a drop in yon receding tide,
   That does not answer to their voiceless lays.

Then how much more should gifted man proclaim
   The greatness of God's overruling power,
When all His works do glorify his name

Eternally, through every fleeting hour?
Teach me, Oh! God, to read thy works aright,
　Fill me with love for all things bright and free,
Grant me, through life to look, by day and night,
　Through all Thy vast creations up to Thee!

THE CHIEFTAIN'S LAST SIGH.

Through the depths of the forest a warrior came,
His look threat'ning death, and destruction, and flame;
Erect and majestic he stood in his pride,
By the graves of his people who fell by his side—
By the graves of the Red Men, for a Red Man was he,
Hunted down like a beast in the Land of the Free!
Pursued, but no longer that Chieftain will fly;
By the graves of his kindred he'll conquer or die.

His eye flashed with rage—there was scorn in its light,
As he called to his band to prepare for the fight;
His tomahawk's keenness he smilingly felt,
And looked to the red scalping-knife in his belt;
Shook the plumes that o'ershadowed his obdurate brow,
Again rallied his band, and repeated his vow.
Now the foe is in sight—hark! that terrible cry
Proves, that here the brave Red Man will conquer or die!

Thick fly the swift arrows, unerring they fly,
Like the bleak winds in Autumn the stricken ones sigh;

And that Warrior-Chief, with a demon possessed,
In the midst of the carnage lays bare his bold breast;
Each blow of his tomahawk, reeking and red,
Like the stroke of a Fate, adds one more to the dead,
And his resolute band, with their wild battle-cry,
Are thronging around him, in numbers, to die.

Yes, to die! but they fall without murmur or groan,
And their death-dealing Chieftain stands firmly—alone!
As the sea, lash'd to fury, rolls on in its might,
So he breasts his foes with a frantic delight;
There's revenge in his look, there is death in his frown,
And he fights like a Chief who upholds his renown;
Overpowered by numbers he yields his last sigh
By the graves of his race, where he wandered to die.

HOLY GROUND.

When thoughtful Contemplation fills
The mind, go, climb the rugged hills,
Down which the crystal-footed rills
    In freedom bound;
The mind, all hope, is upward led,
For every spot on which we tread
    Is Holy Ground.

As homeward turns the shepherd's flock,
Stand on the firmly-rooted rock,
That trembles 'neath the thunder's shock,

With awe profound ;
The spirit erewhile so oppress'd,
Is now the soul's delighted guest—
　　'T is Holy Ground.

Emerging from the leprous town,
We wander where the mountains frown,
Or where the torrent leapeth down,
　　With psalmy sound :
Feelings of inspiration steal
Upon the mind—we own—we feel
　　'T is Holy Ground.

When pondering by the silent shore,
We hear the tortured ocean roar,
Our thoughts beyond its vastness soar,
　　And all around
Delights—uplifts—expands the mind
Where Beauty ever lives enshrined—
　　'T is Holy Ground.

Go, thread the Wisdom-haunted Woods,
Where slave of Mammon ne'er intrudes,
Or seek the sylvan solitudes
　　Where Peace is found ;
Contrast their silence with the strife
And folly of a selfish life—
　　'Tis Holy Ground.

We reverence the marble stone,
That tells us of a spirit flown

To worlds unseen, but not unknown;
    This grassy mound,
Each green blade on whose sacred knoll
Begets sweet feelings in the soul,
    Is Holy Ground.

Not less so is the wood-clad height,
Seen by broad Day or sombre Night;
Each humble view that meets the sight
    Serves to expound
The wholesome truth, that Earth was meant,
Despite Man's peevish discontent,
    For Holy Ground.

PLEASANT MEMORIES.

    Mary, do you Remember—
Do you remember the ancient house,
The moss to its brown roof clinging—
The old open roof, where the swallows each year
Reared their downy broods without let or fear—
    The moss in the eaves,
    And the birds 'mong the leaves,
    The flute-toned Robin and his spouse,
    A vermeil tinge on his rounded breast,
    In the plumb and apple trees singing?
    The yellow-bird's nest
Woven with skill in the forkéd boughs
Of the currant trees in the garden walk,

Where we'd thoughtfully meet, and sparingly talk,
Sometimes aloud, but oftener mute,
Pulling the juicy coral-hued fruit,
Conversing of books, and of learnéd men,
In the grassy walk of the garden then—
  Mary, do you Remember?

Do you remember the hollyhock
That stood at the foot of the garden walk,
  With its rich purple flowers,
  And around it, in showers,
The rose-trees dropping their delicate leaves,
Like the tears shed by Beauty when she grieves;
The hardy rockets, pink, lilac and white,
The morning-glory that clomb in the night
Up the slender rod, as if some spirit bright
  Beckoned it up
  With its dew-filled cup,
To bask in the pale moon's loving light?
The marygold's deep-yellow hue,
The sweet-pea blossoms, red and blue,
The mignonette, scenting the morning air,
With a perfume as sweet as an infant's prayer;
And over them all the humming-bird,
Like a living flower, gold and green,
Pleasing the eye with its glancing sheen,
Scenting the odors, was often heard,
Oft was heard, and oft was seen,
Like a beautiful thought the leaves between—
  These, Mary, do you Remember?

Do you remember the little windmill,
On the long, slim pole, that would never be still?
Ever by night, and ever by day,
In its easy, rolicking, careless way,
Buffing the zephyrs, grave or gay,
Ever warning dull spirits away,
With its clattering, chattering roundelay?
In the warm sunny noon, when the bees were abroad,
  Kissing the flowers,
  Or when the Hours
  Stepp'd down at night,
  Golden and bright,
Gently pressing the warm, green sod,
Chanting the Hymn of Departing Day;
  When the rain fell merrily,
  Or the cricket cheerily
  Chirped its strange melody,
Singing of Home, in the long, green grass;
When the winds piped loud, or the zephyrs sang low,
That mill was scampering fast or slow,
Mocking at sorrow, and winking at woe—
Do you remember that talkative mill?
That wrangling, mischievous, mirth-loving mill?
   Mary, do you Remember?

Do you remember the marsh near by,
Where the winds would moan, and the rushes would
 sigh—
The rushes that grew nearly five feet high,

Screening the houses the muskrats built,
Where the brown-bearded bulrush rose a-tilt,
Ruffling the flowers of purplish blue,
That blossomed and bloomed the summer through?
Do you remember the lilies that grew,
The white water-lilies that grew, and lay
Rocking themselves in the sun all day,
Like a Neriad fleet, along the bay;
And the mossy nest of the saucy wren,
  Swinging and swaying
  All day long; and when
  The hounds' distant baying
Told that the star-watch was set in the skies.
Then, do you remember the fire-flies,
  Startling the air
  With a mystic glare,
Like the Borealis streaming forth
Up the blue skies of the crispéd North,—
Now here—now there—now everywhere?
And strangest of all, the bullfrogs' croaking!
Called you it singing, or vamping, or joking?
For I never can tell, for the life of me,
What these musical wretches sing or say!
   Mary, do you Remember?

Do you remember the meadow-field,
Where the red-ripe strawberries lay concealed,
Close to the roots of the scented grass,
That bowed to let the sunbeams pass

To smile on the buttercups clustering over
The drooping heads of honied clover?
Or the golden dandelions, milky-stemmed,
With which the spring fields were begemmed?
Do you remember the hawthorn hedge,
   In its virginal bloom,
   Breathing perfume
Far along the water-worn ledge;
The crows, with their signals of raven-like caws,
Like Ethiope sentinels over the haws?
    The wild roses flinging
    Their sweets to the breeze,
    While perched on the trees
    The sparrow sat, singing
Its plain, homely melody, and the brown thrush
Flung mellowy peals from thickets of rush,
As the blackbird piped from his vocal throat
His one soft-syllabled, graceful note?
      Gentlier breezes never blew,
      Lovelier roses never grew,
      Honeysuckles nowhere ever
      Had a more delicious flavor,
      Never hedge that ever budded
      Was more delicately studded,
      Never buttercups more yellow,
      Clover sweeter or more mellow,
      Than along this bank of flowers
      Cheered the rosy-pinioned hours,
      Passing o'er the swaying meadow,

Passing, leaving not a shadow,
But bearing odors to the brain,
Binding the senses as with a chain
Of linkéd sounds, that pleased the ears,
Of sights, that charmed the eye to tears!
Do you remember the little snipe,
Whenever surprised how shrill he'd pipe?
A comical, restless, industrious snipe,
With a piccolo-sound to his three-note pipe—
Mary, do you Remember?

Do you remember the old school-room
That seemed little else than a solemn tomb?
Though on looking back
On life's beaten track,
Those hours were happier far than they seemed,
Dearer than ever we thought or dreamed!
Do you remember, each holiday,
When old Winter came, muffled up to the ears,
Like a frigid old fellow, his eyes all tears,
Congealed as they fell—a sparkling chain
Of frost-pearls, clanking a cold refrain—
How the schoolboys would skate o'er the frozen bay,
Making old Boreas as tricksy at play
As the liveliest sprite of a summer's day?—
Old Boreas that killed all the delicate leaves,
Dried the moss in the eaves,
Withered the rushes, and trampled the flowers
Raised by the spring in her sunniest hours,

Whitened the bosom of valley and hill—
But he never could quiet that little wind-mill,
    That winter and summer
      Was its own drummer,
Playing one season out, and another one in,
A perfect young Topsy for mischief and din!
Do you remember the fine old bell,
That warned us home with its silvery knell?
    Mary, do you Remember?

Do you Remember! Yes.—The slave at the oar
Of the galley he knows he can quit nevermore,
No chain can more firmly, more hopelessly bind,
Than time has enwoven those scenes with thy mind;
And more that in memory's heart will remain,
More than these, too, are struggling in memory's chain:
Happy faces that met you in life's happy dawn,
Of her that is living, and they that are gone;
Happy faces that cluster, like hopes, round you still,
Like the sunbeams that linger the last on the hill;
And though sad or though pleasant these memories be
They are fraught with the noblest of lessons to thee.

MY KITTEN.

    Playful, kind, mischievous thing!
    Like a stream meandering
    Through the sun-enamored glade,
    Frisking when its course is stayed;

MY KITTEN.

Leaping joyously along,
With thy unassuming song,
Delighted with the thought of living,
Caring little how deceiving
Is the world, with all its joys,
Blighted hopes and false decoys.

Teasing, saucy little pest!
Will you never be at rest?
Romping in and out the house,
Chasing tabby for a mouse,
Climbing nimbly up the door,
Strewing papers round the floor,
Prancing up and down the roof,
Giving, every moment, proof
That all living things should strive
To be happy while alive.

Life to thee is but a play,
Invented to pass time away;
Earth is not a house of grief;
Our existence is too brief
To yield up a single hour
To that grim, obtrusive power,
Melancholy, with his brow
Ever black as night with wo!
I'd much rather be a kitten,
With a love for humor smitten,
Then be doomed to live on earth,
And not have my share of mirth.

Puss! I'd rather have it said
That your waggish little head
Rested archly on my shoulders,
Making fun for all beholders,
Than be forced to live for life
With the world of gloom and strife.
Yes—much rather would I be
Full of merriment like thee,
Than a gloomy misanthrope,
Without any earthly hope
E'er to live, as was designed,
Happy both in heart and mind.

THE FROST KING'S REVEL.

It was a night of terror—fiercely bleak!
The winds like haggard demons leaped along
The whitened fields. Far o'er the piney hills,
Far up among the mountain fastnesses,
Their horrid laughter and avenging tones,
Shook the red granite to its base. The trees
Sprang from the frozen ground in fear, and fell
Death-doomed to earth. Indifferent were they,
These unrelenting and malignant winds,
What poor misguided wretch they scourged to death;
Whether he struggled onward clad with rags,
The sport and playthings of the spiteful breeze,
That as it filled his very bones with chills

And heartfelt tremblings, whistled as it passed.
A merry tune; or whether favored less
By some capricious messenger of Fate,
His weary limbs refused to carry him
To where a scanty shelter might be found,
And he was forced to hug the ground and die,
A victim to the Frost King's Judas kiss—
'T was all the same.—The subtle winds swept down
On all who madly ventured forth to dare
Their rugged blasts that night. Theirs was the task
To swell the almost endless catalogue
Of those who perished by their cruel aid:
A countless multitude, whose names were traced
Upon a scroll the hoary Frost King held
In his firm grasp, as, seated on a cloud
Of snowy vapour, he was wafted through
The skies, by winds that loved to do him homage.

Onward he sped, attended by his train
Of tyrannous dependents: Winds that pierced
And froze the marrow in men's bones, that chilled
The blood, so that it nourished not the frame,
But crept, cold and unnatural, in slow
And sluggish motion through the heart; vapours
That quenched the stars and darkened all the air,
Bearing their frozen spray o'er many a league
Of country. These obeyed their monarch's nod,
Joyed in his frowns, and watched his meteor-eye
To catch an icy look of cool approval,

As they performed their ærial manœuvres,
Or sprinkled showers of snow upon the earth,
Or laid some miserable hovel low,
Leaving its inmates in the cold to perish.

  The merry monarch held his boisterous way
Through mid-air, marshaling his blackest clouds,
Devising cruel schemes wherewith he might
Descend, and torture some unconscious wretch,
Who, unsuspecting, lay upon his couch,
Dreaming of happiness. His keen eyes gleam,
Like rival stars, that through the wintry night
Flash hatred on each other; his gaze is fixed
On earth; and shouting a triumphant shout,
That strikes the echoes dumb in the hill sides,
He claps his deathly hands, as, smilingly,
He marks some scene of suffering below,
On which his heartless look is fixed. The winds
Gather their fiercest blasts; the vapoury car
Restrains its airy flight; and hastening down
To view the fearful scene and claim his rights,
The Frost-King comes. It is a sight of awe,
From which, and justly too, the sensitive mind
Recoils with terror. Flames are seen to rise,
Mouthing the shrinking air with feverous lips,
Scorching the raven locks from night's dark brow,
And showering up swift, burning-pointed darts,
That rend the tortured bosom of the sky,
And rive the clouds in twain. Affrighted cries,

And shrieks of thrilling anguish and despair,
Resound abroad; the mother clasps her babes,
And flies the shelter of her burning roof,
With scarce a tatter snatched up in her haste,
To shield them from the cold. Their humble home
Is soon reduced to ashes. 'Tis the dead
Of night. The winds unmercifully beat
Against their naked forms. For many miles
No human dwelling can be found, wherein
They might obtain a refuge from the storm,
That with its breath inclement, sharp and cold,
Shrivels the tender skin, and numbs the flesh
Of these poor houseless ones. No strength have they
To move their stiffened joints. Their breath departs,
With many a groan, light-breathed, inaudible,
And they a group of corses strew the ground.

  Blow on, stern tyrants! death-leagued winds that come
From out the north's bleak chambers, vent your rage!
Above, below, on earth, and in the sky,
Gather your forces; set the deadliest parts
Of your destructive, dread machinery
In motion, and the hoary Prince of Cold
Bear far away from the appalling view
Of this too-tragic picture! Now unrolls
The fatal scroll. The Frost King writes thereon
The names of his last victims, and ascends,
With triumph in his eye, to seek new haunts

Where he can exercise his brief authority,
And make his arbitrary presence felt.

Across wide tracts of country sped the car.
As quick as thought the surly king was borne
Over primeval forests, where the trees,
Like those in hardy Lapland, hid in snow,
Scarce shewed their leafless tops; o'er deserts wide,
Where roamed the Indian and the trapper, free
Joyous and unconstrained, as if they trod
The grassy sod of Summer; o'er the gay
And populous city, where luxurious Ease
And Plenty dared his ghostly train to enter.
No passion had he for the glories of
The tropics, or the blooming of the south;
Brazilian forests, or the slumberous lakes
Of Guinea, or the bamboo-covered banks
Of the immortal Ganges; or the woods
And prairies of the unfathomed ocean deeps;
Italian sunsets; the delicious skies
Of Greece; where'er continual Summer reigned;
Or where Mozambique or Arabian gales
Scent the fine air a furlong out at sea:
On these his spectre vision rested not.

But like a fiend he hastened to the Cape,
Where reigns eternal winter; to the plains
Bordering on the Icy Sea; across
Norwegian hills, or o'er the desert bleak
Where the brave sons of Sweden, years ago,

Fell patriot victims to the northern blast;
Nor stayed to pluck a single Alpine rose,
That, like a cherub in the midst of death,
Peered in sweet beauty o'er the icy mass.
Now, he beheld the gleaming palaces
Of Russia's tyrant realm; and now, he swept
Over Siberian deserts; or reviewed,
A moment after, Greenland's frost-bound plains,
Which, in interminable fields of ice,
Lay stretched in vastness. Hast'ning back he comes,
With rage impatient, furious with delay,
To tread his old haunts o'er and o'er again,
In search of death. The Northern skies grow dark
At his approach; the poor his presence dread,
Though tremblingly submit, with many a sigh,
To all his rude, tyrannic pleasantries.
High on the cold bleak hills, on mountain peaks,
That rear their whitened summits to the skies,
He, watchful, sits. High up above the Alps,
He listens to the echoes whooping through
The snow-bound defiles, like a troop of wolves
Howling among the hills. Swiftly he flies,
As the last echo fells the avalanche,
And sweeps the venturous traveller to his doom;
Records his victims; mounts his car again,
And like a universal spirit-thought,
Circles the world. His eagle eye is strained,
To catch an early glimpse of dire mishaps,
And rude disasters; and his lengthening scroll

Is oft unrolled and furled, and op'd again,
As he inscribes the name of many a youth
And buxom dame, o'ertaken by the storm,
That yield to his embrace—the clasp of Death!

Here, the too happy swain, returning home
From the exciting dance, with some fair girl,
His chosen partner and affianced bride,
Drives the impatient horse o'er the frail ice,
That bends beneath their weight, when down they sink,
Beyond the reach of help. And here, from some
Vile brothel, rank with pestilence and crime,
The senseless Drunkard reels, uncertain where
To seek the home he might have made a heaven,
And where his wife, a-weeping o'er her babe,
Like a drenched lily o'er a budding rose,
Patiently droops, awaiting his return—
Return!—Long has the wily Frost King marked
That senseless and inebriated fool,
Who, sinking 'neath his weight of wretchedness,
Extends himself upon the ground, and dies!
These, from his high retreat, and thousands more,
Well pleased, the rugged Frost King sees expire.
Thus is his dreaded reign, from year to year,
Pregnant with death. His icy sceptre sways
These Northern wilds for months; until the Spring—
Creation's first-born — comes through the smiling
    heavens,
And hurls the tyrant monarch from his throne.

G

ENGLAND AND AMERICA.

Greatest twain among the nations,
   Bound, alike, by kindred ties—
Ties that never should be sundered
   While your banners grace the skies—
But, united, stand and labor,
   Side by side, and hand in hand,
Battling with the sword of Freedom,
   For the peace of every land.
Yours the one beloved language,
   Yours the same religious creed,
Yours the glory and the power,
   Great as ever was the meed
Of old Rome, or Greece, or Sparta,
   When their arms victoriously,
Proved their terrible puissance
   Over every land and sea.

Let the Son respect the Sire,
   Let the Father love the Son,
Both unitedly supporting
   All the glories they have won :
Thus in concert nobly wrestling,
   They may work the world's release,
And when having crushed its tyrants,
   Stand the Sentinels of Peace—
Stand, the mighty twin Colossus',
   Giants of the latter days,

Straight'ning for the coming kingdom
    All the steep and rugged ways,
Down which many a lofty nation—
    Lofty on the scroll of fame—
Has been swept to righteous judgment,
    Naught remaining but its name.

What! allied to Merrie England,
    Have ye not a noble birth?
Yours, America, her honors,
    Yours her every deed of worth.
Have ye not her Norman courage?
    Wear ye not her Saxon cast?
Boast ye not her love of Freedom?
    Do ye not revere the Past?
When her mighty Men of Genius—
    Chaucer, Shakespeare, Milton, Pope,
Glorified that selfsame language,
    Since become your pride and hope?
Do ye not respect the council
    Where her living statesmen sit?
Would ye blot the fame of Walpole?
    Dare ye slight the name of Pitt?

Did not Locke, and Hume, and Smollett,
    All conspire to make thee great
In the priceless pearls of Wisdom
    Which such gifted minds create?

Did not Cranmer suffer for thee?
　　Boldly dying at the stake,
When the mitred Roman Pontiff
　　Scourged him for his conscience' sake!
Did not Latimer and Ridley
　　Perish for the very creed
Which your free-born sons would fight for
　　In the bitter hour of need?
Did not Luther triumph for thee,
　　In that dear Religion's cause?
That strong prop that now supports thee—
　　Did not Alfred frame thy Laws?

And not less is thine the glory,
　　England, of thy daring son;
Webster, Cooper, Clay, and Irving,
　　Thine the fame which they have won;
Thine the fame of Western Genius—
　　Bryant, Hoffman, Whittier, Read;
Wisdom's words by them are garnered,
　　They have sown the precious seed
Which thy sons in future ages—
　　Thine and theirs—for ye are one—
Shall be proud to reap the fruit of—
　　Jewels set in Wisdom's Sun!
These, where'er thy tongue is spoken,
　　Will add splendor to thy name,
And thy wisest tongues pronounce them,
　　Worthy of enduring fame.

There will come a time, my Brothers,
    And a dread time it will be,
When your swords will flash together,
    For your Faith in jeopardy.
Not for crowns, or lands, or sceptres,
    Will the fight be fought and won,
Not for fame, or treaties broken,
    But for God, and God alone :
For the mind with which he bless'd us,
    That a false creed would keep down,
Shackle—bind it to its purpose—
    To uphold a falling crown.
See that then ye fail not, Brothers!
    Set the listening skies aglow
With such deeds as live in heaven,
    If your Faith be worth a blow.

Proud, then, of each other's greatness,
    Ever struggle side by side;
Noble Son! time-honored Parent!
    Let no paltry strife divide
Hearts like yours, that should be mindful
    Only of each others' worth—
Mindful of your high position
    'Mongst the powers of the earth.
Mightiest twain among the nations!
    Bound, alike, by kindred ties—
Ties that never should be sundered,
    While your banners grace the skies;

Hearts and dest'nies once united,
   Steadfast to each other prove,
Bind them with enduring fetters—
   Bind them with the Bonds of Love.

THE WRECK.

"When the steamer HOME was wrecked upon the beach at Ocracoke, N. C., they rang the bell incessantly until she went to pieces on the breakers; and that melancholy sound was heard at a distance, above the noise of the waves."

   Hark! hark to the knell
   Of that wild-voiced bell,
That rings o'er the surging waves,
   Each tone doth sweep
   O'er the troubled deep,
Like a voice from the seamen's graves!

   While borne to the shore,
   Is the breakers' roar,
And the elements' wild halloo,
   The dismal sound
   Of its voice hath drowned
The shouts of the struggling crew.

   Swiftly the wreck,
   Like a stricken speck
On the wild upheaving main,
   Sinks through the deep,

With a sudden sweep,
Like a pang through a tyrant's brain.

But the last wild sound
On that deep profound,
Heard high o'er the winds and waves,
Is the startling knell
Of that loud-voiced bell,
Passing down to the seamen's graves.

And each struggling form
In that fearful storm,
As he gasps for a parting breath,
Feels a sudden thrill,
As that warning shrill
Tolls him down to the Ship of Death.

And so when the world
From its place is hurled,
Like a speck will it pass away,
And all ears shall hear,
O'er the crash severe,
The knell of the Judgment Day.

THE LOFTY AND THE LOWLY.

There's not a page of nature's book
O'er which the thoughtful eye may look,
  But fills the mind with praise;
There's not a plant that springs below,

E'en to the lowliest shrubs that grow
   Beneath the sun's bright rays,
But claims a more than passing share
Of admiration and of care.

With pride we view the stately oak,
Feel, when it meets the woodman's stroke,
   As for a friend cut down;
While the sweet daisy by its side,
In all its unassuming pride,
   By the same stroke o'erthrown—
How few lament its sudden fate—
Our sympathy is with the great!

Thus does the world about us feel
For an ambitious statesman's weal,
   Whereas a poor man's woe
Is seldom either known or felt,
Although he may, perhaps, have dealt—
   For aught strict worldlings know—
More good in his small circle than
His more important fellow-man.

I've seen a fawning parasite,
The pliant tool of men of might,
   Attended to his grave
By troops of friends, who'd shared his gold,
Which made his virtues manifold—
   A good man of a knave;
And I've seen men of sterling worth
Borne rudely to their parent earth,

Because, forsooth! they died so poor
That all their worth could not procure
   The friendship of the world :
They were the daisies which had grown
Uncared for, and in part unknown,
   And those the oak trees, hurled
By some rude blast of fortune down,
But miss'd—for they had smelt renown !

I DREAMED I MET THEE.

I dreamed I met thee, with the glow
   Of Girlhood fresh upon thy cheek,
As when thy voice, serene and low,
   In love's undying tones did speak ;
And through my heart, and to my brain,
   Rushed life's warm current wildly-free,
As memory brought back again
   My Boyhood's earnest love for thee.

'Twas midst a gay and brilliant throng,
   Where dancers glided to and fro,
And where the wild, impassioned song,
   Brought to each eye love's burning glow ;
But we had strayed apart from all
   The gayer spirits that had met—
Some to enjoy the festal ball,
   Others to banish deep regret.

Our lips moved not, we did not seek
  By words to tell some love-lorn wile,
Secrets, which words could never speak,
  Were told by an impressive smile.
But there was language in each look,
  That could a kindred mind control,
Language the impatient could not brook—
  The silent commune of the soul.

Thus would I meet thee, fairest one!
  If there the power should be given
To know each other, where the Sun
  Of Love forever shines, in Heaven.
Oh! joy beyond what earth can give!
  To see thee and to know thee, where
The good in endless pleasures live—
  'Twere heaven, indeed, if thou wert there.

THE CHANGES OF A NIGHT.

Midnight had set her star-emblazoned seal
Upon the slumbering world. I could not sleep.
Thoughts flashed across my mind at every throb
Of my lone heart; and voices came to me,
From my hushed chamber's solitary depths,
That I'd long loved to listen to. I heard
The merry laugh of one, whose girlhood's heart,
Light as the spotted fawn's in summer woods,

THE CHANGES OF A NIGHT.

Beat proudly when I smiled upon her love.
I saw her glide mysteriously past,
And felt the pressure of her heart-warmed hand.
The same rich music floated from her lips,
As when, in happier days, she sung to me
The tender ballads of a far-off land:
Her very breath was song, her words were odes,
That set the pulses of the heart aglow
With a divine exuberance of love,
As pure as starbeams round the throne of night.
My soul was flooded with a bounding joy—
Surely 'tis love that quickens us for heaven,
As day-break heralds the impassioned sun!
The heavy clouds that draped my spirit's skies,
And hung like opiate slumbers on my brain,
Had burned to rose-hues in the flame of love.
She spake; my sense expanding like the rose
That opens to the song o' the nightingale,
And buoys on wings of perfume every note,
Meeting the silvery breathings of the stars
Midway from heaven. And sweet sleep came not.
My palpitating brain was burning with
The mountain-thoughts that crushed me with their weight,
And laid me panting on my restless couch.
I staggered forth and drank the cooling breeze
That swept with gentle motion through the air.
The dew of heaven lay upon the grass,
A mimic star-world on a ground of green,
And on the trembling leaves of the young trees,

It glistened, like the globes of rain that lodge
Upon them after a refreshing shower.

   Silence was on my soul; and silence wrapt
The lucid atmosphere. I looked above:
The stars were shining on the brow of night,
Like diamonds pendent from a sapphire dome,
And blazing planets glittered on her breast,
As jewels deck a queen. There Venus burned
Her vestal lamp; and there Orion gleamed,
To cheer the mariner upon his way
Across the midnight waters; and along
The milky way a gauzy light was thrown,
Through which the bright stars glimmered, like the eyes
Of some fair beauty underneath her veil,
That cannot hide their dazzling brilliancy.
In the far west the moon was gliding down
To soothe the restless billows at her feet,
That wrapped their gray heads in her silver robes,
Leaving the untold myriads of stars
That syllable the praises of the night,
To sing their parting hymns ere they put on
Their robes of ether, or retire into
Their air-suspended chambers, hung aloft
By the strong arm of the Invisible.
The river, like a tired Palmer, lay
Dreaming of endless quiet; but afar,
In the now darkened distance, which the eye
Could dimly penetrate, the noise of waves

Was heard distinctly, as they rolled along
In dead, unbroken swells: They heralded
The coming storm. The rivulet that dashed
Its molten amber-drops of cooling water
Against the rocks that dallied with its course,
Like red-haired giants toying with a child,
Mingled its precious tribute with the stream
That lay extended many a sullen mile,
But which regarded not the offering
Which evermore the streamlet ministered
To her insatiable thirst. The breeze
Sprang down and loosed the white manes of the waves,
That, startled, moaned along the echoing shore,
Like snow wreaths scudding from the borean blast,
Shrieking aloud for fear. These lashed the cliffs
Far up the mountain-side. The unchained winds
Laid the old trees, that had withstood the gales
Of half a century, prostrate on the earth.
This sudden change the various passions of
The human mind resembled. Quietness,
And Peace, and blissful Calm usurp the breast,
Until some unexpected power arise,
To force them from their place. Shades dark and light
Are ever flitting o'er the mind. These are
The ebb and flow—the evil and the good
Of human nature, that forever strive
Within us, each at times predominant.
In haste I sought my solitary home;
And as the morning had not dawned, I threw

Myself upon my couch, and meditated
On what had passed. Delicious slumber came
Unbidden, and I sank into repose,
And dreamed of happy faces and bright forms
That used to mingle with my boyhood's sports.

TO REV. JAMES G. WITTED.

ON THE SUDDEN DEATH OF HIS BROTHER.

Death ever snatching up some valued friend,
Sudden as the vexed lightning strips the boughs
Of the strong oak! Oh! will it never end?
This scourge, that fades the crimson from my Rose
Of Life! Will heaven never interpose,
And stay its shafts, till the last arrow cleave
My own lashed heart, and my eyes forever close
Their weary watchings? For my Friend I grieve.
He, for his Brother-Friend, while I, in Sorrow, weave

A wreath of Cypress for the sable Urn
Of Grief, in which the tears of Memory
Are shrined, as well as in the hearts they burn,
With their slow, withering intensity.
Far o'er the wave, how many souls there be
Who feel the stroke that has surprised us here!
But not of Friends alone—the agony
That rends the bosom of the wife; the tear
That scalds the orphan's cheek: these fill Grief's gloomy
       sphere.

TO REV. JAMES G. WITTED.

When he, with his strong frame, and manly glow
Of robust health, gave waiting death his hand,
Who may expect exemption from the blow
That thus strikes down the ablest in the land?
Our spirits, too, my Friend, at Death's command,
Must follow his, that the deep mysteries,
That lie beyond the scope of man, may stand
Disrobed before us, and with soul-like ease
We may peruse the secrets of the infinities.

The dead are ever with us: ever round
About us hovering, like rainbows o'er
The cloud. There's not a foot of ground
On which we tread, where Truth has gone before,
That is not hallowed thence, for evermore,
By the blest footprints of the souls we love.
There is no death. The Shape that guards the shore
Where Life's frail journey ends, is Mercy's dove,
That brings us renewed life from life's great source above.

Well may'st thou grieve! A noble manhood sat
Upon his brow; and in his eye, a true
Nobility of Soul—an eye whereat
Friendship might light her paling lamp anew.
He found a milder home than that which drew
His footsteps from that dear beloved strand,
With the fond Brother of his youth, to view
The boundless garden of the Western land,
Pleased with its generous clime, its breezes soft and bland.

Not far from where the Mississippi's wave
Rolls its rich freightage through the fertile West,
The hands of Stranger-Friends have made his grave,
And borne his body to its shrouded rest.
God oft removes the friends whom we love best:
That through Affliction we may nearer come
To Him and them. Through suffering are we blest,
And purified; surmount life's darkest gloom.
He, Friend, perchance, was called, to bring thee nearer
  home!

EDITH TO HAROLD

AT HIS CORONATION.

Life of my life! joy of my inmost soul!
Whose life and death are destined to control
My spirit's being: let me think of thee,
Possessor of my heart's idolatry!
Bright was the day with sunlight from above,
When first you whispered of long-cherished love;
When that stout heart that beats for England's weal,
Was bound by chains as strong as chains of steel;
When that strong arm with tender fondness press'd
My yielding form against your throbbing breast;
When that calm eye, in danger's hour serene,
Gazed on my brow as on your future Queen;
When that loud voice, deep as the trumpet's sound,
Rang in my ears, and made my spirit bound

With feelings such as they can never know
Who spurn the blind God as men spurn a foe.

  I do not weep, nor think the less of thee,
That thou prefer'st thy country's weal to me,
The fates absolve thee, Harold, from thy vow,
And to my cruel destiny I bow,
Content to know none other name but mine
Will be inscribed on that firm breast of thine,
Save hers, thy country's—England's—with whose fame
Will ever live King Harold's noble name.

  Oft do I think upon our childhood's hours,
When day by day we culled the wildwood flowers.
What holy joy inspired us when we met!
Our partings, too, how saddened with regret!
Until a childish kiss relieved the pain,
And vows were pledged that we should meet again.

  I think of thy long sojourn in the land
Of strangers; and of thy return, to stand
By the decree of thy Country and thy King.
One name to every English lip did spring,
One name was shouted by both Thegn and Ceorl;
That name was Harold's—Harold, England's Earl!
I think on the love-consecrated knoll,
Deep in the forest glade, where love's control
Held in soft bonds your manly heart and mine,
And you confessed your love and called me thine.
And I was happy; and my spirit yearned

For thee; and blushes—maiden blushes—burned
My cheeks, as, gazing on thy noble form,
I knew thy love, more resolute and warm,
Was still as pure as in those childish days,
When on your brow I placed the verdant bays,
Calling each one a Crown, and thee—a King!
Strange that such prophecies should ofttimes bring
Their own fulfilment; and that time will make
The jests of lisping childhood oft partake
Of truthfulness. These sinless days have pass'd—
Oh! that their sweetness could forever last!

When war, like an avenging spirit, rose,
And thou pursuedst thy country's daring foes,
My soul was with thee. In thy adverse hour,
I felt as if heaven had given me the power
To rescue thee from danger: for I knew—
By the sweet feelings understood by few—
The blending of our spirits—when the arm
Of the proud foe was o'er thee. Not the charm
Devised by Hilda with such secret care,
Availed thee more than Edith's humble prayer.
It was the prayer of Love; and Love is strong,
And triumphs, ev'n as Right must conquer Wrong,
And Truth o'erpower Falsehood. Not only then,
When in fair fight you met your fellow-men,
Did my prophetic soul the dangers see—
As in a mirror—which encompassed thee;
But when thou wentest to the Norman's land,

I saw thy fleet endangered on the strand,
And prayed for thy release. In pain I wept,
When William, the ambitious Norman, kept
England's great hero at that pompous court
Against his will: and sought with Norman sport,
And glittering festivity, to find
Some hidden inlet to thy giant mind;
Some secret entrance still unfortified
Against the fopperies of Norman pride.

But England's name was written on thy heart,
For England's fame you gently bore the smart,
And treasured up the insult in that soul
That never yet was swayed by man's control,
Nor artifice nor insult long could brook
From a deceitful foe. Yet one more look
Upon that Kingly brow, and on thy Queen,
Who sits where I—thy Edith—might have been,
Had heaven willed it so; and I retire
For ever from the world, but to aspire
To an immortal heritage—a throne,
Not so uncertain, Harold, as thine own.
Once in my humble cell, my prayers shall be
Employed in meek sincerity for thee.

Beloved Harold! Joy of my heart's joy!
Mainspring of my existence! From a boy,
Sweet partner of my soul! my bosom's lord!
Here and in heaven my constancy's reward—
Farewell!—But not forever be it said:

Once more I'll meet thee, where the ransomed dead
Of this world win that immortality
Which such bright minds as thine, from error free,
Aspire to. One look more, and then—farewell!
Thou hast thy Throne, and Edith has—her Cell!

SONG OF THE NEW YEAR.

I come, I come on untiring wing,
   As swift as a ray of light;
From the far off realms of immensity,
   I come to claim my right.
As the blushing Morn is newly born
   From the depths of startled Night,
Even so do I, Phœnix-like, arise,
From the last faint breath the Old Year sighs.

I come, I come to rule o'er a world
   Of mingled Joy and Woe;
The former alone 't is mine to bring,
   Of the latter ye've had enow!
Choose, then, ye millions of thinking souls;
   Who wills it can bestow
A share of the joy that is needed here,
To banish the ills ye hold so dear.

Choose, choose, ye vessels of mighty thoughts
   That are given from God to man;
Would ye revel in black iniquity

Through life's uncertain span!
Or lay before heaven those acts of love
   That Angels are pleased to scan?
Choose—choose—in that choice are the Future's
    seeds,
I am here as a witness to all your deeds.

I know but little of earthly strife,
   And less of earthly care,
But I must study the dark of life,
   As well as the bright and fair,
Though I come of a mild, celestial race,
   That has never known despair,
From a land where a million suns are known
To shed their light on our monarch's throne.

And much of that light travels down to earth;
   The Sun and the Moon on high,
And the Stars, from their silent watch-towers,
   Spread it round through the tranquil sky;
And the wings of Angels that come unseen,
   But are ever hovering nigh,
Are evermore bringing, by day and night,
To the dwellers on earth, that celestial light.

I, too, on my mission of peace, bring down
   The light of the living day,
To illume the path of earth's hopeless ones,
   Who in evil have gone astray,
As well as to guide the steps of those

Who are walking in wisdom's way;
Oh! spurn it not, nor quench its beams
In the evil that runs through earth's foul streams.

Like you, ye dwellers on earth's fair soil,
   I, also, must sojourn here,
Till, having performed my appointed task,
   I am winged to another sphere,
Where I will meet—in the vast beyond—
   The ghosts of each by-gone year,
Where the waters of Time's unfathomed sea
Roll on to the shores of Eternity.

And many who now are flushed with health,
   Will I meet on that distant strand,
For well will I know my own fair flowers,
   When they bloom in the spirit-land,
Where each glad year that has wandered here,
   Is chief of the goodly band
That during his stay has been called away
To the realms that smile in endless day.

I come, I come on untiring wing,
   As swift as a ray of light,
From the far off realms of immensity
   I come to enforce my right.
Let there be Joy through the universe,
   And let Sorrow feel its might,
For in Joy there is Wisdom, and Strength and
   Love,
And Sorrow lives not in the realms above.

SOUL, THOU ART LONELY.

Soul, thou'rt lonely—calm and lonely,
   Lonely as the stricken deer,
Waiting for its lost companions
   Slaughtered in the distant mere,
Sadness is thy earthly portion,
   Sadness that beclouds the mind,
Scarce a single vestige leaving
   Of God's glorious light behind.
Yes, my soul, thou'rt sad and lonely.
   Be thou to thy lot resigned.

Couldst thou but forget the moments,
   Few in number, that have pass'd
O'er thee, like the light of evening,
   Leaving all in gloom at last;
Could some gently-rolling Lethe
   Wash remembrance from the mind,
Blotting out the golden day-dreams
   Those fond moments left behind;
Then, my soul, how shouldst thou triumph!
   Then thou mightest be resigned.

But so long as memory looketh
   With regret upon the past,
Feasting on the priceless treasures
   Then, in brighter days, amassed,
Will the sweet remembrance foster
   This drear loneliness of mind,
Though my best resolves should prompt thee,

Like true friends with counsel kind,
  To shake off thy chains of bondage,
    And be to thy lot resigned.

Yes, my soul, thou'rt sad and lonely,
  Lonely as the mateless dove,
When the cruel blasts of winter
  Have deprived it of its love.
Could fond Hope resume its empire
  Over my deserted mind,
And retouch the fading day-dream
  Dim within my thoughts enshrined,
Then couldst thou shake off this sadness,
  To thy future lot resigned.

PEACE, FOND SOUL.

Peace, fond soul, the restless fancies
  Ever flitting o'er my mind,
Must not mar thy weal eternal,
  Must not strike thy Reason blind!
Fortune still may frown upon thee,
  Disappointment's sable wings
May, as ever, hover o'er thee,
  Shadowing all lovely things,
But do thou, my Soul, be pressing
  Where no ills shall bid thee mourn,
Ever onward—ever upward—
  Upward to thy certain bourne.

What are all the earthly pastimes,
　　All the joys that thou couldst win,
In this world of joy and sorrow,
　　In this Pleasure-house of Sin—
What are they—the sweetest of them,
　　Likened to a moment's space
Of that clime where thou art hast'ning,
　　Of that Treasure-house of Grace?
Like a single drop of water,
　　Falling in the ocean-wave,
Swallowed up and gone forever,
　　Buried in a boundless grave!

Ropes of sand! they cannot bind thee,
　　Thou art strong, and should prevail;
Mount, then, on Faith's golden pinions,
　　Gird thee on thy coat of mail,
Place the helmet on thy temples,
　　Take the sword in thy right hand,
Stand on Truth's eternal mountains,
　　Battling for the Holy Land;
And no earthly ills will daunt thee,
　　No opponent bid thee quail,
For thy God will make thee victor,
　　Thou art strong, and shalt prevail.

But beware, in this thy conflict
　　With the world, its cares and pelf,
That thy zeal does not undo thee—
　　Learn to conquer, first, thyself:

Then thou may'st go forth and prosper,
  Nerved with power from above,
Battling for thine own salvation,
  With a christian zeal and love;
And, with humble firmness, shaking
  Off the griefs that bade thee mourn,
Thou shalt reach the Eternal City,
  Reach thine own eternal bourne.

MERRY CHRISTMAS.

"Christmas, Merry Christmas!"
  Cries the proud man at his board,
As he thinks upon his larder,
  With the choicest dainties stored;
"Christmas, Merry Christmas!"
  Grunts the gourmond by his side,
Till his sluggish soul is gladdened,
  And his bosom swells with pride.

"Christmas, Merry Christmas!"
  Shouts the toper o'er his glass;
"Here's a health to Merry Christmas—
  Toast it quickly, ere it pass!"
"Christmas, Merry Christmas!"
  Shouts his friend with drunken glee,
Though to him this Merry Christmas
  Is a day of misery.

MERRY CHRISTMAS.

"Christmas, Merry Christmas!"
   Growls the miser o'er his gold,
As he counts the glowing treasures
   For which happiness was sold.
"Christmas, Merry Christmas?"
   Whispers conscience in his ear,
And he thinks of happier moments,
   And, perchance, he sheds a tear.

"Christmas, Merry Christmas!"
   Laughs the maiden in her mirth,
As she stands beside her mirror,
   The most artless one on earth.
"Christmas, Merry Christmas!"
   Sings her lover, with a smile,
As he takes the kiss of welcome,
   In the good old Christmas style.

"Christmas, Merry Christmas?"
   Asks the beggar, as he goes
On his daily round of sorrow,
   To rehearse his train of woes;
"Christmas, Merry Christmas?"
   Shrewdly asks his starving wife,
As mad hunger grasps her infant,
   And assails its parent's life.

Yes, "Merry, Merry Christmas!"
   Shriek the suff'ring in despair,
"Merry Christmas to the Wealthy,

Strangers to both Want and Care!"
"Yes, Merry, Merry Christmas!"
   Cries the Rich Man at his door,
While weak voices shriek around him:
   "Merry Christmas for the Poor!"

Ye favored Sons of Affluence!
   With Health and Plenty bless'd,
Think of the sick and suffering,
   The needy and distressed;
Turn not back, at this glad season,
   The beggar from your door,
For an open hand can ease the heart,
   And your charities insure
A blessing on your works, and bring
   A Merry Christmas to the Poor.

A PLEA FOR THE WOODS.

To the woods! to the woods! where the flowers are springing;
Their flight through the forest the wild birds are winging;
Come on, Child of Nature, who lovest the streams
That dance through this land of thy fanciful dreams,
Come, roam through the wildwood, fair creature! with me,
Where the Anthem of Nature is chanted for thee;
Away to the Woods! for fresh beauty we'll seek,
While the soft summer breezes lend health to thy cheek.

A PLEA FOR THE WOODS.

To the Woods! to the Woods! there is life in the
    breeze,
That bears on its wings the sweet balm of the trees;
There is health in the depths of the intricate wild
Of the dark, embrowned wilderness; off then, my child:
Gay Nymph of my Fancy! away, sweet! away!
Indulge in thy pastimes, and health shall repay
The toil of thy journey, though far be thy flight;
And return when thy bosom is warmed with delight.

There is health in the odor that comes from the soil
That is furrowed and ploughed by the husbandman's
    toil;
There is health on the mountain, and health in the vale,
Where the breeze is not laden with sorrow and wail.
The Indian, who lives as his forefathers did,
In the thick-branching woods, where his wigwam is hid,
Knows nothing of trouble, or sickness, or care,
For the forest supplies him with life-giving air.

To the Woods! to the Woods, then, nor scorn to be seen
With the Child of the Forest, whose dignified mien
Is that of a Chief, unrestricted and free
As the breezes that sweep o'er a mid-summer sea.
Away to the Woods! for the Goddess of Health
Stands inviting us thence, to partake of her wealth;
Away, then, away, where no plodding knave broods
O'er dark schemes of revenge—to the Woods! to the
    Woods!

LITTLE LIBBY.

Child of the sunny brow! mysteriously beautiful
Are those radiant eyes of thine, so full of hidden meanings.
From their depths of blue enigmal voices speak
In language fraught with silent eloquence and love,
That cannot be interpreted.   Dost thou live in the Ideal?
Thou, so young in years that the mild dawn of infancy
Dwells yet upon thy rosy features.   Dost thou dream of worlds
Where spirits like thine own—extremes of purity,
And models of young Innocence, do dwell?
Or, are thy dreams of earth? child of the thoughtful eye,
Of earth, and all the wild realities
That throng our sinning, lovely world?
Or wherefore gazest thou, as if the deep reflections
Of the happy spirits of the sunny skies
Were centred all in thee?   Mysterious are those eyes,
Brimful of unspoken mystery, and lovely as the stars!

  Child of serene beatitude!
  Almost thou claimest our idolatry.
  Child of my heart's unselfish love!
  Bright type of angelic simplicity
  Sent hither from above;
  Earth holds nought lovelier than thee,
  Child of the polished brow and laughing eye!
  The glory of the Eternal rests upon thee;

Thou art spotless as heaven's azure sky,
And gentle as the dove.

Child of the thoughtful eye, the sunny, curl-kissed brow!
Fair as an evening moonbeam is the soft sweetness
Of thy angelic features—the truthful mirror that reflects
The celestial brightness of thy unerring soul,
Even as in the river's face the stars are nightly glassed.
Perfection seated on its loftiest eminence,
Where the transient beauty of this world wings not
Its daring flight, cannot compare with thee,
Or vie with the heavenly intellectuality
Of thy serene and faultlessly-moulded countenance.

    Type of the truly beautiful!
    Figure of the truly happy and the pure!
    Fair and unsurpassable creation!
    Wast thou sent hither to endure
    Such trials as may furrow that calm brow,
    And bedim those lustrous eyes,
    That surpass all bright things? thou peerless one!

Child of the early morning! child of the sunny brow!
On which the spirit's divine immortality
Forever sits; scarce can I deem thee of this earth,
For God has given thee the likeness of an angel,
And left the unmistakable impress of a divine hand
Upon thee. Thou art softer than the holy radiance
Of the immortal stars, that love to look on thee,
Thou art so like to them in brightness, and thou seem'st
To have enticed from the planetary fields

Two of their most beautiful and lustrous ornaments.
Child of the blooming cheek! the marble brow!
Thou wast surely born to love; to learn love's various
    teachings.
We admire thee when thou art rapt in wakeful
    dreamings;
We watch the eloquent expression of thy mild features;
And listen to the innocent prattle of thy fairy lips.
All these bespeak thee a child of love. Love supremely
    reigns
In all thy looks, and in thy magic whisperings;
A love that purifies and elevates the heart;
Thy voice is delectable music, that stirs the inmost soul.
Would that thou wert not doomed to earthly sorrows!
They are inseparable from love. They give the visions
Of the bright mind a tinge of gloom, and mar its soft
    enjoyment.
Sorrow and Love, alas! go hand in hand. They are
Twin issues of the one fate—the one unrelenting destiny.

    Child of the blooming cheek!
    Where young Love tends the delicate rose,
    Sorrow and Love may both be thine?
    God keep thy gentle spirit meek,
    Breathe on thee with breath divine,
    And shield thee from Love's woes!

Child of the rose-tinged cheek! Child of the lily brow!
Let the selfish Atheist approach, and gaze upon thy
    beauty.

Dare he deny that thou wilt live hereafter?
Dare he deny that on thy Celestial countenance
Is stamped the impress of the soul's bright immortality?
Will he not there trace the right hand of Omnipotence?
The breathings of a Divine Creator visible in every
    lineament?
There speaks the undying soul; there the spirit's throne
    is erected;
There the intent of our earthly pilgrimage may be read.
If such a proof as thou art do not impress his mind
With the full certainty of man's eternal destiny,
Let him begone from hence and herd among the brutes!
Child of the placid brow! child of the laughing lip!
Child of the eloquent, thoughtful, dreamy eye!
Child of the musing look — the look of unchildish
    earnestness,
Wherefore wast thou made so beautiful?
The loveliest rose must fade; the lily lose its whiteness,
And the mild eye of the blue violet must close in death!
Thy brow will yet lose its polished, alabaster beauty;
Thy cheek will blanch and wither beneath the breath of
    time;
Thine eye, where sits the God-like Spirit of Language,
Will become dim as the years pass o'er thee in their
    swiftness;
Those golden curls will whiten and lose their velvet
    softness;
And thy dear form is doomed to moulder in the tomb.
Alas! that beauty such as thine should come to this!

Alas! that thy light-bounding heart, whence springs thy
    merry laughter,
Should wither in that gentle bosom and grow cold—
Cold as the pale snows in the bleak church-yard,
That cover the icy bosoms of the dead.

THE YELLOW CURL.

"I send you one of little Libby's curls."—Letter.

    To others, valueless,
To me, a most inestimable prize,
    That doth possess
    True loveliness.
It speaks of childish joy, and manhood's sighs.
At quiet evening, when my work is done,
    I love to look upon
        That Yellow Curl.

    I look on it, and, lo!
My better feelings quicken at the sight,
    For well I know
    How soft time's stream doth flow
Around thy path, dear, gentle child, and bright,
Whose graces, though in absence, I review,
    And that fair head, where grew
        That Yellow Curl.

THE YELLOW CURL.

A rose-bud on a stream,
A twittering swallow first upon the wing,
   A warm sunbeam:
    Such, sweet one! dost thou seem,
First floweret of the early budding spring,
That, 'mongst the many joys it brings to man,
    Hath nothing fairer than
        That Yellow Curl.

   A gift from Fairy land,
A gem from Beauty's casket, dearly prized,
   A golden sand
    From distant Ophir's strand;
Lovelier than Earth's perfections harmonized:
Ev'n so art thou, fair child, and such to me
    Shall ever, ever be
        That Yellow Curl.

   A lily in the wild,
A beauteous Thought amongst a Sea of Words,
   A zephyr mild:
    Such seem'st thou, gifted child;
A gentle lamb chosen from many herds;
A vast idea, concentrated to
    A point. Go! let me view
        That Yellow Curl.

   And I will hoard the gem,
Will keep the golden treasure as secure
   As a rare diadem;

Blossom from a graceful stem;
I look on it, and know that thou art pure.
Thoughts crowd on thoughts, and fancies, strange and new,
    Love to do homage to
        That Yellow Curl.

  I look on it, and all
The evil in my nature seems to die;
    One glance doth call
    Forth peace, and disenthrall
My pent-up fancies. Mount, my thoughts, yon sky,
And there select some graceful cherub's face,
    And faultless head, to grace
        That Yellow Curl.

LET THEM BOAST AS THEY WILL.

Let them boast as they will of the world's giddy pleasures,
  I've tried them, and found them both wanting and vain;
And so will each Truth-seeking mortal, who measures
  The good by the evil—the joy by the pain.
Let him rove through the bowers where Love stands to lure him,
  Let him climb Pleasure's height till he vexes his brain,
And every step that he takes will assure him
  That all gilded delights are both shallow and vain.

Let him sip from the cup where perdition is sowing
  Her tares, that will poison youth's promising grain,
And while the red wine in the goblet is glowing,
  He'll find that earth's pleasures are shallow and vain.
Let him mix in the waltz, where, with beauty to lure him,
  He can revel in smiles till he gladdens his brain,
But the morning will dawn, both to vex and assure him
  That all earthly pleasures are fleeting and vain.

Let him bow down to Fashion, an idol enslaving
  The minds of her votaries, who dare not complain;
Insatiate—peevishly, sinfully craving
  For pleasures, the vainest of all that are vain.
Let him feed upon dishes, whose savors allure him
  To grasp at a pleasure that addles his brain,
Till nature, o'ertaxed, groans aloud, to assure him
  That the pleasure at best was both hurtful and vain.

But Pleasure is useful. It teacheth the wisest
  That, from joys which are sweetest 'tis well to abstain,
While he who the lowliest lessons despisest,
  Will learn to his cost that earth's pleasures are vain.
Thrice happy is he, who, when false pleasures allure him,
  Repels the proud tempter with christian disdain,
And calls on calm Reason, to haste and assure him
  That Love, Truth, and Heaven, alone are not vain.

LIMERICK CATHEDRAL BELLS.

A remarkable and touching story is connected with the "Limerick Cathedral Bells." They were originally brought from Italy, where they had been manufactured by a young Italian, who devoted a long period of his life to the accomplishment of his darling task. He afterwards lived for many years in the vicinity of the convent for which they were purchased. Civil war at length fell like a withering blight upon the land: the convent was razed to the ground, and the bells removed. The Italian, broken hearted, and no longer young, travelled over the greater part of Europe in search of them; until at length, having sailed for Ireland, and proceeded up the Shannon, the vessel anchored off Limerick; and as the small boat, in which he was, approached the shore, from St. Mary's steeple came the cheering music of his long-lost bells. The effect was too much for him: the first peal smote him to the heart, and when they landed, he was found not only dead, but cold as marble.

In fair and sunny Italy, beneath its heavenly sky,
A young and stately Artisan on a mossy bank doth lie;
A light spreads o'er his features, and his darkly flashing eye—
Is it because his lovely wife and children all are nigh?

No—no—but on his ear there falls, from a neighboring convent tower,
The pleasant chime of vesper bells, that proclaim the evening hour;
And every morn, and every eve, for years it was his pride
To listen to the blending of their tones at eventide.

For they were of his handicraft—his ears first heard the tone
That had become a part of him as those happy years had flown;

Each note had been a joy to him, to other hearts unknown,
He would not exchange their music for the honors of a Throne.

But lo! the brand of civil war is flaming o'er the land—
He sees his treasures borne away by the marauder's hand;
And though old and silver-headed now, he leaves Italia's plain,
And deigns to tread the wide world o'er to hear their sounds again.

  Upon St. Mary's turret
   An old man keeps his eye,
  For there his long-lost idols,
   His earthly treasures lie;
  The boat moves on serenely,
   The happy shore is nigh,
  Bathed in the softening radiance
   Of a summer evening sky.

  The old man sits reflecting,
   Perchance on happier times,
  When from the Italian convent
   First pealed those silvery chimes
  That on his ear, incessantly,
   From youth to age did fall,
  Soothing his ravished senses
   With their heaven-ascending call,

For years he had not heard them,
  For years he had not known—
Save in his secret memory—
  Their sweetly sounding tone;
For in a foreign country,
  While he had weary grown,
Strange ears drank in the melody
  That once was all his own.

And now the aged wanderer
  Nears the desired shore,
Fain would he clasp his treasures,
  Fain hear their peals once more,
When, lo! as if to welcome him,
  Each with the other vied;
He heard their silvery voices,
  He heard their tones—and died!

LOVE'S GUIDING STAR.

In happier hours, Love's star was beaming
  About my path by day and night,
Ev'n when my mind was wrapped in dreaming,
  I felt the fervor of its light.
And when my soul was dark with sorrow,
  Its brightness quenched in mental pain,
I looked with hope towards the morrow,
  For I knew that star would shine again.

But now, the hours are sad and dreary,
   Love from my heavenward path is flown,
And Hope is crushed, and I am weary
   In living for myself alone :
No guiding star to cheer me onward,
   To wing my better thoughts to God,
But dark Despair impels me downward.
   I see my grave beneath the sod!

Oh! is it to be thus forever?
   And must that guardian spirit's light
Illume my darkened footsteps never,
   Or quicken this eternal night?
Fool that I was! to madly sever
   That bright link in my being's chain—
To quench that holy light for ever!—
   For I cannot hope 'twill shine again!

THE ANGEL'S GIFT.

"Maiden of the sunny soul!
   Heaven build life's skies above thee,
     Pure and bright
     As her own light,
   Faithful as the hearts that love thee!
As the stars do shine upon
   Earth's pure spirits while they're sleeping,
     Filled with love

From heaven above,
Angels have thee in their keeping!"

Thus a Minstrel-Poet sung,
  O'er a maiden's peaceful slumbers,
    She slept on,
    As sleeps the dawn,
Soothed by Morning's golden numbers.
But through all his harp strings swept
  Airs, that mortal fingers never
    Yet did fling
    From dulcet string!—
Still the sounds came bounding ever.

Till a radiant Angel stood
  With a glowing harp before him,
    Hers the lyre
    Whose Orphean fire
Trilled in burning numbers o'er him.
"Have thy wish," the angel said,
  "Heaven approves thy pure emotion;
    In thy care
    I place the fair,
Guard her with thy heart's devotion."

Smiling like the blue-eyed dawn,
  Waked the radiant-minded Maiden,
    Blissful gleams
    Had sunned her dreams,
Her blue eyes were beauty-laden.

Leaped for joy her yearning heart,
At the vision bending o'er her,
Well she knew
Her dreams were true,
Her Love's brave Knight knelt before her.

LOVE'S SIGNET RING.

I stood and watched the wild Chaudiere,*
Its waters to the cauldron leaping,
When in my mind awoke the fair
Whose spirit in my heart was sleeping.
"Behold!" I said, "how swift and strong
The current strikes the foaming basin!
So in my heart, for thee, love's song
Hymns its eternal diapason.

"And as yon clouds of vapor roll
Above the seething foam to heaven,
So floats love's incense up my soul,
To God, for thee, at morn and even.
The iris, blushing far below
The bosom of the bounding river,
Is Love's bright Signet Ring, a bow
Of promise in life's sky forever!"

Sweet memories of that wild Chaudiere
Within my mind are gaily leaping;

* The magnificent Falls of the Chaudiere, Bytown—now Ottawa.

And in my thrice-bless'd heart, that fair,
  Belovéd spirit, still is sleeping;
And when dark clouds their shadows fling
  Across life's swiftly bounding river,
I look upon Love's Signet Ring—
  The Bow is there—I bless the Giver!

MARY'S TWENTIETH BIRTHDAY.

One of the Fourscore years, Mary,
  Has passed like a dream away,
A dream of laughter and tears, Mary,
  Like a showery summer's day,
    With its rainbow bright,
    In the warm twilight,
  Fair pledge of a happier day, Mary,
  God's pledge of a happier day.

Swiftly the seasons roll, Mary,
  Like the waves o'er a mighty sea,
Searching the depths of the soul, Mary,
  With their power and mystery.
    Every hour that flies,
    Tells in distant skies
  The words that it heard from thee, Mary,
  The deeds that are done by thee.

See that the tale be pure, Mary,
  That the Hours may have to tell;

Goodness and Truth, we are sure, Mary,
　Heav'n loveth exceeding well;
　　And the beauteous mind
　　Where Truth is shrined,
Glows bright as a sunny dell, Mary,
Glows bright as a sunny dell.

More of the Fourscore years, Mary,
　Must pass like the first away,
Each, as its turn appears, Mary,
　May not be a summer's day;
　　But Hope's rainbow bright,
　　With its smile, will light
The close of a happier day, Mary,
The dawn of Eternal Day.

LOVE'S MORNING LARK.

The Lark mounts up to greet the dawn,
　Midway between the earth and sky,
The glad morn yearns and smiles upon
The bright-winged spirit, whose song fills
The pulsing air with music rills,
　Glad'ning the Angels that pass by.

For never morn comes down to earth,
　That is not borne on Angels' wings;
Music is of celestial birth,
And like the Lark, with voice of love,

Pure as God's light, it soars above,
    When Woman from her full heart sings.

So, Maiden, thou shalt be the Lark,
    And I, the long-expectant Morn;
Bring back the lost Dove to its Ark,
And let my mateless heart be bless'd,
My being in thy soul find rest,
    And my new life be Music-born.

SONG—THE BANNER OF OLD ENGLAND.

SONG FOR THE QUEEN'S BIRTHDAY—1858.

    Raise high the broad Banner!
    Old England's broad banner!
That waves its Red Cross over every sea;
    With hearts firm and loyal,
    Cheer loud for the Royal—
The famed Royal Standard, the Flag of the Free!
And where its loved folds are triumphantly seen,
Let the rallying cry be: "GOD SAVE ENGLAND'S QUEEN!"

    God prosper that Banner!
    That red Saxon Banner!
'Tis England's—'tis ours; far away though we be
    From that Isle of the Ocean,
    Our heart's fond devotion
Is with her—with England—the Home of the Free!

That Flag makes the moments of Danger serene,
For it floats o'er the Home of VICTORIA OUR QUEEN!

  Long flourish that Banner!
  That proud Saxon Banner!
When Nations and Kingdoms go down to decay;
  May Peace aye surround it,
  As Valor has crowned it,
When foemen unnumbered were smote with dismay.
Three cheers—three times three—for the time-honored
  sheen
Of that Banner, the Flag of VICTORIA OUR QUEEN!

  Then up with the Banner!
  Our broad Red Cross Banner!
The banner renowned by both Saxon and Gael;
  Brave Celts fought victorious,
  On fields hot and glorious,
Beneath that broad Banner, on mountain and vale.
Let ALL gather round its loved, conquering screen,
With a true British cry for "VICTORIA OUR QUEEN!"

SONG—THE HEROES OF THE ALMA.

  The Heroes of the Alma!
   Right gallantly they fought!
    No flinching knave,
    Or craven slave,
   For coward quarter sought!

But manfully, and zealously,
    Each hero struck, that day,
        As up the height
        The arm of might
    Impelled the strong array.

The heroes of the Alma!
    Intrepidly they stood,
        As stood of old
        Their Fathers bold,
    On Cressy's field of blood.
Right manfully, and zealously,
    They pressed the swerving foe—
        Not all his might
        Could hold the height
    Against so firm a blow.

The heroes of the Alma!
    Exultingly they trode;
        Though every breath
        Was fraught with death,
    Loud swelled the Battle-Ode.
Right manfully, and thrillingly,
    Uprose the Victor-Psalm,
        As on the height,
        With arm of might,
    The Allies grasped the palm.

The Heroes of the Alma!
    Well may their pæans flow:

For never yet
  Was tyrant met
With more decisive blow!
Right manfully, intrepidly,
  Each Briton proved his might,
    And every Gaul
    Stood up a Saul,
  Upon that groaning height.

Brave Heroes of the Alma!
  Each man a Victor-God!
    Your noble dead,
    Who fought and bled,
  Cry vengeance from the sod!
Right manfully, and zealously,
  Uphold your high renown,
    And heav'n will aid
    Each righteous blade
  To strike the Tyrant down!

THE TWOFOLD VICTORY—AN ALMA LYRIC.

By the famous Alma River
  Knelt a Warrior, brave and young,
Through his veins ran Death's cold shiver,
  On his lips his last breath hung;
Far above him rolled the battle,
  Downward rolled to Alma's wave,
Downward, through the crash and rattle,
  Came the cheering of the brave.

"Comrades," said he, rising slowly,
  Kneeling on one bended knee,
"Comrades," said he, feebly, lowly,
  "Is that cheer for Victory?"
"Yes!—they fly!—the foe is flying!"
  "Comrades," said he, ardently,
"Cheer for me, for I am dying,
  Cheer them on to Victory!"

By that blood-encrimsoned River
  Cheered they with a martial pride,
Death's last shaft had left its quiver,
  And the Warrior, smiling, died.
Faintly his last cheer was given,
  Feebly his last breath went free,
And his spirit passed to Heaven
  On the wings of Victory!

SONG OF THE BRITISH MARINER.

Launched once more on the ocean wave,
  Where my careless boyhood found me;
Free to roam where the wild winds rave,
  And the billows roll, around me.
Oh! there's joy on my restless home,—
  Joy for the daring seamen!
    Though landsmen shrink
    When on danger's brink,

Not the rocky shore,
Nor the breakers' roar,
Can daunt old Ocean's Freemen.

Hearts as free as the winds that sweep
  The breast of the trackless ocean,
Have the sons of the mighty deep,
  When the gallant ship's in motion.
Toss'd on waves that roll mountains high,
  What cares the dauntless seaman?
    His heart beats warm,
    Both in calm and storm,
    For there's not a breeze
    That sweeps the seas,
Can daunt old Ocean's Freemen!

Long as the Red-Cross Banner flies
  High over the heaving billow,
Will the tar tempt the fiercest skies
  That frown on his restless pillow.
Long as Old England's Ensign waves
  Over her dauntless seamen,
    Not the midnight breeze
    That sweeps the seas,
    Nor the hostile shore,
    Nor the battle's roar,
Can daunt her Ocean Freemen!

THE INDIAN SUMMER.

It is not like the Spring-time, bright
   With budding leaves and opening flowers,
But there's a glory in its light,
Softer than that which falls by night
   On lovers' bowers.
There is a mellow tint on every tree,
And nature's breath is sweet, and all is harmony.

It is not like the Summer time,
   Enlivened by a brilliant sun,
It savors of a purer clime
Than Summer, in its earliest prime,
   E'er smiled upon.
There is a light serene on everything,
Half veiled, and blushing, like a Bride in Spring.

Thou com'st in Autumn, when the trees
   Have doff'd their florid livery,
Ere Winter sweeps, with blighting breeze,
And fetters strong, to bind the seas—
   All hail to thee!
To thee, whose subtle charms no pen can trace,
To whom the artist's skill imparts no flattering grace.

THE BETRAYAL.

Into the bower young Osmond came,
  Into the bower where Annie was sleeping;
Softly he whispers the maiden's name,
  She awakes—her eyes are moist with weeping.
  Wherefore doth Annie sigh?
    What cruel pangs doth move her?
  Wherefore that tearful eye?
    Osmond—does he not love her?
    Annie is poor and fair,
      No paltry gems array her,
    But she deigns to love the princely heir,
      Though he comes but to betray her.

There is a magic in woman's tears,
  Each glittering drop a charm possesses,
And Osmond trembles with guilty fears,
  As the charming girl to his breast he presses.
  Wherefore doth Annie smile?
    What sudden change doth move her?
  How woman's tears beguile!—
    Young Osmond swears to love her!
    Annie is young and fair,
      Rich gems will soon array her,
    She will shortly wed the princely heir,
      Whose young heart would not betray her.

There is a Bridal at Osmond Hall,
  And beautiful forms the revels are keeping,

But Annie has wandered apart from all,
  The Maid of the Bower again is weeping!
Why weeps the fair-one now?
  What hasty pledge is broken?
Does she repent the vow—
  The solemn vow—just spoken?
No—'tis dear woman's plan,
  Let joy or grief waylay her,
If she miss, or catch, some simple man,
  Her tears will at once betray her!

THE IMPATIENT LOVER.

Haste hither, my love, the river
  Is tinged with the pale moonlight,
The leaves of the dark trees quiver,
  And throb in the parting night.
Why linger, my love, why linger?
  Swift fly the hours away,
And soon will Aurora's finger
  Point to the dawning day.

The Spirit of Morn doth hover
  Above the horizon dark,
'T is time that both Maid and Lover
  Were safe in their waiting bark;
Then hasten to meet me, dearest,
  Why does my true-love stay?

Oh! haste, and your loved-one nearest,
   We'll leave ere the dawn of day.

As the Spring-time awaits the Summer,
   With longing I wait for thee;
All graceful the gay new comer
   Trips smilingly o'er the lea;
As Summer the Spring embraces,
   So chide I thy long delay;
Now we'll leave ere Aurora chases
   The mists from the waking day.

THE GRAPE.

The Grape! the Grape! the lovely Grape!
   'T is the staff of the idiot brave;
      It supports them where
      The grim fiend Despair
Beckons on to an early grave.
Then, a joy to the Grape!—the lovely Grape!
   The staff of the truly brave;
      For its juice hath wrought
      What the brave have bought—
A right to the Drunkard's Grave.

The Grape! the Grape! the luscious Grape!
   How it glows in the sparkling bowl!
      How the ruby wine
      From the tempting vine

Doth gladden the Drunkard's soul!
But a curse on the Grape! the luscious Grape,
As it glows in the treacherous bowl;
    For a scorpion lurks
    In its juice, and works
The Doom of the Drunkard's Soul.

A THOUSAND FACES.

A thousand faces, and not one like hers.
I looked upon them all. I looked, and felt
That every feature had its worshippers.
But there were none to whom my heart had knelt,
To offer its devotion; none were there
That made me tremble, as the idol stirs
The feelings of its devotee; no eyes
With their dark beauty, to inflame the soul,
And make it risk its portion in the skies,
One welcome look of their soft light to share.
Oh! if the ransomed spirits, from their goal
In Paradise, did yearn to visit earth,
Enslaved by loveliest maids of mortal birth;
If woman's eyes seduced them down from heaven,
Surely weak, erring man, may sometimes dare
To worship too, and hope to be forgiven!

THE PAST.

Erase it from my memory! for, lo!
As I look backward on the devious track,
Unhappy images are seen to pass,
Like the wild shapes in a Magician's glass,
Making the brain grow dizzy as they go
And come again, as if employed to rack
The human mind, and cause the tears to flow
From Life's own fountain. Yes, erase the Past!—
But, no!—not all—for some green spots are there;
Small, twinkling stars, out-peering through the gloom;
Warm gleams of sunlight, which do sometimes cast
Their mellow tints within. These will entomb
Each sullen shadow in its secret lair,
And Hope may make the future prospect fair.

Yea; let them rest! I would not banish one
Stern recollection from its chosen cell.
Thick clouds may for a moment hide the sun,
But lessen not his glory; even so,
We hold within us what of dark and bright
By our own wills have been implanted there.
And we can purge from the mind's crucible
The scum of Error that excludes the light
Of Truth. Experience teacheth us to know
That light and darkness—moral day and night—
Are incident to mortals here below.
Yes; let me rather muse on errors past,
The silent monitors that bring us peace at last.

IMAGINATION.

Off through the world with the lightning's velocity,
   Darting through space with electrical speed,
Loosed are the reins of thy impetuosity,
   Roam where thou wilt, then, my beautiful steed.
Fleeter art thou than the fairest of Araby's
   High-mettled, swift-footed steeds of the plain,
Perfect as theirs is thy beautiful symmetry,
   Petulant, fanciful steed of my brain.
Regions more wild than the sun ever shone upon,
   Cycles and worlds of unbounded delight,
Andes of Thought, towering grandly-majestical,
   Reaching to heaven's indefinite height;
Swiftly ascending some Alpine acclivity,
   Plunging, unscathed, to the abyss below,
Thence to the fields where the sword of the conqueror
   Reddens the soil with the blood of the foe;
Mounting again on the breath of the hurricane,
   Upward and onward, through tempest and storm;
Thus, wheresoever abideth sublimity,
   There shalt thou wander, thou beautiful form.

Maid of my soul! though my thoughts were Ubiquitous,
   Ranging unshackled through earth, air and sea,
Fancy were swayed in its wildest imaginings,
   Evermore, evermore turning to THEE.

Breasting the ocean, high-heaving, tempestuous,
   Down through its deepest and costliest cell,

Where the fair Nymphs in their crystalline palaces,
    Where the bright Naiads harmoniously dwell.
Threading, unseen, its dark caves subterranean,
    Glowing with coral, and gleaming with gems,
Forests of sea-weed, and groves, where the emerald
    Lieth half hidden beneath the green stems.
Upward and off on some billowy mountain-top,
    Heavenward borne where the thunderstorm sings,
Tracking the lightning, and finding its dwelling-place
    Cradled to sleep on the proud eagle's wings.
Awed by the psalm of some deep-toned Niagara,
    Scorched by the flashes from Etna's red flame,
Rising again in thy flight subitaneous,
    Shouting aloud an ecstatic acclaim:
Thus my fond steed, with the lightning's velocity,
    Dart'st thou through space like the beam of a star,
Loosed are the reins of thy impetuosity,
    Roam where thou wilt, with thy glittering car.

Maid of my soul! though my thoughts were Ubiquitous,
    Ranging forever unshackled and free,
Still would they turn in their highest imaginings,
    Hurrying evermore downward to THEE.

Circling the Night, when Darkness is hovering
    Over the world, like a spirit astray,
Thy presence illumines each dark-seeming labyrinth,
    Shedding around it perpetual Day.
Making one moment a glowing millennium,

Brimming with pleasures untasted and pure,
  Crowding millenniums into moments of ecstacy,
Brief as the lightning's flash over the moor.
Upwards, through worlds that no mortal e'er looked
    upon,
  Upwards, all gracefully, speedily on;
Up through the stars with thy wondrous celerity,
  Travelling restlessly up to the sun.
Sweeping across the deep void of the universe,
  The ether thy robe, and a star for thy bark,
Backward to earth, to thy dwelling mysterious,
  Gently, but swift, like the dove to its ark.

Maid of my soul! though my thoughts were Ubiquitous,
  Swift as the thunderbolt, deep as the sea,
Fancy were reined in its boldest imaginings,
  Tremblingly, joyfully hast'ning to THEE.

THE SPIRIT OF THE WOODS.

Gently wanders he
Where no human foot intrudes,
Joyously,
Fancy-free,
The Spirit of the Woods.
Singing through the trees,
Playing with the breeze,
Laughing at the seas
As they roll,

With sullen roar,
To the shore,
Rushing evermore
To their goal.

Softly wanders he
Where no human foot intrudes,
More fancy-free
Than the sea,
The Spirit of the Woods.
Up and down the hill,
By the leaping rill,
On towards the mill
In the vale;
Upwards through the sky,
Where he seems to die,
Breathing forth a sigh
To the gale.

Quietly wanders he,
Through the deep solitudes;
Who so free
There, as he,
The Spirit of the Woods?
By the silent bower,
When the heavens lour,
Nestling in the flower,
Snug and warm;
Darting out again

O'er the grassy plain,
With the merry rain
  Through the storm.

Daringly wanders he
Where no human foot intrudes,
    Recklessly,
    Laughingly,
The Spirit of the Woods.
  Up the snowy steep,
  To the topmost heap,
  As the bleak winds sweep
    Down its sides;
  From the rocky height,
  Through the stormy night,
  Laughing with delight,
    Back he glides.

Recklessly wanders he
Where no human foot intrudes,
    Dauntlessly,
    Fancy-free,
The Spirit of the Woods.
  In the zephyr mild,
  Watching o'er the child,
  Lost in the wild,
    Lest it fear;
  In the lion's den,
  In the marsh with the wren,

Through the dismal fen
With the deer.

Thus wanders he, eternally,
Where no human foot intrudes,
Playfully,
Fancy-free,
The Spirit of the Woods.
Rambling everywhere,
Through the woodland air,
Distancing dull care,
As he flies:
Like him, eternally,
Pure thoughts wander free,
Over earth and sea,
To the skies.

LOVE'S NEW ERA.

There's a wild joy within my heart,
Hope's sunlight warms my brain,
And my thirsty soul drinks Gladness in,
As the earth drinks summer rain;
Flushed Health is leaping through my veins,
My blood is all aglow,
Each pulse has a loud and a stately beat,
And my thoughts are like the snow.

For Woman's Voice of Love hath burst
Like a meteor on my way,

And I live in smiles, like the Sun's bright Isles,
   That bask in Eternal Day.
Life never came to me till now,
   But pass'd like a restless dream,
Where Love for evermore wandered by,
   Like a rose upon a stream.

FAITH.

Faith is the Christian's Pisgah. Here he stands
Enthroned above the world; and with the eye
Of full Belief looks through the smiling sky
Into the Future, where the Sacred Lands
Of Promise, though extending ev'n beyond
His half-ubiquitous vision, are brought nigh,
And he beholds their beauty. Faith is strong;
It is the giant arm that puts aside
The mountain-tops of Error. 'Tis the bond
Indissoluble, that unites man to
His God; the trusty, Omnipresent Guide
That wings him with electric speed along
The intervening space that screens the view
Of that high heaven where the Sons of Faith abide.

FROM QUEENSTON HEIGHTS.

Eleven.   Welcome to the Sabbath bells!
A blessing and a welcome!   At this hour
One prays for me at home, two hundred miles
From where I lounge along the grassy knoll,
Far up upon this classic hill.   The air
Hath a delicious feeling, as it breathes
Its autumn breath upon me; air so calm,
One cannot feel the beat of Nature's pulse.
No, not a throb.   The heav'nly influences,
Hearing that maiden's prayer, lean down and move
My being with their answerings of love.
The myriad-tinted leaves have gravely paused
To listen to the spheral whisperings—
The unvoiced harmonies that few can hear
Or feel, much less interpret faithfully;
And the swift waters of the dizzy gorge,
Stunned with their recent plunge against the crags
That hide Niagara's iris-circled feet,
And lashed to very madness as they wound
Their circling way past rocks and fretted banks,
Melt into calm in the blue lake beyond,
As starlight melts into the distant sea.

Those ancient willows have a solemn droop;
You scarce can see the dwelling they adorn:
Behind them rest the grain-denuded fields.
Here, to my left, an unpretending town;

There, to my right, another; like two friends,
Each thanking heaven for the Sabbath-pause,
And the brief respite from man's curse of toil.
The church bells pealing now and then a note,
Swell the bless'd Pæan with their silver tongues.
The very tombstones yonder, near the church,
Look whiter for the eloquent Repose.

  A few short paces through the cedar trees,
Where the pert chipmunks chatter, and the birds
Select and melodize their sweetest notes,
And I have gained the level. Toward the lake,
The cloudlike points of land are seen
Blending with old Ontario, and the gorge
Hurries its whirling current past the banks
That glass their fair proportions in the stream.

  Here is the Monument. Immortal BROCK,
Whose ashes lie beneath it, not more still
Than is the plain to-day. What have we gained,
But a mere breath of fame, for all the blood
That flowed profusely on this stirring field?
'T is true, a Victory; through which we still
Fling forth the meteor banner to the breeze,
And have a blood-sealed claim upon the soil.
'T were better than Defeat, a thousand times.
And we have rightly learned to bless the name
Of the Old Land, whose courage won the day—
We, the descendants of her Victor-sires.
But dearer than a hundred victories,

With their swift agony, the earnest Calm,
That, like a Blessing from the lips of God,
Rests on the classic plain, o'er which my feet
Tread lightly, in remembrance of the dead—
My Brothers all, Vanquished and Victors both.
And yet my heart leaps up, poor human heart!
As I lean proudly, with a human pride,
Against this pillar to a great man's name.
Yet I would rather earn that maiden's prayer,
Than all the fame of the immortal dead.

There may be furrows still upon the field,
Ploughed up with the wild hurricane of war
On that eventful day. Here, certainly,
An angry missile grooved this honored rock.
Though nearly half a century has pass'd,
The fissure still is here, and here the rust
Left by the iron messenger of death,
As it sped forward like an angry fate,
Sending, perhaps, ten human souls to hell.

There, there was pain. Here, where the wondrous skill
Of the mechanic, with this iron web
Has spanned the chasm, the pulse beats hopefully,
And thoughts of peace sit dove-like in the mind.
Heav'n bridge these people's hearts, and make them one!

FANNY.

Silence knelt praying in the room,
   And timid forms on tiptoe walked,
   And timorous voices lowly talked,
Like whisperings passing through the gloom.
      The world was lulled to sleep;
      The stars looked down upon the deep,
        Gravely and chill; and the flesh did creep;
The cold winds bleached the tint from off the rose.

Life's taper burned into the dust,
   Pale-flickering for a solemn while,
   Life's Angel, pausing with a smile,
Re-lit it with Eternal Trust!
      Warm hearts were filled with pain;
      Like flowers drenched by a wintry rain,
        Though they hear not the bleak winds complain,
The wretched weight strikes deeper than the blast.

Grief robbed each feature of its glow,
   The weary watchers watched no more,
   For death stood sentinel at the door,
And filled each entering heart with woe.
      The corse is white and cold,
      Like winter on the frozen wold;
        The grievers gaze with a grief untold,
But with a certain hope that ends in heaven.

The dismal coffin and the shroud!
   The mourners with their half-sealed lips!

A little while, and death's eclipse
Will vanish from that silent crowd.
    Remembrance wakes and weeps
    In a few hearts; life's action sweeps
    Over the many, whose unstirred deeps
Harbor that human thing—Indifference.

Along the straight and dusty road,
    And through the shadowy grove of pines,
    The long procession moves and twines;
And down into her dim abode
    The Mother and the Wife
    Is lowered, gently as her life
    Was gentle, ever through the strife
Of the harsh world, a patient-minded soul.

How like a curse it seems, to see
    The summer flowers bloom and die;
    How like a tenfold curse, to sigh
When death removes triumphantly
    A human form from earth!
    In kindness is the arm stretched forth,
    What seemeth Death is a Victor-Birth,
The unsealing of God's hidden mysteries.

LAMENT OF SHINGWAKONCE.

In the year 1849 some difficulty occurred between the Provincial Government, and the Indians on Lake Superior, in consequence of the sale of the lands in that region, to a certain Mining Company, by which the Indians were most unfairly dealt with, and almost driven from the occupation of lands to which they had the strongest possible claim. The chiefs of the Chippewas, headed by Shingwakonce, despatched a very strong remonstrance to the Government, in view of which these lines were written. They do not, however, contain a particle of the address, but grew out of the occasion, as it were.

I.

Where are the Hunting Grounds,
   O'er which we chased
The wild deer and buffalo?
   All laid waste!
By the White Man made desolate,
   Where shall we go
To hunt down the bison,
   Or the wild roe?
Away from the sacred mounds,
   To the far west,
From the graves of our fathers,
   We travel, oppress'd.
Back, back to the desert,
   Where the Pale Face has never
Set the print of his footsteps:
   Thus shall it be ever!

II.

Far from the tangled brakes,
Far from the sunny lakes,

Where the Red Man's rifle wakes
  The wild bird at morn;
Far from our chosen home,
Friendless, unfed, we roam,
    Hungered—forlorn!
  Far from the lands
Which the Great Spirit gave us,
  Driven by hands
That should stretch out to save us;
Far from our Wigwams rude,
To the deep solitude
Of the untrodden wood,
    Evermore driven!
    Hear it Oh! Heaven!
    Witness, ye Sun,
    That lights us at noon,
    And thou, restless Moon;
Ye witnesses all
  Of the Great Unseen Spirit,
When shall the Red Man
  His lost rights inherit?
Shall he be driven thus,
  Backward, forever?
  Never—Oh! never!

III.

Why, then, do we suffer
  The wrongs that surround us?
Why this barefaced injustice

Submit to for aye?
Why? Because we believed them,
   When they promised to own us
For Friends and for Brothers—
For such they have found us
   In battle and fray.
   But, alas! for the day
When we kindly received them!
   Alas! for the day
When our weapons retrieved them
From destruction and danger;
   From threatening foes,
Who harassed their ranks,
   Till the Red Man arose!
   A curse on the day!
If this be their boasted
   Support and protection:
To suffer marauding bands
   To hold in subjection
Our hard-fought-for lands—
Bands of Long Knives, who never
   Befriended, or served us,
But who would have scattered,
   Destroyed us—unnerved us,
   At once and forever!

IV.

Oh! for the time, when we
Could dot the stormy sea

With our birchen fleet!
Then we were strong and proud,
With a nation's strength endowed;
Then we roved the prairie vast,
Thinking it would ever last;
Then we were united all,
Mustering at the Great Chief's call! :
  Then we had the feet
Of the bounding antelope,
Full of buoyant life and hope;
Then we were determined,
  As brave men should be;
As the oaks we stood firmly,
  As the winds we were free;
We had food in abundance,
  And fish from the sea;
We warred not for others,
  Of woes, we had none,
And we rested securely
  When our hunting was done.

v.

But the Pale Faces saw us,
  They envied the lot
Of the Sons of the Forest,
  Who doubted them not;
They came with professions
  Of kindness and love,
And the Red Men believed

They were sent from above;
They came to despoil us
　Of every right
Which we long had enjoyed,
　Came, disputing our might;
They came to divide us,
　They sought to enslave
A race, that, when injured,
　Could learn to be brave!
We fought—we were victors,
　But more Pale Faces came,
And murdered our Nations
　With thunder and flame;
We fought—we were scattered
　Abroad through the land,
To seek a new shelter
　On some distant strand.

VI.

More Pale Faces came,
　From a far-foreign isle,
They came not to waste us,
　Came not to revile;
But by their broad banner,
　The Red Cross they bore,
They vowed to protect us—
　What could they do more?
Their battles we fought,
　When the Long Knives oppress'd them,

Their battles we won,
    When the Great Spirit bless'd them;
Our rights they respected,
    As brothers we shared
The bountiful country,
    With faith unimpaired.
For this we have loved them,
    For this we have stood
Battling danger and death,
    Both by land and by flood;
For this, when the terrible
    War-cry uprose,
Did we bare our breasts
    To the stroke of their foes!

VII.

And shall they who have owned us
    For brothers so long—
Shall they break their promise?
    Shall they do us wrong?
No! by that sacred Banner
    We looked on of yore,
When our friendly White Brothers
    First stood on our shore;
By the faith we then pledged,
    By their prowess and might!
We know they are willing
    To serve us aright.
Why, then, do they barter

Our rich lands away
  To the Long Knives, who hate us,
    As thieves hate the day?
Why suffer us backward
  By our foes to be driven?
The wrong calls for mercy,
  For justice from heaven!

VIII.

Rise, then, my Red Brothers!
  Speak aloud for your own,
For the Right has a voice,
  Like the thunder's loud tone;
Rise, not in deep anger,
  But firmly demand
That your White Brothers purchase
  Their right to our land:
Then, though we must wander
  Through forests unknown,
'T were better than famish
  On lands not our own.
Rise! Sons of Tecumseh!
  Ojibwas, arise!
Let the voice of the Mohawks
  Ascend to the skies!
Rise! tell our Great Father
  The wrongs we sustain,
And He, who loves Justice,
  Will heal them again.

IX.

Where are our mighty Chiefs,
  Whose deeds of war
Spread from this fertile land
  To climes afar?
Where are our stalwart sons,
  Our nations strong,
Who in our memories live,
  And in the White Man's song?
Spread like the autumn leaves
  Before the blast
Of the cold winds of winter—
  Their day has pass'd!
Behold! how few survive
  Of that countless host
Of brave and stern-faced warriors
  We once could boast!
Some perished by the White Man's hand,
  In mortal strife,
When the war whoop rose and fell
  With each chieftain's life!
Others, in peace were borne
  To the blest Hunting Grounds,
Whese the Red Men's spirits live,
  Where the war cry never sounds.

X.

Come, then, my brothers few,
  Let us depart,

Though we leave the wilds we love,
    With a heavy heart.
There are lands where the White Man's feet
    May never press,
Where the wild fowl still abound—
    In the deep wilderness;
There are rivers wide,
    Where the birch canoe,
As of old, can glide
    O'er the waters blue;
There are forests deep,
    Where the deer are found,
There are lands untrod—
    These are Freedom's ground,
Where we can live, till the Great Spirit calls
    The last of our tribes away,
    To hunt from day to day,
    From year to happier year,
In the blest Hunting Grounds
    Which the Red Men revere;
There to live evermore,
    Where death shall not sever
The loved from the loving,
    Through ages, whose vistas
    Stretch onward forever,
Where the White Man's unholy oppression shall cease,
And strife be unknown in those regions of Peace.

ABSENCE.

Oh! this continued absence from thy side!—
When will it cease? When will this lonely heart
Know thy companionship? When will thy breast
Pillow this aching head, and set at rest
The crowds of tantalizing fantasies
That throng my brain? Stern edict! to divide
The worshipper from his idol, or to part
The olive and the vine in their embrace!
Ev'n as the heavens are mirrored in the seas,
So in my mind reflected is thy face:
I look into its depths, and there I trace
Thy image unmistakably impressed—
Love's true daguerreotype. But even there
Thou art not—yet thou art—I joy, and I despair.

FESTUS.

Not strictly orthodox; but brimming full
Of the divinest meanings—good intents.
Thoughts flash like starbeams through it, which if sown
In man's concentral heart, will overrule
The earthliness of his nature; make him one
With God and Heaven; and the elements
Of his degenerate manhood purify;
As gold by fire, or sin by God's free-will.
Read, mark and learn. Extract herefrom the pearls,

And leave the dross untouched.   Up through Infinity,
And down through Hell, alike, behold the skill
Of the bright mind that planned the genial tale.
With him visit the infinitude of worlds,
Like him, in all thy acts let Love and Truth prevail.

SONNET.

Dark-eyed one! when I first beheld thy face,
My soul was gladdened.   Many years I'd sought
A living semblance to the bright Ideal
Imagination drew.   It was not all unreal,
That pleasing dream, nor was it all a vision;
For looking on thee now, my mind can trace
A faultless likeness 'tween that form and thee.
In my prophetic dreamings I had caught
The true impression.   Angelo or Titian
Could not have wrought a happier imagery;
And less enduring—Theirs will end with Time;
But mine—what human skill! what art sublime!
Will live forever! theirs will cease to be,
While mine, in thee, will live to all eternity.

HOPE.

A gentle messenger is Hope; a trusty friend,
That finds in every breast a welcome home.
Room for the Angel! let her radiant wings
Surround me evermore. The syren flings
Her magic mantle o'er me, and I roam
Through sunny realms that seemeth without end.
Onward and upward on Hope's rosy pinions
My thoughts are borne. What visions can transcend
The wondrous view of these her fair dominions,
Extending everywhere! Above—below,
Where'er she smiles, the landscape wears a glow
Of calm serenity. Her skill doth blend
Heaven's hues with those of earth. Weak and undone
Were man, without this gift of the Eternal One.

THE TRIO.

It was a summer's eve, on which I first
Beheld thee. As I looked into thine eyes,
And saw them flashing with the consciousness
Of their attractive power, the Love God
Spread his wings o'er me. From that hour I nursed
A pleasing form that to my bosom flew,
Seeking admittance. Not till then I knew
That Love and Hope were friends. Could I despise
The teachings of the rosy twain? Not less
Welcome was Love's companion than himself.

How kind was Hope! But Love—deceitful elf!
Called Sorrow in, who with his heavy rod
Chastised me. There the three remain:
Hope soothes when Love or Sorrow brings me pain.

THE ONE IDEA.

Oh! how it burns the brain, and tramples down
All other thoughts that struggle to be freed
From their imprisonment, driving them back
With its stern mandate, or its sterner frown;
And ruling from its heaven-exalted throne
The meaner serfs that form the motley herd!
In vain do they attempt to intercede—
Presuming slaves, that cross their monarch's track—
Death to them all! The menial tribes have stirred
The anger of their king. Degenerate pack!
Cringe—kneel—before this giant of the mind,
This reigning thought, which liveth there enshrined!
Thoughts that did once at my mere bidding move,
Are now the vassals of the tyrant—LOVE!

UNCURBED PASSION.

A human Niagara, plunging from the height
Of vain presumption to the sea of wrath
Below. An Alpine avalanche, in its might,
Strewing the giddy traveller's upward path
With devastation; whirling him adown
Into the steep abyss. The unchained bolt
Of sin's dread electricity. The revolt
Of judgment. Agent of the arch-traitor's frown.
The midnight tempest on a stormy sea.
Reason's eclipse. The Mephistophiles
That points the murderer's weapon: Like to these,
And in its headlong fury ever thus,
Is Passion unrestrained: The simoom's breath—
The entrance to the whirlpool, and to death.

PEACE.

  The Plague of War is stayed.
God's brightest Angel has stretched forth his hand,
And like a blessed light, from land to land
  Glides Peace, the mild-eyed maid.

  From th' sunny realm of France,
To England, chosen Mistress of the Sea,
O'er Russia's Northern Steppes, she moves, to free
  War's satyrs from their dance.

With voices jubilant,
And trembling lips, that burn with earnest prayer,
A million whispers, rising through the air,
    Storm heaven with a chant

    Of joy and thankfulness.
And human life is sacred, now, once more:
The fame of Inkerman, of Alma's shore,
    Of Balaklava's wild excess,

    Sufficeth us at last.
War with its brazen tongue! Peace with its smile!
Peace shedding halos over Briton's isle,
    War slumbering with the past.

    How long?—a single breath
May rouse the monster from his lair to-morrow,
And he allied with us in joy and sorrow,
    Strew England's shores with death.

    "In peace prepare for war."—
Time-honored maxim of an honored chief;
The gallic eagle's slumbers may be brief;
    Let England's hearths beware.

BERTRAM AND LORENZO.

A DRAMATIC FRAGMENT.

BERTRAM AND LORENZO.

A DRAMATIC FRAGMENT.

SCENE I.

A picturesque Valley. A range of Mountains in the back-ground. Cascade, falling into a waveless Lake at the base of the Cliff. Time, Evening.

BERTRAM.

This is a lonely place.

LORENZO.

    Call it not lonely;
Say, rather, that the God of Nature hath
Peopled these wilds with spiritual forms,
With which the man of an exalted mind
Can hold sweet converse in his studious hours.
Survey these hills! mark the immensity,
The wild sublimity, of those high mountains,
That with their purple summits pierce the skies,
Ev'n to the heavens above them, till they seem
Divested of their earthly coloring,
And clothed with an ethereal loveliness,
Soft as the drapery of the twilight robe
Thrown o'er the shoulders of voluptuous eve.
Behold the cataract, panting with alarm,
Leaping with frantic bound from rock to rock,
As leaps the lama o'er Peruvian hills,

When at its heels the mountain-hunter comes,
His quiver filled with death.   Struggling with fate,
The tortured waters pause upon the verge
Of yonder rock, then spring into the gulf,
Rejoicing at the bound, as, all adorned
With gold-bedrizzled locks, the stricken flood
Shakes its white mane, and speeds adown the stream,
Like to an expert swimmer, hale and young,
Stunning the billows with his manly limbs.
See how the Iris blushes at its feet,
Enveloped in the white arms of the spray,
Through which, ghost-like, its delicate pulse is seen
To throb responsive to the heaving breast
Of the pale vapour spirit, in whose arms
It lies, all blushes, like a timid maid
Enfolded in her lover's chaste embrace.
The trees that nod upon the piney height;
The humble shrubbery that men pass by
Unnoticed; the soft moss that grows upon
The flinty granite; the pale, meek-eyed flower,
Half hidden by the rank, luxuriant weeds,
Like full-blown Innocence in a world of Sin;
The unformed buds; the golden-veinéd leaves
That strew the brown soil of the autumn woods;
The birds that nestle closely in the grass,
Or chirrup forth a note for every beat
Of their impulsive, overflowing hearts;
Do each and all possess a powerful claim
Upon the sober mind.

BERTRAM.

              Give me the town,
Old man; its gay delights are more to me
Than all the paltry beauties of this place,
Which thou so much admirest. I would die
If I were banished to a place like this,
So lonely that my very nature shrinks
Within me at the thought of being here.
For thee, it may have charms enough to please
A spirit like to thine, bowed down with age;
To me, the prospect is most terrible;
'Tis lonely as a world without one's fellows
Can be.

LORENZO.

        Young man, thou dost not know the peace
That falls upon the spirit in these wilds,
Like gentle dew upon the parchéd leaf.
Learn to aspire to God; clutch at the stars;
Give thy ambition wings; from world to world
Mount bravely upwards, until, like the lark,
Thou disappearest in the infinity
That ends in heaven. Make the stars thy friends
Soar to their brilliant homes on wings of thought,
Or mould them to thy will upon the earth,
By careful study; like the falcon, mount,
And strike the quarry in the circling air,
Though it quadruple thee in magnitude.
Then wilt thou feel the noble aspirations
Which I am yearning for; then wilt thou pause,

Ere thy sense give permission to thy tongue
To say—this place is lonely. None dread more
Than I the thought of utter loneliness;
It is a treacherous cankerworm that feeds
Upon the flowery garden of the mind,
And leaves it seared and blighted; has its home
In the dark cell of the lean anchorite,
Who for some crime would torture his poor body
To purge his soul. But to be lonely here,
Where every breeze that passeth by interprets
God's everlasting, all-pervading truths
Unto our inmost souls; where we can feast
Our hungry mind's eye on the rich repast
Which the wild wilderness contains; is to
Be blind—insensible—to all the beauty
Which nature hath in vast profusion strewn,
With an unsparing hand, about our path.
Give me the place where I can hold communion
With Nature and with Nature's God; where I
Can analyze the secrets of my mind,
And pluck therefrom the rank, luxuriant weeds,
Which from my birth have been implanted there,
And sow some healthy seedlings in their stead,
From which will spring a ripe ambrosial fruit
That angels might partake of.

BERTRAM.

                      Singular mortal!
Why! I would rather tread the pleasing halls
Where such light-hearted fellows as myself

Had learned to kill the pleasure-wingéd hours
With dance and song, than listen to the ravings
Of an enthusiast. I'd rather be
A playful kid—a kitten—a young widow,
Be anything that trips it joyously
Over the many ups and downs of life,
Than an ascetic mortal like to thee.

LORENZO.

Yet all of these which thou hast named, are prone
To aspire to certain ends: The kid will climb
The steepest rocks, and 'mid the grandest scenes
Of nature live, forgetful of its fellows;
The kitten, sporting by its mother's side,
Will leave her to ascend the tottering pole,
While tabby purs below, and gravely scans
Th' ambitious feats of her young progeny;
The gay young widow wears a pleasing face,
And aims at winning a becoming mate,
To ease her poignant sorrow. But for thee,
Thou dost aspire to nothing! hast no aim,
But that of being pleased with endless dances—
The ball room is the goal of thy ambition!
This is trifling too much with thy existence.
In early youth I shared in all the joys
Which thou hast named, but took no real pleasure
In them. Ever before my eyes there stood
The ladder of my thoughts, where angels came
And went, like the Aurora in the North,
And by whose aid I had resolved to climb

To something greater than I yet had been,
And step by step to struggle to the top,
Or tumble headlong from the wild ascent.
I'd many lofty thoughts, but one there was,
Like snow-crowned Jura 'mongst his subject Alps,
Catching the sun's first rays; the moon and stars
Sent down their silver-pluméd messengers,
Whose smiles did keep it in perpetual light,
While all else lay in twilight: one great thought,
A kingly oak within a field of shrubs.
If thou wouldst be a Teacher, school thyself;
The Mind of Man is as a crucible
Which the Great Giver fills with golden Thought,
Tis Human Nature which supplies the dross;
But the same nature with that aid divine
Which all must seek who would live nigh to God,
Is a most subtle Alchymist, whose skill
Turns Error's dross to Truth's refinéd gold.
Seek Truth in time. The well is deep, my friend.
See that she pass thee not upon the way.
Man never sought for Truth and found her not.
The diver may not seize the largest pearl
At the first dip, nor yet in many years,
But every hair of his devoted head
Flings back a pearl into the deep again,
As full of beauty as the one he sought,
While he, all resolute, re-seeks the gem.
In searching for the one great Truth, beware
Lest thou reject the lesser truths which heaven

Profusely scatters in thy daily path.
I'd rather mould one burning Star of Thought,
Whose light would centre in some darkened mind,
Make some lone heart a peopled universe,
Lit by the smile of God's immeasured love,
Than sway the sceptres of an hundred thrones,
Or boast the wealth of Crœsus ten times told.

BERTRAM.

Old man! Your words, like sparks from stubborn flint,
Descend in brilliant showers on my brain,
Which like the earnest tinder cannot fail
To catch therefrom some gleams of inspiration,
Almost unwillingly. Already do
I wander in my purpose, to begone
To the ephemeral sports that make my life
One round of giddy pleasure. Did I stay,
I might forget the utter loneliness
Of the place, while confounded by thy speech;
I must away at once.

LORENZO.

Not yet awhile.
I've a surprise in store for thee, if thou
Canst bear it. I would fain convince thee, friend,
That God sits throned upon these lofty wilds,
And prove to thy half-unbelieving mind
That the still voice of august nature speaks
Audibly and incessantly to man.
Let's to the mountains.

BERTRAM.

    Well; to please thee, yes.
Age has its whims, which youth must knuckle to,
Or bide by the displeasure of its seniors.

SCENE II.

Midway up a rugged Mountain. Pathway rough and wearisome.

BERTRAM.

Old man, I'm tired! How can you foot it so
Over these rough and dangerous crags? my life
Upon it, I'll not be so easily caught
Another time.

LORENZO.

    Rebellious boy! dost think
The things that are worth seeking for
Can be procured without a little trouble?—
An extra thought, perchance—a step or two.
And yet, the worldly man, in peevish plight,
Frets, if the attainment of most perfect bliss
Would lead him off the paltry jig-jog path
Of every-day life. Dost thou hope for heaven?

BERTRAM.

Yes. But why ask a question of such import?
We all do hope to reach that bourne at last.

LORENZO.

Prepare then to encounter many obstacles
During thy journey thither. There's a vale
Darker than death, through which we needs must pass,
Where spirits from the abodes of wretchedness
Contest the passage with each weary pilgrim
Who enters it. Scorn not to learn from this,
That, to ensure our happiness, we must
Submit to all the sad perplexities
That lay before us. We must learn to conquer
Each evil thought and passion that waylay us,
'T will make the bliss laid up in store for us
The richer gain when earned by our good deeds.

Enter several Peasants on their way up the Mountain.

FIRST PEASANT.

Ha! our old friend! whither away so late?
Dost come to spend the night with us?

LORENZO.

      Many thanks.
This youth and I return again, so soon
As we have learned our lesson. Good even, friends!

 [*Salutes the other Peasants, who return it warmly.*

FIRST PEASANT.

See, brothers, how the red-hot sun goes down,
Burning a steep path through the hissing wave,
That flames around him with a torrid heat,

Like a huge cauldron boiling o'er with gold
And purple foam. I remember, when a boy,
Climbing with desperate effort to the top
Of the mountain, to watch him rise and set.

SECOND PEASANT.

It is a blessed sight.

THIRD PEASANT.

But, brothers, see
How yon small cloud is spreading o'er the sky!
And, hark! the distant thunder warns us home.

FOURTH PEASANT.

To our homes, then; our homes and happy hearths.

ALL THE PEASANTS.

Yes, to our homes; our homes and happy wives.
Farewell kind friends.
     [*To* BERTRAM *and* LORENZO.
    Beware the coming storm.
      [*Exeunt Peasants.*

BERTRAM.

Who are these men?

LORENZO.

    The dwellers in the mountains,
As happy fellows as the sun e'er shone on.
But haste; the gath'ring storm may overtake us,
Ere we can reach the place I had intended
To lead thee to.

BERTRAM.

   Where wouldst thou lead me, friend?

LORENZO.

To happiness.

BERTRAM.

      The distance is too great.
I rather would return.

LORENZO.

          There's but one road
To happiness—the upward path, by which
We must ascend the often dreamed-of height,
And gaze exultingly on all below.

BERTRAM.

The moth, by struggling upward to the taper,
Scorches its wings, and often perisheth
While searching for the light.

LORENZO.

          And so wouldst thou
Risk life and limb, if thou shouldst venture downwards.
As for thine image of the moth, 'tis like
As if a man, who, standing on the brink
Of a steep precipice, should sway his arms,
And springing upwards try to clutch the sun;
Or one, who, leaning o'er Vesuvius' edge,
Should seek to leap across its gaping mouth
By one bold spring, and perish like a fool.
A little further up, and we are safe.
The storm will surely come. These shepherds are
Unfailing oracles.

BERTRAM.

If we must go,
Lead on, old man. How all my witty friends
Would hurl their puns and pointed epigrams
At me, if they but knew the foolish journey
I am performing, half against my will;
For there's a something in this old man's manner
That make me think both well and ill of him;
I'll either hate or love him by and by. (*Aside.*)

SCENE III.

*The summit of a high mountain, looking Westward.—
Time, Sunset.*

LORENZO.

Come, let us rest awhile, since we have gained
The summit of the mountain. See, the sun
Is disappearing through the western wave,
Like a strong diver going down for pearls,
Or a young bridegroom eloquent with joy,
Seeking the chamber where his soul's beloved
Sits in her bridal robes. A moment more
He will have canopied some other clime
With his rich tent of gold, and drawn aside
The sable curtains of polluted Night
From some fair country that we wot not of.

BERTRAM.

But what has this to do with our journey
Hither? And where is the surprise you had

In store for me ?   I will be getting lonely,
And insist on returning ere the night
Sets in.

LORENZO.

Impossible !   You cannot find
Your way.   The path is rough and intricate
By which we came ; and to return by that,
You would require a guide, to whom these wilds
Had grown familiar, to conduct you safely
To the plain.   Stay for a little moment here.
We will return together.   Hark ! the thunder.

BERTRAM.

There are no clouds above us, yet I hear
The thunder rolling in tremendous volleys,
But muffled, as if passing through the hills.

LORENZO.

Let us approach the mountain's edge, and look
Upon the storm.
              [*They approach the verge of the
                      mountain, and look down.*

Observe the passionate clouds,
Struggling like giant wrestling-groups in all
The grandeur of an elemental strife !
See how yon mass of fiery vapour writhes
In agony, like a flame-enveloped fiend,
And bursts asunder with a fearful crash,
That fills the pitying heavens with alarm,
And shakes the massive crag on which we stand.

Mark well the conflict—nay, you need not shrink,
Methought I saw you tremble as you gazed;
There is no danger here. The eagle builds
Its solid eyrie far above the storm,
And round about us sits the Roman bird,
Watching the air-drawn battle, as when perched
Upon the flaunting standards once upraised
On Carthagenian fields. The storm is far
Beneath us. I can call to mind the time—
The very day—the heaven-pilfered hour,
When my young soul first left its body-load,
And made it wings and mingled with the storm,
Ev'n as the headlong warrior leaps in
Where dangers threaten, thick as summer rain,
Each charged with death. A sublime awe swept o'er me;
I trembled with delight; shouted for joy;
The lightning's kiss was hot upon my cheek;
The thunder pealed its anthems in my ears,—
Deep, sublime melodies! and my spirit felt
Ethereal, as if a veil of light,
By angels borne from God's remotest home,
Had clothed it ready for a joy eterne.
Awed by the fervency of my wild thoughts,
I knelt, and with uplifted hands poured out
My unspoken prayers to God. My thankful soul
Was filled with an unstudied eloquence,
Which my lips dared not utter. The profound
And many-voicéd thunder; the red waves,
That spewed forth lightning, as a furnace fire;

The charging squadrons of impatient clouds,
Those burning steeds and riders of the storm,
That neighed in thunder and breathed breaths of flame,
Conspired to fill me with intense delight,
As boundless as the rapture of the winds,
Seated at midnight on the tempest car,
When heaven lifts her white hands to her face
To hide her eyes. Upon this very spot
I stood with vacant, greedy looks, and watched
The mighty conflict going on below:
And yet, thou'dst rather dance a tiresome measure
To a crack'd violin, than read the precious truths
Of these romantic wilds. Are they not lonely?
These mountain summits and deep forests, where
You seem to catch the echoings of strains
That were rehearsed in heaven at the birth
Of the old world, of which this earth, mayhap,
Is but a fragment. Oh! those glorious songs!
Their echoes cannot die, but seem to float,
Like vapours, through the air for evermore.
The poet seizes oft their wondrous plaint,
And ever after earth has one voice more
To magnify the Author of all Good.

BERTRAM.

Old man, you mock me. I can now discern
How such a soul as thine is elevated
Above the world and its ephemeral pleasures.
Henceforward I'll participate with thee

In these ethereal blessings. I'll be all
That thou couldst wish for in an amateur;
And you will find me a devoted pupil,
If you will lead me in the way to wisdom.
Oft have I heard of a discreet old man,
With whom the peasants had conversed, who lived,
Or rather had been seen, upon the mountain.
I wondered how their kindly hearts did warm,
And they grew eloquent, in praise of thee;
But now my doubts are gone, and I can well
Appreciate the generosity—
For such I deemed it—of these simple rustics.
If I become a ready listener
To the immortal truths that thou canst teach me,
Must I relinquish all the harmless pleasures
That I had previously indulged in?

LORENZO.

                            No,
Not one of them. Use them in moderation.
Devote some moments of thy little life
To learning what may be of benefit
To thee hereafter. But I would not ask
That thou shouldst ape the moody devotee,
And live apart from all thy fellow men.
Far rather would I have thee still remain
A trifling mortal, pleased with empty show,
And gilded vanity, than encourage thee
To be a soulless hermit. There are times

When gaiety is useful to the wisest;
And cheerfulness is fraught with many blessings,
If we survey it rightly.   See! the storm
Is over, and the heavens are bent down
Beneath the weight of their bejewelled robes.
The moon, like to a royal traveller,
Her silver chariot axle-deep in stars,
Rides the burning labyrinth of worlds,
A queen amongst her subjects; while the sea
Beyond us is irradiated with
The silver sparkles from her eloquent eyes,
That make a path of light from heaven to earth.
The solemn glories of the sun and moon,
The silver-dappled heavens, the huge sea—
These thou must learn to study, for their wealth
Of earnest truth, sublimity and love,
When I initiate thee into all
My plans of happiness.   Now for the surprise.
Look at the Old Man now.
       [*Removes a disguise.*

BERTRAM.
    My friend Lorenzo!

LORENZO.

Thy youthful friend, whom thou didst call a bookworm,
Because he would not always be a trifler,
And loved to ponder on the intrinsic lore
Of poets and philosophers.   I am
The solitary Hermit of the Hills,

As these warm-hearted peasants choose to call me;
And I would have thee be a hermit, too,
Occasionally. Thou shalt come with me,
And see the free-born mountaineers at eve,
Offering up their earnest, heart-felt thanks,
To the Supreme Intelligence of Heaven;
Shalt hear their old men read the sacred Word;
Their manly youths, and rosy-featured maidens,
Blending their voices in an evening hymn;
Shall see the happiest mortals upon earth,
And learn to imitate them—if thou wilt.

 See yonder cottage in the dreamy vale,
On which the moonlight, like the smile of God,
So sweetly rests. There dwells a Poet-soul;
One who has pass'd through stern Affliction's blaze,
And had his great heart purified by pain.
He was a Monarch in the Halls of Love.
Love crowned him as a nation crowns a King.
His queen, a rural beauty, by his side,
What wonder if he looked from his high throne
Upon the world, and claimed it as his own?
She loved him for his uncoined wealth of words,
That lay in the rich mine of his brain, like pearls
That hoard their lustre in a cave o' the sea.
He had great soul-thoughts floating in his eyes,
Like ships gem-laden on an Indian ocean,
And soft-voiced messengers, with gentle wings,
Soared through his mind, and made him rich in fancies,
As is a miser o'er his wealth of gold.

She loved to mark the lightning of his eye,
And list the mighty thunder of his speech,
That followed the electric fancy-storm,
Even as loves the hardy mountaineer,
Trained amid God's glory-haunted hills,
To trace the storm that rides the Appenines,
And bursts in fearful splendor at his feet.
She hung upon his lips, as hangs the bee
Upon the trembling rose-bud, flushed with sweets,
Like Beauty leaning forward for the kiss,
Of some impassioned lover, nectar-wild,
Quaffing his honied breath. Her fingers toyed
With his long locks of gold, that lay like waves
Of yellow sun-curls dancing on the lea,
Decking the bust of evening: and in each,
With true-love's spiritual, dreamy eyes,
She seemed to trace some intellectual thought,
Some beauteous reflex of his glowing soul,
In which his Prophet-spirit, Titan-like,
Loomed up majestic, clothed with Virtue's robes,
And he, the Adam of her Eve-like heart,
To her eyes, seemed the embodiment of all
The sterling mental manhood of the time,
A golden mouthed Chrysostum, brimmed with Truth,
And revelations of a coming age
Replete with saving glory and deep Love.
These Alpine heights were his, for he had struck
From out their flinty sides a flame of song,
That burned within the breasts of mountaineers,

And made them love their country more and more.
But while he sung, triumphant as the lark,
The tongue of Slander struck his spirit dumb—
For these young Poets are as sensitive
To pain, as the warm morning cloudlets are
To the consuming splendor of the sun.
Curs'd be the tongue that hurled the sland'rous shaft!
Withered the lips that spake the sland'rous tale!
For then his mind was strong, and in its strength
He gloried, as a giant o'er the thew
And sinew of his limbs. The sland'rer spake,
And, lo! the stately man became a child!
His mind, once full of bright imaginings,
Became as gloomy as the murkiest eve
That ever mingled with November's fog.
Thoughts that had ransacked heaven fell to earth,
Enfeebled with the fall. The eye that look'd
Fearlessly on the virtuous of the world,
That gazed admiringly upon the stars,
And drank their wondrous beauty in deep draughts,
Till it was drunken with delight, now quailed,
And sought the ground. And yet the tale was false.
But there was one who did believe it true;
One who had leaned upon his heart of hearts,
Like Innocence on Love. She thought it true.
And he was left alone with his crush'd heart,
To crawl mind-wounded through a cheerless world,
Like a lost planet through infinity,
Tortured with its unrest. He could have borne

The curses of the world, and borne them well;
He could have grasped his troubles by the heel,
And hurled them from him; but for that one thought,
That he was deemed unworthy of her love.
But there are sunbeams in the icicles,
Caloric in snow, and animalculæ
In the hard rock; and in one single germ
Lie all creation's works in miniature:
So in his heart one pulse of hope still beat,
One solitary spark still burned beneath
The ashes of his grief—her woman's love
Had merely flickered in the world's foul breath.
And knowing this, his heart was up again,
Like a stout wrestler whom some sinewy arm
Had humbled to his knees. The tale was false,
And he had proved it in the sland'rer's teeth
To be an upas offshoot, that had sprung
From the fierce cravings of a jealous mind,
And well nigh poisoned all their mutual hopes.
As leaps the sun above the clouded morn,
So rose the Poet-spirit of my friend
Once more into the hopeful skies of day,
From out the night of his intense despair.
And there they live, content, in yonder vale;
Their dwelling is an altar reared to Faith;
'T is built upon the spot which witnessed first
The sweet reünion of their steadfast love.

Again, seest thou yon distant roof-top peer
Above the cedars on the mountain side?

Thence soared a noble soul unto his rest,
While the strong throes of hope and future fame
Passed through his mind like summer o'er the earth.
To live, until the heart is warmed with youth,
And then, like to a suddenly blasted flower
In summer-time, to die and pass away—
Oh! 't is a bitter and a solemn thought!
What glowing hopes lay folded in the breast,
Like honey in the fair, expanding bud!
What burning thoughts leap through the throbbing brain,
Like lightnings hidden in the noon-day cloud!
So passed my student-friend unto his rest,
In the warm summer of his manly youth.
His springtime had been rich in blossoming,
Giving great promise of his harvest days,
When, with a vigorous will, and mind matured,
The golded fruitage of his well-spent hours
Would have been gathered in. Not his the fate
That buffets with the stern and iron world,
And winneth length of days; that wrests from fame
The guerdon that awaits the victor-mind;
That wrestles with great truths, till they become
The ministers of his Titanic will;
The buoyant wave that laves some fair, green isle,
And passing on, strands on a granite rock,
Flinging its wealth of pearl into the air,—
This, rather was his doom. But he had won
The meed of praise that waits the studious soul,
Won the fond friendship of his fellow peers.

He was a Man, in all that constitutes
The truest Manhood, in its strictest sense—
A Man in the full stature of his mind.
Religion was a well-spring in his breast,
Whose waters were as pure as waves of light
Rolling in volumes from the gleaming stars.
His thoughts soared ever upward towards God,
As soars the purifying flame to heaven.
Philosophy, and heaven descended poesy,
Within the sunny chambers of his mind
Met, like fair handmaids, who had come to stay,
And by their presence keep his spirit pure,
And meet for the high calling unto which
He would have given all his earthly days.
But in the midst of Life, the spoiler, Death,
Like a stern tyrant on his heartless round,
Struck down the noble youth, and robbed his friends
And fellow Students of their store of hopes.
Far from his home he died.—No parent's eye
Saw the last struggle of his manly breast;
No sister's voice into his closing ears
Poured the sad music of a last farewell.
But there were loving hands to close his eyes;
And there were loving hearts around, to feel
The grief that enters at the door of death;
And there were loving lips to pour the balm
Of consolation on his chastened mind.
He died, as dies the summer's crimson eve,
When the rich sunset hangs its banners out

Above its palaces of cloud and sky—
A death upon whose brow a radiant life
Sits crowned,—the white-winged messenger of hope,
Whose path is flashing with a sheen of gold.

BERTRAM.

I am ashamed to think you've caught me thus.
You're an accomplished trapper.

LORENZO.

                        When I please.
But not a word upon the subject now;
The secret shall be kept. We will return;
There is a merry-making at the village,
At which I must be present; and to-morrow,
You will commence your schooling, and become
My fellow-student. Nature for our guide,
Depend upon it we will learn far more
Than any pair of beardling adepts did
In those cold, formal universities,
Where young men's heads are crammed like Christmas
      turkeys,
Making them passive as a sweating group
Of listless Dutchmen o'er their meerschaum pipes
That deaden all their faculties of mind.

Index of Titles

THE ST LAWRENCE AND THE SAGUENAY
AND OTHER POEMS

A Plea for the Woods	180
A Poet's Love	66
A Thousand Faces	208
Absence	231
Annie By My Side A Sitting	120
Aurelia	81
Autumn	125
Bertram and Lorenzo	239
Beyond the Grave	118
Canadian Sleigh Song	118
Death of the Old Year	92
Despondency	94
Edith to Harold	168
Elegy	101
Elizabeth's Birth	113
England and America	154
Evening Scene	87
Faith	216
Fanny	220
Festus	231
From Queenston Heights	217
Gentle Mary Ann	90
Henry's Grave	115
Holy Ground	137
Hope	233

I Dreamed I Met Thee	161
Imagination	210
Let Them Boast as They Will	188
Lament of Shingwakonce	222
Light in Darkness	77
Limerick Cathedral Bells	190
Little Annie	130
Little Libby	182
Love's Guiding Star	192
Love's Morning Lark	197
Love's New Era	215
Love's Signet Ring	195
Mary's Twentieth Birthday	196
Merry Christmas	178
Morning in Summer	103
My Kitten	145
Password — Truth is Mighty	110
Peace	235
Peace, Fond Soul	176
Pity's Tear Drop	119
Pleasant Memories	139
Pretty Faces	117
Remembrances	129
Rideau Lake	78
Snow Drops	116
Song of the British Mariner	202
Song of the New Year	172
Song — The Banner of old England	198
Song — The Heroes of the Alma	199

Sonnet	86
Sonnet	232
Soul, Thou Art Lonely	175
Spring	63
Sun, Moon and Stars	133
The Angel's Gift	193
The Betrayal	205
The Changes of a Night	162
The Chieftain's Last Sigh	136
The Fine Old Woods	98
The Frost King's Revel	147
The Grape	207
The Impatient Lover	206
The Indian Summer	204
The Kneeling Heart	124
The Lofty and the Lowly	159
The Name of Mary	122
The One Idea	234
The Past	209
The Spirit of the Woods	212
The St Lawrence and the Saguenay	9
The Trio	233
The Twofold Victory — An Alma Lyric	201
The Voice of God	95
The Whirlwind	112
The Wreck	158
The Yellow Curl	186
To Rev. James G. Witted	166
Uncurbed Passion	235

Hesperus

and Other Poems and Lyrics

HESPERUS,

AND

Other Poems and Lyrics.

BY CHARLES SANGSTER,

AUTHOR OF "THE ST. LAWRENCE AND THE SAGUENAY, AND OTHER POEMS."

Montreal:
JOHN LOVELL, ST. NICHOLAS STREET.
Kingston:
JOHN CREIGHTON, KING STREET.
1860.

Entered, according to the Act of the Provincial Parliament, in the year one thousand eight hundred and sixty, by CHARLES SANGSTER, in the office of the Registrar of the Province of Canada.

THESE

Poems and Lyrics

ARE

DEDICATED

TO

My Niece,

CARRIE MILLER,

OF

SANDWICH, C. W.

CONTENTS.

	PAGE.
Dedicatory Poem	9
Hesperus	11
Crowned	29
Mariline	30
The Happy Harvesters	40
Falls of the Chaudière, Ottawa	53
A Royal Welcome	59
Malcolm	61
The Comet, October 1858	63
Autumn	65
Colin	68
Margery	70
Eva	76
The Poet's Recompense	77
The Wine of Song	78
The Plains of Abraham	80
Death of Wolfe	83
Brock	84
Song for Canada	86
Song.—I'd be a Fairy King	89
Song.—Love while you may	91

CONTENTS.

	PAGE.
The Snows, Upper Ottawa	92
The Rapid	94
Lost and Found	96
Young Again	99
Glimpses	100
My Prayer	102
Her Star	104
The Mystery	107
Love and Truth	109
The Wren	111
Grandpere	113
England's Hope and England's Heir	114
Rose	116
The Dreamer	118
Night and Morning	119
Within thine eyes	120
Gertrude	121
Flowers	122
The Unattainable	123
Yearnings	124
Ingratitude	125
True Love	126
An Evening Thought	127
A Thought for Spring	128
The Swallows	129
Song.—Clara and I	130
The April Snow Storm, 1858	132
Good Night	134
Hopeless	135
Into the Silent Land	139

CONTENTS.

SONNETS:—

	PAGE.
Proem	159
Sonnet I	162
II	163
III	164
IV	165
V	166
VI	167
VII	168
VIII	169
IX	170
X	171
XI	172
XII	173
XIII	174
XIV	175
XV	176
XVI	177
XVII	178
XVIII	179
XIX	180
XX	181
XXI	182
XXII	183
Au Revoir	184

POEMS.

DEDICATORY POEM.

Dear Carrie, were we truly wise,
And could discern with finer eyes,
    And half-inspired sense,
    The ways of Providence:

Could we but know the hidden things
That brood beneath the Future's wings,
    Hermetically sealed,
    But soon to be revealed:

Would we, more blest than we are now,
In due submission learn to bow,—
    Receiving on our knees
    The Omnipotent decrees?

That which is just, we have. And we
Who lead this round of mystery,
    This dance of strange unrest,
    What are we at the best?—

Unless we learn to mount and climb;
Writing upon the page of time,
    In words of joy or pain,
    That we've not lived in vain.

DEDICATORY POEM.

We all are Ministers of Good;
And where our mission's understood,
    How many hearts we must
    Raise, trembling, from the dust.

Oh, strong young soul, and thinking brain!
Walk wisely through the fair domain
    Where burn the sacred fires
    Of Music's sweet desires!

Cherish thy Gift; and let it be
A Jacob's ladder unto thee,
    Down which the Angels come,
    To bring thee dreams of Home.

What were we if the pulse of Song
Had never beat, nor found a tongue
    To make the Poet known
    In lands beyond his own?

Take what is said for what is meant.
We sometimes touch the firmament
    Of starry Thought—no more;
    Beyond, we may not soar.

I speak not of myself, but stand
In silence till the Master Hand
    Each fluttering thought sets free.
    God holds the golden key.

KINGSTON, C. W., *May 1st*, 1860.

HESPERUS:

A LEGEND OF THE STARS.

PRELUDE.

The Stars are heaven's ministers;
    Right royally they teach
God's glory and omnipotence,
    In wondrous lowly speech.
All eloquent with music as
    The tremblings of a lyre,
To him that hath an ear to hear
    They speak in words of fire.

Not to learnèd sages only
    Their whisperings come down;
The monarch is not glorified
    Because he wears a crown.
The humblest soldier in the camp
    Can win the smile of Mars,
And 'tis the lowliest spirits hold
    Communion with the stars.

Thoughts too refined for utterance,
    Ethereal as the air,
Crowd through the brain's dim labyrinths,
    And leave their impress there;

As far along the gleaming void
    Man's tender glances roll,
Wonder usurps the throne of speech,
    But vivifies the soul.

Oh, heaven-cradled mysteries,
    What sacred paths ye've trod—
Bright, jewelled scintillations from
    The chariot-wheels of God!
When in the spirit He rode forth,
    With vast creative aim,
These were His footprints left behind,
    To magnify His name!

We gazed on the Evening Star,
    Mary and I,
    As it shone
    On its throne
      Afar,
    In the blue sky;
Shone like a ransomed soul
In the depths of that quiet heaven;
    Like a pearly tear,
    Trembling with fear
On the pallid cheek of Even.

And I thought of the myriad souls
Gazing with human eyes
    On the light of that star,
    Shining afar,
In the quiet evening skies;

Some with winged hope,
Clearing the cope
Of heaven as swift as light,
Others, with souls
Blind as the moles,
Sinking in rayless night.

Dreams such as dreamers dream
Flitted before our eyes;
Beautiful visions!—
Angelo's, Titian's,
Had never more gorgeous dyes:
We soared with the angels
Through vistas of glory,
We heard the evangels
Relate the glad story
Of the beautiful star,
Shining afar
In the quiet evening skies.

And we gazed and dreamed,
Till our spirits seemed
Absorbed in the stellar world;
Sorrow was swallowed up,
Drained was the bitter cup
Of earth to the very lees;
And we sailed over seas
Of white vapour that whirled
Through the skies afar,
Angels our charioteers,
Threading the endless spheres,

And to the chorus of angels
Rehearsed the evangels
The Birth of the Evening Star.

I.

Far back in the infant ages,
Before the eras stamped their autographs
Upon the stony records of the earth;
Before the burning incense of the sun
Rolled up the interlucent space,
Brightening the blank abyss;
Ere the Recording Angel's tears
Were shed for man's transgressions:
A Seraph, with a face of light,
And hair like heaven's golden atmosphere,
Blue eyes serene in their beatitude,
Godlike in their tranquillity,
Features as perfect as God's dearest work,
And stature worthy of her race,
Lived high exalted in the sacred sphere
That floated in a sea of harmony
Translucent as pure crystal, or the light
That flowed, unceasing, from this higher world
Unto the spheres beneath it. Far below
The extremest regions underneath the Earth
The first spheres rose, of vari-coloured light,
In calm rotation through aërial deep,
Like seas of jasper, blue, and coralline,
Crystal and violet; layers of worlds—
The robes of ages that had passed away,

Left as memorials of their sojournings.
For nothing passes wholly. All is changed.
The Years but slumber in their sepulchres,
And speak prophetic meanings in their sleep.

FIRST ANGEL.

Oh, how our souls are gladdened,
    When we think of that brave old age,
        When God's light came down
        From heaven, to crown
    Each act of the virgin page!

Oh, how our souls are saddened,
    At the deeds which were done since then,
        By the angel race
        In the holy place,
    And on earth by the sons of men!

Lo, as the years are fleeting,
    With their burden of toil and pain,
        We know that the page
        Of that primal age
    Will be opened up once again.

II.

Progressing still, the bright-faced Seraph rose
From Goodness to Perfection, till she stood
The fairest and the best of all that waked
The tuneful echoes of that lofty world,
Where Lucifer, then the stateliest of the throng
Of Angels, walked majestical, arrayed

In robes of brightness worthy of his place.
And all the intermediate spheres were homes
   Of the existences
   Of spiritual life.
Love, the divine arcanum, was the bond
That linked them to each other—heart to heart,
And angel world to world, and soul to soul.
   Thus the first ages passed,
   Cycles of perfect bliss,
God the acknowledged sovereign of all.
Sphere spake with sphere, and love conversed with love,
From the far centre to sublimest height,
And down the deep, unfathomable space,
To the remotest homes of angel-life,
A viewless chain of being circling all,
And linking every spirit to its God.

    ANGEL CHORUS.

   Spirits that never falter,
   Before God's altar
Rehearse their pæans of unceasing praise;
   Their theme the boundless love
   By which God rules above,
   Mysteriously engrafted
   On grace divine, and wafted
Into every soul of man that disobeys.

   Not till the wondrous being
   Of the All-Seeing
Is manifested to finite man,
   Can ye understand the love

By which God rules above,
Evermore extending,
In circles never ending,
To every atom in the universal plan.

SECOND ANGEL.

Oh, the love beyond computing
Of the high and holy place!
The unseen bond
Circling beyond
The limits of time and space.

Through earth and her world of beauty
The heavenly links extend;
Man feels its presence,
Imbibes its essence,
But cannot yet comprehend.

THIRD ANGEL.

But the days are fast approaching,
When the Father of Love will send
His interpreter
From the highest sphere,
That man fully may comprehend.

III.

Oh, truest Love, because the truest life!
Oh, blest existence, to exist with Love!
Oh, Love, without which all things else must die
The death that knows no waking unto life!
Oh, Jealousy, that saps the heart of Love,

And robs it of its tenderness divine;
And Pride, that tramples with its iron hoof
Upon the flower of love, whose fragrant soul
Exhales itself in sweetness as it dies!
A lofty spirit surfeited with Bliss!
A Prince of Angels cancelling all love,
All due allegiance to his rightful Lord;
Doing dishonour to his high estate;
Turning the truth and wisdom which were his
For ages of supreme felicity,
To thirst for power, and hatred of his God,
Who raised him to such vast preëminence!

SECOND ANGEL CHORUS.

Woe, woe to the ransomed spirit,
 Once freed from the stain of sin,
  Whose pride increases
  Till all love ceases
 To nourish it from within!
Its doom is the darkened regions
Where the rebel angel legions
Live their long night of sorrow;
Where no expectant morrow,
 No mercy-tempered ray
 From the altar of to-day,
Comes down through the gloom to borrow
One drop from their cup of sorrow,
 Or lighten their cheerless way.

FIRST ANGEL.

But blest be the gentle spirit
   Whose love is ever increased
      From its own pure soul,
     The illumined goal
  Where Love holds perpetual feast!

IV.

      Ingrate Angel, he,
To purchase Hell, and at so vast a price!
'Tis the old story of celestial strife—
Rebellion in the palace-halls of God—
False angels joining the insurgent ranks,
Who suffered dire defeats, and fell at last
From bliss supreme to darkness and despair.
But they, the faithful dwellers in the spheres,
Who kept their souls inviolate, to whom
Heaven's love and truth were truly great rewards:
For these the stars were sown throughout all space,
As fit memorials of their faithfulness.
The wretched lost were banished to the depths
Beneath the lowest spheres. Earth barred the space
Between them and the Faithful. Then the hills
Rose bald and rugged o'er the wild abyss;
The waters found their places; and the sun,
The bright-haired warder of the golden morn,
Parting the curtains of reposing night,
Rung his first challenge to the dismal shades,
That shrunk back, awed, into Cimmerean gloom;
And the young moon glode through the startled void
With quiet beauty and majestic mien.

SECOND ANGEL.

Slowly rose the dædal Earth,
    Through the purple-hued abysm,
    Glowing like a gorgeous prism,
Heaven exulting o'er its birth.

Still the mighty wonder came,
    Through the jasper-coloured sphere,
    Ether-winged, and crystal-clear,
Trembling to the loud acclaim.

In a haze of golden rain,
    Up the heavens rolled the sun;
    Danae-like the earth was won,
Else his love and light were vain.

So the heart and soul of man
    Own the light and love of heaven;
    Nothing yet in vain was given,
Nature's is a perfect plan.

V.

The glowing Seraph with the brow of light
Was first among the Faithful. When the war
Between heaven's rival armies fiercely waged,
She bore the Will Divine from rank to rank,
The chosen courier of Deity.
Her presence cheered the combatants for Truth,
And Victory stood up where'er she moved.
And now, in gleaming robe of woven pearl,
Emblazoned with devices of the stars,
And legends of their glory yet to come,

The type of Beauty Intellectual,
The representative of Love and Truth,
She moves first in the innumerable throng
Of angels congregating to behold
The crowning wonder of creative power.

THIRD ANGEL CHORUS.

Oh, joy, that no mortal can fathom,
    To rejoice in the smile of God!
      To be first in the light
      Of His Holy sight,
    And freed from His chastening rod.
Faithful, indeed, that soul, to be
The messenger of Deity!

FIRST ANGEL.

This, this is the chosen spirit,
    Whose love is ever increased
      From its own pure soul,
      The illumined goal
    Where Love holds perpetual feast.

VI.

With noiseless speed the angel charioteers
In dazzling splendour all triumphant rode;
Through seas of ether painfully serene,
That flashed a golden, phosphorescent spray,
As luminous as the sun's intensest beams,
Athwart the wide, interminable space.
Legion on legion of the sons of God;
Vast phalanxes of graceful cherubim;

Innumerable multitudes and ranks
Of all the hosts and hierarchs of heaven,
Moved by one universal impulse, urged
Their steeds of swiftness up the arch of light,
From sphere to sphere increasing as they came,
Till world on world was emptied of its race.
Upward, with unimaginable speed,
The myriads, congregating zenith-ward,
Reached the far confines of the utmost sphere,
The home of Truth, the dwelling-place of Love,
Striking celestial symphonies divine
From the resounding sea of melody,
That heaved in swells of soft, mellifluous sound,
To the blest crowds at whose triumphal tread
Its soul of sweetness waked in thrills sublime.
The sun stood poised upon the western verge;
The moon paused, waiting for the march of earth,
That stayed to watch the advent of the stars;
And ocean hushed its very deepest deeps
      In grateful expectation.

SECOND ANGEL.

Still through the viewless regions
    Of the habitable air,
Through the ether ocean,
    In unceasing motion,
Pass the multitudinous legions
    Of angels everywhere.

Bearing each new-born spirit
    Through the interlucent void

To its starry dwelling,
Angel anthems telling
Every earthly deed of merit
To each flashing asteroid.

THIRD ANGEL.

Though the realms sidereal,
Clothed with the immaterial,
Far as the fields elysian
In starry bloom extend,
The stretch of angel vision
Can see and comprehend.

VII.

Innumerable as the ocean sands
The angel concourse in due order stood,
In meek anticipation waiting for
The new-created orbs,
Still hidden in the deep
And unseen laboratory, where
Not even angel eyes could penetrate:
A star for each of that angelic host,
Memorials of their faithfulness and love.
The Evening Star, God's bright eternal gift
To the pure Seraph with the brow of light,
And named for her, mild Hesperus,
Came twinkling down the unencumbered blue,
On viewless wings of sweet melodious sound,
Beauty and grace presiding at its birth.
Celestial plaudits sweeping through the skies
Waked resonant pæans, till the concave thrilled

Through its illimitable bounds.
With a sudden burst
Of light, that lit the universal space
As with a flame of crystal,
Rousing the Soul of Joy
That slumbered in the patient sea,
From every point of heaven the hurrying cars
Conveyed the constellations to their thrones—
The throbbing planets, and the burning suns,
Erratic comets, and the various grades
And magnitudes of palpitating stars.
From the far arctic and antarctic zones,
Through all the vast, surrounding infinite,
A wilderness of intermingling orbs,
The gleaming wonders, pulsing earthward, came;
Each to its destined place,
Each in itself a world,
With all its coming myriad life,
Drawing us nearer the Omnipotent,
With hearts of wonder, and with souls of praise:
Astrea, Pallas, strange Aldebaran,
The Pleiads, Arcturus, the ruddy Mars,
Pale Saturn, Ceres and Orion—
All as they circle still
Through the enraptured void.
For each young angel born to us from earth,
A new-made star is launched among its peers.

FULL ANGEL CHORUS.

Dreamer in the realms aërial,
Searcher for the true and good,

Hoper for the high, ethereal
Limit of Beatitude,
Lift thy heart to heaven, for there
Is embalmed thy spirit-prayer :
Not in words is shrined thy prayer,
But thy Thought awaits thee there.
God loves the silent worshipper.
The grandest hymn
That nature chants—the litany
Of the rejoicing stars—is silent praise.
Their nightly anthems stir
The souls of lofty seraphim
In the remotest heaven. The melody
Desends in throbbings of celestial light
Into the heart of man, whose upward gaze,
And meditative aspect, tell
Of the heart's incense passing up the night.
Above the crystalline height
The theme of thoughtful praise ascends.
Not from the wildest swell
Of the vexed ocean soars the fullest psalm ;
But in the evening calm,
And in the solemn midnight, silence blends
With silence, and to the ear
Attuned to harmony divine
Begets a strain
Whose trance-like stillness wakes delicious pain.
The silent tear
Holds keener anguish in its orb of brine,
Deeper and truer grief
Than the loud wail that brings relief,

As thunder clears the atmosphere.
But the deep, tearless Sorrow,—how profound !
Unspoken to the ear
Of sense, 'tis yet as eloquent a sound
As that which wakes the lyre
Of the rejoicing Day, when
Morn on the mountains lights his urn of fire.
The flowers of the glen
Rejoice in silence; huge pines stand apart
Upon the lofty hills, and sigh
Their woes to every breeze that passeth by;
The willow tells its mournful tale
So tenderly, that e'en the passing gale
Bears not a murmur on its wings
Of what the spirit sings
That breathes its trembling thoughts through all the
    drooping strings.
He loves God most who worships most
In the obedient heart.
The thunder's noisome boast,
What is it to the violet lightning thought?
So with the burning passion of the stars—
Creation's diamond sands,
Strewn along the pearly strands,
And far-extending corridors
Of heaven's blooming shores;
No scintil of their jewelled flame
But wafts the exquisite essence
Of prayer to the Eternal Presence,
Of praise to the Eternal Name.
The silent prayer unbars

The gates of Paradise, while the too-intimate,
Self-righteous' boast, strikes rudely at the gate
Of heaven, unknowing why it does not open to
Their summons, as they see pale Silence passing
    through.

VIII.

In grateful admiration, till the Dawn
Withdrew the gleaming curtains of the night,
We watched the whirling systems, until each
Could recognize their own peculiar star;
    When, with the swift celerity
    Of Fancy-footed Thought,
The light-caparisoned, aërial steeds,
    Shod with rare fleetness,
Revisited the farthest of the spheres
Ere the earth's sun had kissed the mountain-tops,
Or shook the sea-pearls from his locks of gold.

    Still on the Evening Star
    Gazed we with steadfast eyes,
        As it shone
        On its throne
        Afar,
In the blue skies.
No longer the charioteers
Dashed through the gleaming spheres;
No more the evangels
  Rehearsed the glad story;
But, in passing, the angels
    Left footprints of glory:

> For up the starry void
> Bright-flashing asteroid,
> Pale moon and starry choir,
> Aided by Fancy's fire,
> Rung from the glittering lyre
> Changes of song and hymn,
> Worthy of Seraphim.

Night's shepherdess sat, queenlike, on her throne,
Watching her starry flocks from zone to zone,
While we, like mortals turned to breathing stone,
Intently pondered on the Known Unknown.

CROWNED.

Her thoughts are sweet glimpses of heaven,
   Her life is that heaven brought down;
Oh, never to mortal was given
   So rare and bejewelled a crown!
I'll wear it as saints wear the glory
   That radiantly clasps them above—
     Oh, dower most fair!
     Oh, diadem rare!
   Bright crown of her maidenly love.

My heart is a fane of devotion,
   My feelings are converts at prayer,
And every thrill of emotion
   Makes dearer the crown I would wear.
My soul in its fulness of rapture
   Begins its millennial reign,
     Life glows like a sun,
     Love's zenith is won,
   And Joy is sole monarch again.

My noonday of life is as morning,
   God's light streams approvingly down;
Uncovered, I wait her adorning,
   She comes with the beautiful crown!
I'll wear it as saints wear the glory
   That radiantly clasps them above—
     Oh, dower most fair!
     Oh, diadem rare!
   Bright crown of her maidenly love.

MARILINE.

I.

At the wheel plied Mariline,
Beauteous and self-serene,
Never dreaming of that mien
Fit for lady or for queen.

Never sang she, but her words,
Music-laden, swept the chords

Of the heart, that eagerly
Stored the subtle melody,
Like the honey in the bee;
Never spake, but showed that she

Held the golden master-key
That unlocked all sympathy

Pent in souls where Feeling glows,
Like the perfume in the rose,
Like her own innate repose,
Like the whiteness in the snows.

Richly thoughted Mariline!
Nature's heiress!—nature's queen!

II.

By her side, with liberal look,
Paused a student o'er a book,
Wielder of a shepherd's crook,
Reveller by grove and brook:

Hunter-up of musty tomes,
Worshipper of deathless poems:

Lover of the true and good;
Hater of sin's evil brood,
Votary of solitude,
Man of mind-like amplitude.

With exhalted eye serene
Gazed he on fair Mariline.

Swifter whirled the busy wheel,
Piled the thread upon the reel—
Saw she not his spirit kneel,
Praying for her after-weal?

Like the wife of Collatine,
Busily spun Mariline.

III.

Hour by hour, and day by day,
Sang the maid her roundelay;
Hour by hour, and day by day,
Spun her threads of white and gray.

While the shepherd-student held
Commune with the great of eld:

Pondered on their wondrous words,
While he watched his scattered herds,
While he stemmed the surging fords.
And he knew the lore of birds,

Learned the secrets of the rills,
Conversed with the answering hills.

Like her threads of white and gray,
Passed their mingled lives away,
One unceasing roundelay—
Winter came, it still was May!

IV.

When the spring smiled, opening up
Pink-lipped flower and acorn-cup;

When the summer waked the rose
In the scented briar boughs;
When the earth, with painless throes,
Bore her golden autumn rows—

Field on field of grain, that pressed,
Childlike, to her fruitful breast—

When hale winter wrapped his form
In the mantle of the storm,
Tamed the bird, and chilled the worm,
Stopped the pulse that thrilled the germ;

As the seasons-went and came,
One in heart, and hope, and aim,

Cheered they each the other on,
Where was labor to be done,
At day-break or set of sun,
Like two thoughts that merge in one.

Dignified, and soul-serene,
Busily spun Mariline.

V.

Brightly broke the summer morn,
Like a lark from out the corn,—
Broke like joy just newly born
From the depths of woe forlorn,—

Broke with grateful songs of birds,
Lowings of well-pastured herds;

Hailed by childhood's happy looks,
Cheered by anthems of the brooks—
Chants beyond the lore of books—
Cawing crows, instead of rooks.

Glowed the heavens—rose the sun,
Mariline was up, for one.

VI.

Like a chatterer tongue-tied,
Lo, the wheel is placed aside!—
Not from indolence or pride—
Mariline must be a Bride!

Fairest maid of maids terrene!
Bride of Brides, dear Mariline!

VII.

Up the meditative air
Passed the smoke-wreaths, white and fair,
Like the spirit of the prayer
Mariline now offered there:

Passed behind the cottage eaves,
Curling through the maple leaves:

Through the pines and old elm-trees,
Relics of past centuries,
Hardy oaks, that never breeze
Humbled to their gnarly knees:

Forest lords, beneath whose sheen
Flowers bloomed for Mariline.

Round the cottage, fresh and green
Climbed the vine, the scarlet bean,
Morning-glories peeped between,
Looking out for Mariline.

Odours never felt before
Tranced the locust at the door,

Vieing with the mignonette
Round the garden parapet,
Whose rare fragrances were met
By rich perfumes, rarer yet,

Stealing from the garden walks,
Sentineled with hollyhocks.

VIII.

What a heaven the cottage seemed!
Love's own temple, where Faith dreamed
Of the coming years that beamed
On them, as pale stars have gleamed

Through unnavigated seas,
To which the prophetic breeze

Whispered of a future day,
When swift fleets would urge their way,
Through the waters cold and gray,
Like the dolphins at their play.

There the future Bride, and he,
Prince of love's knight-errantry,

Whose good shepherd-arms must hold
This pet yeanling of the fold,
Gift of God so long foretold,
Gift beyond the price of gold.

There the parents, aged and hale,
Passing down life's autumn vale,

With a joy as rare and true
As their daughter's eye of blue,
With such hopes as reach up to
Heaven's gate, when, passing through,

Peris, bound for higher skies,
Win the Celestial Paradise.

IX.

Thoughtfully stood Mariline,
Whitely veiled, and soul-serene;
Love's fair world for her demesne,
Never looked she more a queen—

With her maidens by her side,
Smiling on the coming bride.

Her pet lamb, with comic mirth,
Licked her hand and scampered forth;
The fine sheep-dog, on the hearth,
Kindly eyed her for her worth.

X.

Up the air, across the moor,
As they left the cottage door,

Chimed the merry village-bells,
Music-wrapt the neighbouring fells,
Stirred the heart's awakened cells,
Like fine strains from fairy dells.

Past the orchard, down the lane,
By fresh wavy fields of grain,

By the brook, that told its love
To the pasture, glen, and grove—
Sacred haunts, that well could prove
Vows enregistered above.

By the restless mill, where stood,
Bowing in his amplest mood,

The old miller, hat in hand,
Rich in goodness, rich in land,
On whose features, grave and bland,
Glowed a blessing for the band.

Through the village, where, behind
Many a half-uplifted blind,

Eyes, that might have lit the skies
Of Mahomet's Paradise,
Flashed behind the curtains' dyes,
With a cheerful, half-surprise.

Through the village, underneath,
Many a blooming flower-wreath,

Garlanding the arches green
Reared in honour of the queen
Of this day of days serene,
Day of days to Mariline.

To the church, whose cheering bells
Told the tale in music-swells—

Told it to the country wide,
With an earnest kind of pride—
Something not to be denied—
" Mariline must be a Bride !"

XI.

Up the aisle with solemn pace,
Meeting God there, face to face.

Never Bride more chaste or fair
Stood before His altar there,
Her ripe heart aflame with prayer,
Blessing Him for all His care:

Every earthly promise given,
Registered with joy in heaven.

From the galleries looked down
Village belle and country clown,
Men with honest labour brown,
Far removed from mart or town :

Smiling with a zealous pride
On the shepherd and his bride—

Playmates of their early days ;
For their walks in wisdom's ways,
Ever crowned with honoured bays
Of esteem and ardent praise.

XII.

Well done, servant of the Lord !
Grave expounder of His Word,

Who in distant Galilee
Graced the marriage feast, that He,
With all due solemnity,
Might commission such as thee

To do likewise, and unite
Souls like these in marriage plight.

With what manly, gentle pride,
The glad Shepherd clasps his Bride!
Love like theirs, so true and tried,
Ever true love must abide !

XIII.

Ye whose souls are strong and firm,
In whom love's electric germ

Has been fanned into a flame
At the mention of a name;
Ye whose souls are still the same
As when first the Victor came,

Stinging every nerve to life,
In the beatific strife,

Till the man's divinest part
Ruled triumphant in the heart,
And, with shrinking, sudden start,
The bleak old world stood apart,

Periling the wild Ideal
By the presence of the Real:

Ye, and ye alone, can know
How these twain souls burn and glow,
Can interpret every throe
Of the full heart's overflow,

That imparts that light serene
To the brow of Mariline.

THE HAPPY HARVESTERS.
A CANTATA.

I.

Autumn, like an old poet in a haze
Of golden visions, dreams away his days,
So Hafiz-like that one may almost hear
The singer's thoughts imbue the atmosphere;
Sweet as the dreamings of the nightingales
Ere yet their songs have waked the eastern vales,
Or stirred the airy echoes of the wood
That haunt the forest's social solitude.
His thoughts are pastorals; his days are rife
With the calm wisdom of that inner life
That makes the poet heir to worlds unknown,
All space his empire, and the sun his throne.
As the bee stores the sweetness of the flowers,
So into autumn's variegated hours
Is hived the Hybla richness of the year;
Choice souls imbibing the ambrosial cheer,
As autumn, seated on the highest hills,
Gleans honied secrets from the passing rills;
While from below, the harvest canzonas
Link vale to mountain with a chain of praise.
Foremost among the honoured sons of toil
Are they who overcome the stubborn soil;
Brave Cincinnatus in his country home
Was even greater than when lord of Rome.
Down sinks the sun behind the lofty pines
That skirt the mountain, like the straggling lines

Of Ceres' army looking from the height
On the dim lowlands deepening into night;
Soft-featured twilight, peering through the maze,
Sees the first starbeam pierce the purple haze;
Through all the vales the vespers of the birds
Cheer the young shepherds homeward with their
And the stout axles of the heavy wain [herds;
Creak 'neath the fulness of the ripened grain,
As the swarth builders of the precious load,
Returning homewards, sing their Autumn Ode.

AUTUMN ODE.

God of the Harvest! Thou, whose sun
    Has ripened all the golden grain,
We bless Thee for Thy bounteous store,
The cup of Plenty running o'er,
    The sunshine and the rain.

The year laughs out for very joy,
    Its silver treble echoing
Like a sweet anthem through the woods,
Till mellowed by the solitudes
    It folds its glossy wing.

But our united voices blend
    From day to day unweariedly;
Sure as the sun rolls up the morn,
Or twilight from the eve is born,
    Our song ascends to Thee.

Where'er the various-tinted woods,
　　In all their autumn splendour dressed,
Impart their gold and purple dyes
To distant hills and farthest skies
　　Along the crimson west:

Across the smooth, extended plain,
　　By rushing stream and broad lagoon,
On shady height and sunny dale,
Wherever scuds the balmy gale,
　　Or gleams the autumn moon:

From inland seas of yellow grain,
　　Where cheerful Labour, heaven-blest,
With willing hands and keen-edged scythe,
And accents musically blythe,
　　Reveals its lordly crest:

From clover-fields and meadows wide,
　　Where moves the richly-laden wain
To barns well-stored with new-made hay,
Or where the flail at early day
　　Rolls out the ripened grain:

From meads and pastures on the hills,
　　And in the mountain valleys deep,
Alive with beeves and sweet-breathed kine
Of famous Ayr or Devon's line,
　　And shepherd-guarded sheep:

The spirits of the golden year,
    From crystal caves and grottoes dim,
From forest depths and mossy sward,
Myriad-tongued, with one accord
    Peal forth their harvest hymn.

II.

Their daily labour in the happy fields
A two-fold crop of grain and pleasure yields,
While round their hearths, before their evening fires,
Where comfort reigns, whence weariness retires,
The level tracts, denuded of their grain,
In calm dispute are bravely shorn again,
Till some rough reaper, on a tide of song,
Like a bold pirate, captivates the throng:

A SONG FOR THE FLAIL.

A song, a song for the good old Flail,
    And the brawny arms that wield it;
Hearty and hale, in our yeoman mail,
    Like intrepid knights we'll shield it.
        We are old nature's peers,
        Right royal cavaliers!
Knights of the Plough! for no Golden Fleece we sail,
We're Princes in our own right—our sceptre is the Flail.

A song, a song for the golden grain,
    As it wooes the flail's embraces,
In wavy sheaves like a golden main,
    With its bright spray in our faces.

Mirth hastens at our call,
Jovial hearts have we all!
Knights of the Plough! for no Golden Fleece we sail,
We're Princes in our own right—our sceptre is the Flail.

A song, a song for the good old Flail,
　　That our fathers used before us;
A song for the Flail, and the faces hale
　　Of the queenly dames that bore us
　　　　We are old nature's peers,
　　　　Right royal cavaliers!
Knights of the Plough! for no Golden Fleece we sail,
We're Princes in our own right—our sceptre is the Flail.

III.

Fair was the maid, and lovely as the morn
From starry Night and rosy Twilight born,
Within whose mind a rivulet of song
Rehearsed the strains that from her lips ere long
Welled free and sparkling, as the vocal woods
Repeat the day-spring's sweetest interludes.
Her gentle eyes' serenest depths of blue
Shrined love and truth, and all their retinue;
The health and beauty of her youthful face
Made it the harem of each maiden grace;
And such perfection blended with her air,
She seemed some stately goddess moving there:
Beholding her, you thought she might have been
The long-lost, flower-loving Proserpine:

AN AUTUMN CHANGE.

"Oh, dreamy autumn days!
I seek your faded ways,
As one who calmly strays
    Through visions of the past;
I walk the golden hours,
And where I gathered flowers
The stricken leaves in showers
    Are hurled upon the blast."

Thus mused the lonely maid,
As through the autumn glade,
With pensive heart, she strayed,
    Regretting Love's delay;
In vain the traitor flies!
To pleading lips and eyes,
Sweet looks, and tender sighs,
    He falls an easy prey.

"Oh, dreamy autumn days!
I tread your bridal ways,
As one who homeward strays,
    Through realms divinely fair;
I walk Love's radiant hours,
Fragrant with passion-flowers,
And blessings fall like dowers
    Down the elysian air."

Thus mused the maiden now,
With sunny heart and brow,
For Love had turned his prow

Towards the Golden Isles,
Where from Pierean springs
The soul of Music sings
Its sweet imaginings,
Through all the Land of Smiles.

IV.

Up the wide chimney rolls the social fire,
Warming the hearts of matron, youth, and sire;
Painting such grotesque shadows on the wall,
The stripling looms a giant stout and tall,
While they whose statures reach the common height
Seem spectres mocking the hilarious night.
From hand to hand the ripened fruit went round,
And rural sports a pleased acceptance found;
The youthful fiddler on his three-legged stool,
Fancied himself at least an Ole Bull;
Some easy bumpkin, seated on the floor,
Hunted the slipper till his ribs were sore;
Some chose the graceful waltz or lively reel,
While deeper heads the chess-battalions wheel,
Till some old veteran, compelled to yield,
More brave than skilful, vanquished, quits the field.
As a flushed harper, when the doubtful fight
Favors the prowess of some stately knight,
In stirring numbers of triumphal song
Upholds the spirits of the victor throng,
A sturdy ploughboy, wedded to the soil,
Thus sung the praises of the partner of his toil:

THE SOLDIERS OF THE PLOUGH.

No maiden dream, nor fancy theme,
　　Brown Labour's muse would sing;
Her stately mien and russet sheen
　　Demand a stronger wing.
Long ages since, the sage, the prince,
　　The man of lordly brow,
All honour gave that army brave,
　　The Soldiers of the Plough.
　　　　Kind heaven speed the Plough!
　　　　And bless the hands that guide it;
　　　　　　God gives the seed—
　　　　　　The bread we need,
　　　　Man's labour must provide it.

In every land, the toiling hand
　　Is blest as it deserves;
Not so the race who, in disgrace,
　　From honest labour swerves.
From fairest bowers bring rarest flowers,
　　To deck the swarthy brow
Of those whose toil improves the soil,
　　The Soldiers of the Plough.
　　　　Kind heaven speed the Plough!
　　　　And bless the hands that guide it;
　　　　　　God gives the seed—
　　　　　　The bread we need,
　　　　Man's labour must provide it.

Blest is his lot, in hall or cot,
  Who lives as nature wills,
Who pours his corn from Ceres' horn,
  And quaffs his native rills!
No breeze that sweeps trade's stormy deeps,
  Can touch his golden prow;
Their foes are few, their lives are true,
  The Soldiers of the Plough.
    Kind heaven speed the Plough!
    And bless the hands that guide it;
      God gives the seed—
      The bread we need,
    Man's labour must provide it.

v.

Fast sped the rushing chariot of the Hours.
Without, the Harvest Moon, through fleecy bowers
Of hazy cloudlets, swept her graceful way,
Proud as an empress on her marriage-day;
Th' admiring planets lit her stately march
With smiles that gleamed along the silent arch,
And all the starry midnight blazed with light,
As if 'twere earth and heaven's nuptial-night;
The cock crowed, certain that the day had broke,
The aged house-dog suddenly awoke,
And bayed so loud a challenge to the moon,
From the old orchard fled the thievish 'coon:
Within, the lightest hearts that ever beat
Still found their harmless pleasures pure and sweet;
The fire still burned on the capacious hearth,
In sympathy with the redundant mirth;

Old graybeards felt the glow of youth revive,
Old matrons smiled upon the human hive,
Where life's rare nectar, fit for gods to sip,
In forfeit kisses passed from lip to lip.
Be hushed rude Mirth! as merry as the May
Is she who comes to sing her roundelay:

CLAIRE.

Whither now, blushing Claire?
Maid of the sylph-like air,
Blooming and debonair,
 Whither so early?
Chasing the merry morn,
Down through the golden corn?
List'ning the hunter's horn
 Ring through the barley?

" Flowerets fresh and fair,"
Answered the blushing Claire,
" Fit for my bridal hair,
 Bloom 'mongst the barley;
Hark! 'tis the hunter's horn,
Waking the sylvan morn,
And through the yellow corn
 Comes my brave Charlie."

Through the dew-dripping grain
Pressed the heart-stricken swain,
Crushed with a weight of pain,

Drooped like the barley;
Ah! timid shepherd boy!
Man's love should ne'er be coy,
Sweet is Claire's maiden joy,
  Kissing her Charlie!

VI.

A pleasant soul as ever trilled a song
Was hers who warbled "Claire." All the day long
Her voice was ringing like a bridal bell;
Gladness and joy leaped up at every swell;
And love was deeper, warmer, for the tone
That clasped the heart like an enchanted zone.
A youth was there more comely than the rest;
One who could turn a furrow with the best,
Compete for manly strength and portly air,
Or wield a scythe with any reaper there.
The spirit of her voice had moved above
The waters of his soul, and waked his song to Love:

BALLAD.

" Come tell me, merry Brooklet, of a gentle Maid I seek,
Thou'lt know her by the freshness of the rose upon her
  cheek;
Her eyes are chaste and tender, and so serenely bright,
You can read her heart's pure secrets by their warm
  religious light."

"The Maid has not come hither," said the Brooklet in
    reply;
"I've listened for her footfall ere the stars were in the
    sky;
The Fountain has been singing of a Maid, with eyes so
    bright
You may read the cherished secrets of her bosom by
    their light."

"Pray tell me, merry Brooklet, what saith her thoughts
    of one
Who wronged her loving nature ere the setting of the
    sun?
What say they of yon autumn moon that smiles so
    mournfully
On the slowly-dying season, and the blasted moorland
    tree?"

"She sitteth by the Fountain," the Brook replied again,
"Her heart as pure as heaven, and her thoughts without
    a stain;
'Oh, fickle moon, and changeful man!' she saith, 'a year
    ago
All the paths were true-love-lighted where I'm groping
    now in woe.'

"She sitteth by the Fountain, the gentle mists arise,
And kiss away the tear-pearls that tremble in her eyes;
The Fountain singeth to me that the Maiden in her
    dream
Shrinks as the vapours claim her as the Oread of the
    stream."

Off sped the merry Streamlet adown the sloping vale;
The Shepherd seeks the Fountain, where sits the Maiden pale;
And to the wandering Brooklet, through many a lonely wild,
The burden of the Fountain was, that Love was reconciled.

VII.

But soon the Morn, on many a distant height,
Fingers the raven locks of lingering Night;
The last dark shadows that precede the day
Have stripped the splendour from the Milky Way;
And Nature seems disturbed by fitful dreams,
As one who shudders when the owlet screams;
The painful burden of the Whippoorwill,
Like a vague Sorrow, floats from hill to hill;
Along the vales the doleful accents run,
Where the white vapours dread the burning sun;
While human voices stir the haunted air,
One sings " the Plough," another warbles " Claire:"
The Happy Harvesters, a lightsome throng,
Dispersing homewards, prove the excellence of Song.

THE FALLS OF THE CHAUDIÈRE, OTTAWA.

I have laid my cheek to Nature's, placed my puny hand
    in hers,
    Felt a kindred spirit warming all the life-blood of my
        face,
Moved amid the very foremost of her truest worshippers,
    Studying each curve of beauty, marking every minute
        grace ;
Loved not less the mountain cedar than the flowers at
    its feet,
    Looking skyward from the valley, open-lipped as if in
        prayer,
Felt a pleasure in the brooklet singing of its wild
    retreat,
    But I knelt before the splendour of the thunderous
        Chaudière.

All my manhood waked within me, every nerve had
    tenfold force,
    And my soul stood up rejoicing, looking on with
        cheerful eyes,
Watching the resistless waters speeding on their down-
    ward course,
    Titan strength and queenly beauty diademed with
        rainbow dyes.
Eye and ear, with spirit quickened, mingled with the
    lovely strife,
    Saw the living Genius shrined within her sanctuary
        fair,

Heard her voice of sweetness singing, peered into her hidden life,
And discerned the tuneful secret of the jubilant Chaudière:

" Within my pearl-roofed shell,
Whose floor is woven with the iris bright,
Genius and Queen of the Chaudière I dwell,
As in a world of immaterial light.

My throne, an ancient rock,
Marked by the feet of ages long-departed,
My joy, the cataract's stupendous shock,
Whose roll is music to the grateful-hearted.

I've seen the eras glide
With muffled tread to their eternal dreams,
While I have lived in vale and mountain side,
With leaping torrents and sweet purling streams.

The Red-Man's active life;
His love, pride, passions, courage, and great deeds;
His perfect freedom, and his thirst for strife;
His swift revenge, at which the memory bleeds:

The sanguinary years,
When sullen Terror, like a raging Fate,
Swept down the stately tribes like slaughtered deers,
And war and hatred joined to decimate

The remnants of the race,
And spread decay through centuries of pain—
No more I mark their sure, avenging pace,
And forests wave where war-whoops shook the plain.

Their deeds I envied not.
The royal tyrant on his purple throne,
I, in secluded grove or shady grot,
Had purer joys than he had ever known.

God made the ancient hills,
The valleys and the solemn wildernesses,
The merry-hearted and melodious rills,
And strung with diamond dews the pine-trees' tresses;

But man's hand built the palace,
And he that reigns therein is simply man;
Man turns God's gifts to poison in the chalice
That brimmed with nectar in the primal plan.

Here I abide alone—
The wild Chaudière's eternal jubilee
Has such sweet divination in its tone,
And utters nature's truest prophecy

In thunderings of zeal!
I've seen the Atheist in terror start,
Awed to contrition by the strong appeal
That waked conviction in his doubting heart:

' Teachers speak throughout all nature,
  From the womb of Silence born,
Heed ye not their words, O Scoffer?
  Flinging back thy scorn with scorn!
To the desert spring that leapeth,
  Pulsing, from the parchèd sod,
Points the famished trav'ler, saying—
  ' Brothers, here, indeed, is God!'"

From the patriarchal fountains,
　　Sending forth their tribes of rills,
From the cedar-shadowed lakelets
　　In the hearts of distant hills,
Whispers softer than the moonbeams
　　Wisdom's gentle heart have awed,
Till its lips approved the cadence—
　　'Surely here, indeed, is God!'

Lo! o'er all, the Torrent Prophet,
　　An inspired Demosthenes,
To the Doubter's soul appealing,
　　Louder than the preacher-seas:
Dreamer! wouldst have nature spurn thee
　　For a dumb, insensate clod?
Dare to doubt! and these shall teach thee
　　Of a truth there lives a God!'

By day and night, for hours,
I watch the cataract's impulsive leap,
Refreshed and gladdened by the cheering showers
Wrung from the passion of the seething deep.

Pleased when the buried waves
Emerge again, like incorporeal hosts
Rising, white-sheeted, from their gloomy graves,
As if the depths had yielded up their ghosts.

And when the midnight storm
Enfolds the welkin in its robe of clouds,
Through the dim vapours of the cauldron swarm
The sheeted spectres in their whitest shrouds,

By the lightning's flash betrayed.
These gather from the insubstantial vapour
The lunar rainbows, which by them are made—
Woven with moonbeams by some starry taper,

To decorate the halls
Of my fair palace, whence I'm pained to see
Thy human brethren watch the waterfalls—
Not with such rev'rence as I've found in thee:

Too many with an eye
To speculation and the worldling's dreams;
Others, who seek from nature no reply,
Nor read the oral language of the streams.

But of the few who loved
The beautiful with grateful heart and soul,
Who looked on nature fondly, and were moved
By one sweet glance, as by the mighty whole:

Of these, the thoughtful few,
Thou wert the first to seek the inner temple,
And stand before the Priestess. Thou wert true
To nature and thyself. Be thy example

The harbinger of times
When the Chaudière's imposing majesty
Will awe the spirits of the heartless mimes
To worship God in truth, with nature's constancy."

Still I heard the mellow sweetness of her voice at intervals,
    Mingling with the fall of waters, rising with the snowy spray,
Ringing through the sportive current like the joy of waterfalls,
    Sending up their hearty vespers at the calmy close of day.
Loath to leave the scene of beauty, lover-like I stayed, and stayed,
    Folding to my eager bosom memories beyond compare;
Deeper, stronger, more enduring than my dreams of wood and glade,
    Were the eloquent appeals of the magnificent Chaudière.

E'en the solid bridge is trembling, whence I look my last farewell,
    Dizzy with the roar and trampling of the mighty herd of waves,
Speeding past the rocky Island, steadfast as a sentinel,
    Towards the loveliest bay that ever mirrored the Algonquin Braves.
Soul of Beauty! Genius! Spirit! Priestess of the lovely strife!
    In my heart thy words are shrined, as in a sanctuary fair;
Echoes of thy voice of sweetness, rousing all my better life,
    Ever haunt my wildest visions of the jubilant Chaudière.

A ROYAL WELCOME.

By England's side we stand,
We grasp her royal hand,
And pay her rightful homage through her Son;
Thank God for England's care!
Thank God for Britain's heir!
Our hearts go forth to meet him—we are one.

A loyal Province pours
Her thousands to her shores,
From iron-girt Superior to the sea;
We feel our youthful blood
Surge through us like a flood,
There's not a slave amongst us—we are free.

For none but Freemen know
The truly loyal throe
That gives heroic impulse to the Man—
The passion and the fire,
The chivalrous desire:
Our Fathers all were heroes—in the van.

And we, their ardent sons,
Through whom, triumphant, runs
The old intrepid attribute serene,
Would leave our chosen land,
Our homes, our forests grand,
To strike for England's honour and her Queen.

No soulless welcome we
   Dare give to such as thee:
Be thou a bright example to the world;
   Great in thy well-earned fame,
   Beloved in heart and name,
Wherever Britain's banner is unfurled.

   Through all our leafy glades,
   Through all our green arcades,
The living torrents, sweeping in, evince
   That from their manly hearts
   The Yeoman chorus starts:
' Honour to England's Heir!—long live the Prince!'

   Oh, England! in this hour
   We own thy sov'reign pow'r;
To thee and thine our best affections cling;
   And when thy crown is laid
   On Royal Albert's head,
With heart and soul we'll shout—GOD SAVE THE
   KING!

MALCOLM.

Boy! this world has ever been
   A bright, glad world to me;
Through each dark and checkered scene
   God's sun shone lovingly.
But Content I've never known;
   Hoping, trusting that the years,
   With their April smiles and tears,
   Would yet bring me one like thee
      That I could call my own.

With thy soft and heavenly eyes
   In deep and pensive calm,
I seem looking at the skies,
   And wonder where I am!
Something more than princely blood
   Courses in thy tranquil face:
   When she lent thee such a grace,
   Nature lit life's earnest flame
      In her most queenly mood.

Such a sweet intelligence
   Is stamped on every line,
Banqueting our craving sense
   With minist'rings divine.
If thy Boyhood be so great,
   What will be the coming Man,
   Could we overleap the span?
   Are there treasures in the mine,
      To pay us, if we wait?

Doth the voice of Music live
   In that majestic brain,
Waiting for the Hand to give
   Expression to the strain?
Are there wells of Truth—pure, deep,
   Where the patient diver, Thought,
   Finds the pearl that has been sought
Many a weary age in vain,
      Entrusted to thy keep.

Doth the fire of Genius burn
   Within that ample brow?
Or some patient spirit yearn
   For things that are not now?
Hidden in the over-soul
   Of the Future, to be born
   When the world has ceased its scorn,
When the sceptic's heart will bow
      To the divine control.

Patiently we'll watch and hope,
   And wait, alternately;
Trusting that, when time shall ope
   The casket's mystery,
We will be made rich indeed
   With the wonders it contains;
Rich beyond all previous gains;
   Richer for thy thought and thee,
      Beyond our greatest meed.

THE COMET—OCTOBER, 1858.

Erratic Soul of some great Purpose, doomed
To track the wild illimitable space,
Till sure propitiation has been made
For the divine commission unperformed!
What was thy crime? Ahasuerus' curse
Were not more stern on earth than thine in Heaven!

Art thou the Spirit of some Angel World,
For grave rebellion banished from thy peers,
Compelled to watch the calm, immortal stars,
Circling in rapture the celestial void,
While the avenger follows in thy train
To spur thee on to wretchedness eterne?

Or one of nature's wildest fantasies,
From which she flies in terror so profound,
And with such whirl of torment in her breast,
That mighty earthquakes yearn where'er she treads;
While War makes red its terrible right hand,
And Famine stalks abroad all lean and wan?

To us thou art as exquisitely fair
As the ideal visions of the seer,
Or gentlest fancy that e'er floated down
Imagination's bright, unruffled stream,
Wedding the thought that was too deep for words
To the low breathings of inspirèd song.

When the stars sang together o'er the birth
Of the poor Babe at Bethlehem, that lay
In the coarse manger at the crowded Inn,
Didst thou, perhaps a bright exalted star,
Refuse to swell the grand, harmonious lay,
Jealous as Herod of the birth divine ?

Or when the crown of thorns on Calvary
Pierced the Redeemer's brow, didst thou disdain
To weep, when all the planetary worlds
Were blinded by the fulness of their tears ?
E'en to the flaming sun, that hid his face
At the loud cry, " Lama Sabachthani !"

No rest ! No rest! the very damned have that
In the dark councils of remotest Hell,
Where the dread scheme was perfected that sealed
Thy disobedience and accruing doom.
Like Adam's sons, hast thou, too, forfeited
The blest repose that never pillowed Sin ?

No! none can tell thy fate, thou wandering
    Sphinx!
Pale Science, searching by the midnight lamp
Through the vexed mazes of the human brain,
Still fails to read the secret of its soul
As the superb enigma flashes by,
A loosed Prometheus burning with disdain.

AUTUMN.

If seasons, like the human race, had souls,
Then two artistic spirits live within
The Chameleon mind of Autumn—these,
The Poet's mentor and the Painter's guide.
The myriad-thoughted phases of the mind
Are truly represented by the hues
That thrill the forests with prophetic fire.
And what could painter's skill compared to these?
What palette ever held the flaming tints
That on these leafy hieroglyphs foretell
How set the ebbing currents of the year?
What poet's page was ever like to this,
Or told the lesson of life's waning days
More forcibly, with more of natural truth,
Than yon red maples, or these poplars, white
As the pale shroud that wraps some human corse?
And then, again, the spirit of a King,
Clothed with that majesty most monarchs lack,
Might fit old Autumn for his royal rule:
For here is kingly ermine, cloth of gold,
And purple robes well worthy to be worn
By the best monarch that e'er donned a crown.

Proclaim him Royal Autumn! Poet King!
The Laureate of the Seasons, whose rare songs
Are such as lyrist never hoped to fling
On the fine ear of an admiring world.
Autumn, the Poet, Painter, and true King!
His gorgeous Ideality speaks forth

From the rare colors of the changing leaves;
And the ripe blood that swells his purple veins
Is as the glowing of a sacred fire.
He walks with Shelley's spirit on the cliffs
Of the Ethereal Caucasus, and o'er
The summits of the Euganean hills;
And meets the soul of Wordsworth, in profound
And philosophic meditation, rapt
In some great dream of love towards
The human race. The cheery Spring may come,
And touch the dreaming flowers into life,
Summer expand her leafy sea of green,
And wake the joyful wilderness to song,
As a fair hand strikes music from a lyre:
But Autumn, from its daybreak to its close,
Setting in florid beauty, like the sun,
Robed with rare brightness and ethereal flame,
Holds all the year's ripe fruitage in its hands,
And dies with songs of praise upon its lips.

And then, the Indian Summer, bland as June:
Some Tuscarora King, Algonquin Seer,
Or Huron Chief, returned to smoke the Pipe
Of Peace upon the ancient hunting grounds;
The mighty shade in spirit walking forth
To feel the beauty of his native woods,
Flashing in Autumn vestures, or to mark
The scanty remnants of the scattered tribes
Wending towards their graves. Few Braves are left;
Few mighty Hunters; fewer stately Chiefs,
Like great Tecumseth fit to take the field,
And lead the tribes to certain victory,

Choosing annihilation to defeat:
But having run the gauntlet of their days,
This Autumn remnant of some unknown race,
Nearing the Winter of their sad decay,
Fall like dry leaves into the lap of Time;
Their old trunks sapless, their tough branches bare,
And Fate's shrill war-whoop thund'ring at their heels.

COLIN.

Who'll dive for the dead men now,
    Since Colin is gone?
Who'll feel for the anguished brow,
    Since Colin is gone?
True Feeling is not confined
To the learned or lordly mind;
Nor can it be bought and sold
In exchange for an Alp of gold;
For Nature, that never lies,
Flings back with indignant scorn
The counterfeit deed, still-born,
In the face of the seeming wise,
In the Janus face of the huckster race
Who barter her truths for lies.

Who'll wrestle with dangers dire,
    Since Colin is gone?
Who'll fearlessly brave the maniac wave,
Thoughtless of self, human life to save,
Unmoved by the storm-fiend's ire?
Who, Shadrach-like, will walk through fire,
    Since Colin is gone?
Or hang his life on so frail a breath
That there's but a step 'twixt life and death?
For Courage is not the heritage
Of the nobly born; and many a sage
Has climbed to the temple of fame,
And written his deathless name
In letters of golden flame,
Who, on glancing down

From his high renown,
Saw his unlettered sire
Still by the old log fire,
Saw the unpolished dame—
And the dunghill from which he came.

Ah, ye who judge the dead
By the outward lives they led,
And not by the hidden worth
Which none but God can see;
Ye who would spurn the earth
That covers such as he;
Would ye but bare your hearts,
Cease to play borrowed parts,
And come down from your self-built throne:
How few from their house of glass,
As the gibbering secrets pass,
Would dare to fling, whether serf or king,
The first accusing stone!

Peace, peace to his harmless dust!
    Since Colin is gone;
We can but hope and trust;
Man judgeth, but God is just;
    Poor Colin is gone!
Had he faults? His heart was true,
And warm as the summer's sun.
Had he failings? Ay, but few;
'Twas an honest race he run.
Let him rest in the poor man's grave,
Ye who grant him no higher goal;
There may be a curse on the hands that gave,
But not on his simple soul!

MARGERY.

"Truth lights our minds as sunrise lights the world.
The heart that shuts out truth, excludes the light
That wakes the love of beauty in the soul;
And being foe to these, despises God,
The sole Dispenser of the gracious bliss
That brings us nearer the celestial gate.
They who might feed on rose-leaves of the True,
And grow in loveliness of heart and soul,
Catch at Deception's airy gossamers,
As children clutch at stars. To some, the world
Is a bleak desert, parched with blinding sand,
With here and there a mirage, fair to view,
But insubstantial as the visions born
Of Folly and Despair. Could we but know
How nigh we are to the true light of heaven;
In what a world of love we live and breathe;
On what a tide of truth our souls are borne!
Yet we're but bubbles in the whirl of life,
Mere flecks upon its ever-restless sea,
Meteors in its ever-changing sky.
Eternity alone is worth the thought
That we expend upon the passing hour,
Chasing the gaudy butterflies that lure
Our footsteps from the path that leads us home.
We will not see the beacon on the rock;
The prompter is unheeded; and the spark
Of the true spirit quenched in utter night,
As we rush headlong, wrecked on Error's shoals.
Some hearts will never open; all their wards

Have grown so rusty, that the golden key
Of Love Divine must fail to move the bolt
That Self has drawn to keep God's angels out."

So spake the merry Margery, the while
Her fingers lengthened out a filigree,
That seemed to me so many golden threads
Of thought between her fingers and her brain,
Bestrung with priceless pearls; her lightsome mood,
Worn as occasion might necessitate,
Replaced to-night by sober-sided Sense,
That made her beauty like an eve in June,
Just as the moon is risen. I, to mark
My approbation of her present mood,
Rehearsed a rambling lyric of my own,
That seemed prophetic of her thoughts to-night:

    Within my mind there ever lives
        A yearning for the True,
    The Beautiful and Good. God gives
        These, as He gives the dew

    That falls upon the flowers at night,
        The grass, the thirsty trees,
    Because 'tis needful; and the light
        That suns my mind from these—

    Truth—Beauty—Goodness, doth but fill
        A void within my soul;
    And I fall prone before the Will
        Of Him who gave the whole—

The wondrous life—the power to think,
   And love, and act, and speak.
Standing, half-poised, upon the brink
   Of being—strong, yet weak—

Strong in vast hopes, but weak in deeds,
   I lift my heart and pray,
That where the tangled skein of creeds
   Excludes the light of day

From human minds, God's purposes
   May be made plain, that all
May walk in truth's and wisdom's ways,
   And lay aside the thrall

Of enmity, whose clouds have kept
   Their souls as dark as night;
That they whose love and hope have slept,
   May come into the light,

And live as men, with minds to grasp
   Within the sphere of thought
The boundless universe, and clasp
   The good the wise have sought,

As if it were a long-lost dove,
   Or a stray soul returned
To worship in the fane of love,
   That it so long had spurned.

Where'er I gaze, my eyes behold
   Nought but the beautiful.
The world is grand as it is old;
   The only fitting school

For man, where he may learn to live,
　And live to learn that what
He needs heaven will in mercy give.
　　Whatever be his lot,

He shapes it for himself; his mind
　Is his own heaven or hell:
Just as he peoples it, he'll find
　　Himself compelled to dwell

With good or evil.　Good abounds
　In this delightful sphere;
But man will walk his daily rounds,
　　And evermore give ear

To the false promptings that waylay
　His steps at every turn;
Flinging the true and good away
　　For joys that he should spurn,

As being all unworthy of
　His greatness as a man.
Why, man!—why tremble at the scoff
　　Of fools and bigots?　Scan

The mental firmament, and see
　How men in every age,
Who strove for immortality—
　　Whose errand was to wage

Not War, but Peace—men of pure minds,
　Who sought and found the truth,
And treasured it, as one who finds
　　The secret of lost Youth

Restored and made immortal—see
   How they were scorned, because
Their Sphinx-lives spake of mystery
   To those to whom the laws

Of nature are as claspèd books!—
   Poets, who ruled the world
Of Thought; in whose prophetic looks
   And minds there lay impearled,

But hidden from the vulgar sight,
   Such universal truths,
That many, blinded by the light—
   Gray-haired, green-gosling youths,

With whips of satire, looks of scorn,
   And finger of disdain,
Have crushed these harbingers of morn,
   But could not kill the strain

That was a part of nature's mind,
   And therefore can not die.
That which men spurned, angels have shrined
   Among God's truths on high.

And so 't will ever be, till man
   Knows more of Goodness, Truth,
And Beauty—more of nature's plan,
   And Love that brings back youth

To hearts that have grown frail and old
   By groping in the dark
With blinded eyes; their idol, **Gold**,
   And Gain, their Pleasure-bark!

" 'Tis well that nature hath her ministers,"
She said, her voice and looks so passing sweet ;
" Great-hearts that let in love, and keep it there,
Like the true flame within the diamond's heart,
Informing, blessing, chastening their lives.
Man has but one great love—his love for God ;
All other loves are lesser and more less
As they recede from Him, as are the streams
The farthest from the fountain. God is Love.
Who loves God most, loves most his fellow-men ;
Sees the Creator in the creature's form
Where others see but man—and he, so frail
The very devils are akin to him !
There is no light that is not born of love ;
No truth where love is not its guiding star ;
Faith without love is noonday without sun,
For love begetteth works both good and true,
And these give faith its immortality."

We parted at the outer door. The stars
Seemed never half so bright or numberless
As they appeared to-night. Margery's laugh
Tripped after me in merry cadences,
Like the quick steps of fairies in the air
United to the chorus of their hearts
Breathed into silvery music. Happy soul !
Nature's epitome in all her moods.

EVA.

"God bless the darling Eva!" was my prayer.
A pure, unconscious depth of earnestness
Was in her eyes, so indescribable
You might as well the color of the air
Seek to daguerreotype, or to impress
A stain upon the river, whose first swell
Would swirl it to the deep. A calm, sweet soul,
Where Love's celestial saints and ministers
Did hold the earthly under such control
Virtue sprung up like daisies from the sod.
Oh, for one hour's sweet excellence like hers!
One hour of sinlessness, that never more
Can visit me this side the Silent Shore,
To stand, like her, serene, unblushing before God!

THE POET'S RECOMPENSE.

His heart's a burning censer, filled with spice
From fairer vales than those of Araby,
Breathing such prayers to heaven, that the nice
Discriminating ear of Deity
  Can cull sweet praises from the rare perfume.
Man cannot know what starry lights illume
The soaring spirit of his brother man!
He judges harshly with his mind's eyes closed;
His loftiest understanding cannot scan
The heights where Poet-souls have oft reposed;
He cannot feel the chastened influence
Divine, that lights the Ideal atmosphere,
  And never to his uninspirèd sense
Rolls the majestic hymn that inspirates the Seer.

THE WINE OF SONG.

Within Fancy's Halls I sit, and quaff
  Rich draughts of the Wine of Song;
    And I drink, and drink,
    To the very brink
  Of delirium wild and strong,
Till I lose all sense of the outer world,
  And see not the human throng.

The lyral chords of each rising thought
  Are swept by a hand unseen;
    And I glide, and glide,
    With my music bride,
  Where few spiritless souls have been;
And I soar afar on wings of sound,
  With my fair Æolian Queen.

Deep, deeper still, from the springs of Thought
  I quaff, till the fount is dry;
    And I climb, and climb,
    To a height sublime,
  Up the stars of some lyric sky,
Where I seem to rise upon airs that melt
  Into song as they pass by.

Millennial rounds of bliss I live,
  Withdrawn from my cumbrous clay,
    As I sweep, and sweep,
    Through infinite deep
  On deep of that starry spray;
Myself a sound on its world-wide round,
  A tone on its spheral way.

And wheresoe'er through the wondrous space
  My soul wings its noiseless flight,
    On their astral rounds
    Float divinest sounds,
  Unseen, save by spirit-sight,
Obeying some wise, eternal law,
  As fixed as the law of light.

But, oh, when my cup of dainty bliss
  Is drained of the Wine of Song,
    How I fall, and fall,
    At the sober call
  Of the body, that waiteth long
To hurry me back to its cares terrene,
  And earth's spiritless human throng.

THE PLAINS OF ABRAHAM.

    I stood upon the Plain,
    That had trembled when the slain,
Hurled their proud, defiant curses at the battle-heated foe,
    When the steed dashed right and left,
    Through the bloody gaps he cleft,
When the bridle-rein was broken, and the rider was laid low.

    What busy feet had trod
    Upon the very sod
Where I marshalled the battalions of my fancy to my aid!
    And I saw the combat dire,
    Heard the quick, incessant fire,
And the cannons' echoes startling the reverberating glade.

    I saw them, one and all,
    The banners of the Gaul
In the thickest of the contest, round the resolute Montcalm;
    The well-attended Wolfe,
    Emerging from the gulf
Of the battle's fiery furnace, like the swelling of a psalm.

I heard the chorus dire,
That jarred along the lyre
On which the hymn of battle rung, like surgings of the
    wave
When the storm, at blackest night,
Wakes the ocean in affright,
As it shouts its mighty pibroch o'er some shipwrecked
    vessel's grave.

I saw the broad claymore
Flash from its' scabbard, o'er
The ranks that quailed and shuddered at the close and
    fierce attack;
When Victory gave the word,
Then Scotland drew the sword,
And with arm that never faltered drove the brave de-
    fenders back.

I saw two great chiefs die,
Their last breaths like the sigh
Of the zephyr-sprite that wantons on the rosy lips of
    morn;
No envy-poisoned darts,
No rancour, in their hearts,
To unfit them for their triumph over death's impending
    scorn.

And as I thought and gazed,
My soul, exultant, praised
The Power to whom each mighty act and victory are
    due,

For the saint-like Peace that smiled
Like a heaven-gifted child,
And for the air of quietude that steeped the distant
view.

The sun looked down with pride,
And scattered far and wide
His beams of whitest glory till they flooded all the
Plain;
The hills their veils withdrew,
Of white, and purplish blue,
And reposed all green and smiling 'neath the shower of
golden rain.

Oh, rare, divinest life
Of Peace, compared with Strife!
Yours is the truest splendour, and the most enduring
fame;
All the glory ever reaped
Where the fiends of battle leaped,
Is harsh discord to the music of your undertoned
acclaim.

DEATH OF WOLFE.

"They run! they run!"—"Who run?" Not they
    Who faced that decimating fire
      As coolly as if human ire
        Were rooted from their hearts;
They run, while he who led the way
So bravely on that glorious day,
      Burns for one word with keen desire
        Ere waning life departs!

"They run! they run!"—"*Who* run?" he cried,
    As swiftly to his pallid brow,
      Like crimson sunlight upon snow,
        The anxious blood returned;
"The French! the French!" a voice replied,
When quickly paled life's ebbing tide,
      And though his words were weak and low
        His eye with valour burned.

"Thank God! I die in peace," he said;
    And calmly yielding up his breath,
      There trod the shadowy realms of death
        A good man and a brave;
Through all the regions of the dead,
Behold his spirit, spectre-led,
      Crowned with the amaranthine wreath
        That blooms not for the slave.

BROCK.
October 13th, 1859.*

One voice, one people, one in heart
    And soul, and feeling, and desire!
    Re-light the smouldering martial fire,
    Sound the mute trumpet, strike the lyre,
    The hero deed can not expire,
        The dead still play their part.

Raise high the monumental stone!
    A nation's fealty is theirs,
    And we are the rejoicing heirs,
    The honored sons of sires whose cares
    We take upon us unawares,
        As freely as our own.

We boast not of the victory,
    But render homage, deep and just,
    To his—to their—immortal dust,
    Who proved so worthy of their trust
    No lofty pile nor sculptured bust
        Can herald their degree.

No tongue need blazon forth their fame—
    The cheers that stir the sacred hill
    Are but mere promptings of the will
    That conquered then, that conquers still;
    And generations yet shall thrill
        At Brock's remembered name.

* The day of the inauguration of the new Monument on Queenston Heights.

Some souls are the Hesperides
    Heaven sends to guard the golden age,
    Illuming the historic page
    With records of their pilgrimage;
    True Martyr, Hero, Poet, Sage:
        And he was one of these.

Each in his lofty sphere sublime
    Sits crowned above the common throng,
    Wrestling with some Pythonic wrong,
    In prayer, in thunder, thought, or song;
    Briareus-limbed, they sweep along,
        The Typhons of the time.

SONG FOR CANADA.

Sons of the race whose sires
Aroused the martial flame
    That filled with smiles
    The triune Isles,
Through all their heights of fame!
With hearts as brave as theirs,
With hopes as strong and high,
    We'll ne'er disgrace
    The honoured race
Whose deeds can never die.
    Let but the rash intruder dare
      To touch our darling strand,
        The martial fires
        That thrilled our sires
      Would flame throughout the land.

Our lakes are deep and wide,
Our fields and forests broad;
    With cheerful air
    We'll speed the share,
And break the fruitful sod;
Till blest with rural peace,
Proud of our rustic toil,
    On hill and plain
    True kings we'll reign,
The victors of the soil.
    But let the rash intruder dare

To touch our darling strand,
    The martial fires
    That thrilled our sires
Would light him from the land.

Health smiles with rosy face
Amid our sunny dales,
    And torrents strong
    Fling hymn and song
Through all the mossy vales;
Our sons are living men,
Our daughters fond and fair;
    A thousand isles
    Where Plenty smiles,
Make glad the brow of Care.
But let the rash intruder dare
    To touch our darling strand,
        The martial fires
        That thrilled our sires
    Would flame throughout the land.

And if in future years
One wretch should turn and fly,
    Let weeping Fame
    Blot out his name
From Freedom's hallowed sky;
Or should our sons e'er prove
A coward, traitor race,—
    Just heaven! frown
    In thunder down,
T' avenge the foul disgrace!

But let the rash intruder dare
To touch our darling strand,
The martial fires
That thrilled our sires
Would light him from the land.

SONG.—I'D BE A FAIRY KING.

Oh, I'd be a Fairy King,
  With my vassals brave and bold;
    We'd hunt all day,
    Through the wildwood gay,
  In our guise of green and gold;
And we'd lead such a merry, merry life,
  That the silly, toiling bee,
    Would have no sweet
    In its dull retreat,
So rich as our frolic glee.
    I'd be a Fairy King,
      With my vassals brave and bold;
        We'd hunt all day,
        Through the wildwood gay,
      In our guise of green and gold.

At night, when the moon spake down,
  With her bland and pensive tone,
    The fairest Queen
    That ever was seen
  Would sit on my pearly throne;
And we'd lead such a merry, merry life,
  That the stars would laugh in show'rs
    Of silver light,
    All the summer night,
To the airs of the passing Hours.
    I'd be a Fairy King,
      With my vassals brave and bold;
        We'd hunt all day
        Through the wildwood gay,
      In our guise of green and gold.

We'd talk with the dainty flow'rs,
    And we'd chase the laughing brooks;
        My merry men,
        Through grove and glen,
    Would search for the mossy nooks;
And we'd be such a merry, merry band,
    Such a lively-hearted throng,
        That life would seem
        But a silvery dream
In the flowery Land of Song.
        I'd be a Fairy King,
            With my vassals brave and bold;
                We'd hunt all day,
                Through the wildwood gay,
            In our guise of green and gold.

SONG.—LOVE WHILE YOU MAY.

Day by day, with startling fleetness,
    Life speeds away;
Love, alone, can glean its sweetness,
    Love while you may.
While the soul is strong and fearless,
While the eye is bright and tearless,
Ere the heart is chilled and cheerless—
    Love while you may.

Life may pass, but love, undying,
    Dreads no decay;
Even from the grave replying,
    "Love while you may."
Love's the fruit, as life's the flower;
Love is heaven's rarest dower;
Love gives love its quick'ning power—
    Love while you may.

THE SNOWS.
UPPER OTTAWA.

Over the snows,
Buoyantly goes
The lumberers' bark canoe;
Lightly they sweep,
Wilder each leap,
Rending the white caps through.
Away! away!
With the speed of a startled deer,
While the steersman true,
And his laughing crew,
Sing of their wild career:

"Mariners glide
Far o'er the tide,
In ships that are staunch and strong;
Safely as they,
Speed we away,
Waking the woods with song."
Away! away!
With the flight of a startled deer,
While the laughing crew
Of the swift canoe
Sing of the raftsmen's cheer:

"Through forest and brake,
O'er rapid and lake,
We're sport for the sun and rain;
Free as the child
Of the Arab wild,
Hardened to toil and pain.

Away! away!
With the speed of a startled deer,
While our buoyant flight,
And the rapid's might,
Heighten our swift career."

Over the snows
Buoyantly goes
The lumberers' bark canoe;
Lightly they sweep,
Wilder each leap,
Tearing the white caps through.
Away! away!
With the speed of a startled deer;
There's a fearless crew
In each light canoe,
To sing of the raftsmen's cheer.

THE RAPID.

ST. LAWRENCE.

All peacefully gliding,
The waters dividing,
The indolent bátteau moved slowly along,
The rowers, light-hearted,
From sorrow long parted,
Beguiled the dull moments with laughter and song:
"Hurrah for the Rapid! that merrily, merrily
Gambols and leaps on its tortuous way;
Soon we will enter it, cheerily, cheerily,
Pleased with its freshness, and wet with its spray."

More swiftly careering,
The wild Rapid nearing,
They dash down the stream like a terrified steed;
The surges delight them,
No terrors affright them,
Their voices keep pace with their quickening speed:
"Hurrah for the Rapid! that merrily, merrily
Shivers its arrows against us in play;
Now we have entered it, cheerily, cheerily,
Our spirits as light as its feathery spray.'

Fast downward they're dashing,
Each fearless eye flashing,
Though danger awaits them on every side;
Yon rock—see it frowning!
They strike—they are drowning!
But downward they speed with the merciless tide:

No voice cheers the Rapid, that angrily, angrily
Shivers their bark in its maddening play;
Gaily they entered it—heedlessly recklessly,
Mingling their lives with its treacherous spray!

LOST AND FOUND.

In the mildest, greenest grove
  Blest by sprite or fairy,
Where the melting echoes rove,
  Voices sweet and airy;
    Where the streams
    Drink the beams
    Of the Sun,
    As they run
    Riverward
    Through the sward,
A shepherd went astray—
E'en gods have lost their way.

Every bird had sought its nest,
  And each flower-spirit
Dreamed of that delicious rest
  Mortals ne'er inherit;
    Through the trees
    Swept the breeze,
    Bringing airs
    Unawares
    Through the grove,
    Until love
  Came down upon his heart,
  Refusing to depart.

Hungrily he quaffed the strain,
  Sweeter still, and clearer,
Drenched with music's mellow **rain,**
  Nearer—nearer—dearer!

Chains of sound
Gently bound
The lost Youth,
Till, in sooth,
He stood there
A prisoner,
Raised between earth and heaven
By love's divinest leaven.

Was there ever such a face?
 Was it not a vision?
Had he climbed the starry space,
 To the fields Elysian?
  Through the glade
  The milk-maid
  With her pail,
  To the vale
  Passed along,
  Breathing song
 Through all his ravished sense,
 To gladden his suspense.

"Love is swift as hawk or hind,
 Chamois-like in fleetness,
None are lost that love can find,"
 Sang the maid, with sweetness.
  "True, in sooth,"
  Thought the Youth,
  "Strong, as swift,
  Love can lift

Mountain weights
To the gates
Of the celestial skies,
Where all else fades and dies."

Lightly flew the sunny days,
　Joy and gladness sending;
Life becomes a song of praise
　When true hearts are blending.
　　Guileless truth
　　Won the Youth,
　　Kept him there,
　　A prisoner;
　　While dear Love
　　From above
Poured down enduring dreams,
In calm supernal gleams.

YOUNG AGAIN.

Young again! Young again!
  Beating heart! I deemed that sorrow,
With its torture-rack of pain,
  Had eclipsed each bright to-morrow;
  And that Love could never rise
  Into life's cerulean skies,
  Singing the divine refrain—
    "Young again! Young again!"

Young again! Young again!
  Passion dies as we grow older;
Love that in repose has lain,
  Takes a higher flight, and bolder:
  Fresh from rest and dewy sleep,
  Like the skylark's matin sweep,
  Singing the divine refrain—
    "Young again! Young again!"

Young again! Young again!
  Book of Youth, thy sunny pages
Here and there a tear may stain,
  But 'tis Love that makes us sages.
  Love, Hope, Youth—blest trinity!
  Wanting these, and what were we?
  Who would chant the sweet refrain—
    "Young again! Young again!"

GLIMPSES.

Sounds of rural life and labour!
Not the notes of pipe and tabour,
Not the clash of helm and sabre
    Bright'ning up the field of glory,
Can compare with thy ovations,
That make glad the hearts of nations;
E'en the poet's fond creations
    Pale before thy simple story.

In the years beyond our present,
King was little more than peasant,
Labour was the shining crescent,
    Toil, the poor man's crown of glory;
Have we passed from worse to better
Since we wove the silken fetter,
Changed the plough for book and letter,
    Truest life for tinsel story?

Up the ladder of the ages
Clomb the patriarchal sages,
Solving nature's secret pages,
    Kings of thought's supremest glory;
Eagle-winged, and sight far reaching—
Are we wiser for their teaching?—
Wrangling creeds for gentle preaching!
    Falsest life for truest story!

Man is overfraught with culture,
Virtue early finds sepulture,
While our vices sate the vulture

We misname a bird of glory;
Life is blindly artificial,
Rarely pass we its initial,
All our aims are prejudicial
    To its earnest, simple story.

Hail, primeval life and labour!
Martial notes of pipe and tabour,
Gleam of spears and clash of sabre,
    Hero march from fields of glory,
All the thundering ovations
Surging from the hearts of nations,
Poet dreams and speculations,
    Pale before thy simple story!

MY PRAYER.

O God! forgive the erring thought,
　　The erring word and deed,
And in thy mercy hear the Christ
　　Who comes to intercede.

My sins, like mountain-weights of lead,
　　Weigh heavy on my soul;
I'm bruised and broken in this strife,
　　But Thou canst make me whole.

Allay this fever of unrest,
　　That fights against the Will;
And in Thy still small voice do Thou
　　But whisper, "Peace, be still!"

Until within this heart of mine
　　Thy lasting peace come down,
Will all the waves of Passion roll,
　　Each good resolve to drown.

We walk in blindness and dark night
　　Through half our earthly way;
Our clouds of weaknesses obscure
　　The glory of the day.

We cannot lead the lives we would,
　　But grope in dumb amaze,
Leaving the straight and flowery paths
　　To tread the crooked ways.

MY PRAYER.

We are as pilgrims toiling on
   Through all the weary hours;
And our poor hands are torn with thorns,
   Plucking life's tempting flowers.

We worship at a thousand shrines,
   And build upon the sands,
Passing the one great Temple, and
   The Rock on which it stands.

O, fading dream of human life!
   What can this change portend?
I long for higher walks, and true
   Progression without end.

Here I know nothing, and my search
   Can find no secret out;
I cannot think a single thought
   That is not mixed with doubt.

Relying on the higher source,
   The influence divine,
I can but hope that light may dawn
   Within this soul of mine.

I ask not wisdom, such as that
   To which the world is prone,
Nor knowledge ask, unless it come
   Direct from God alone.

Send down then, God! in mercy send
   Thy Love and Truth to me,
That I may henceforth walk in light
   That comes direct from Thee.

HER STAR.

When the heavens throb and vibrate
  All along their silver veins,
To the mellow storm of music
  Sweeping o'er the starry trains,
Heard by few, as erst by shepherds
  On the far Chaldean plains:

Not the blazing, torch-like planets,
  Not the Pleiads wild and free,
Not Arcturus, Mars, Uranus,
  Bring the brightest dreams to me;
But I gaze in rapt devotion
  On the central star of three.

Central star of three that tingle
  In the balmy southern sky;
One above, and one below it,
  Dreamily they pale and die,
As two lesser minds might dwindle,
  When some great soul, passing by,

Stops, and reads their cherished secrets,
  With a calm and godlike air,
Luring all their radiance from them
  Leaving a dim twilight there,
Something vague, and half unreal,
  Like the Alpha of despair.

Gazing thus, and holding converse
  With the silence of my heart,
I would speak with famed Orion,
  I would question it apart,
Wrest her love's strange secret from it,
  If there's strength in human art.

And there come to me sweet whispers,
  Half in answer, half in thought:—
"Be but strong, impassioned mortal!
  Love will come to thee unsought;
Love is the divine Irēnē,—
  It is given, and not bought.

Strong of heart. Be wise, be steadfast,
  Learn, endeavour, and endure;
Blest with strength and light, in wisdom
  Make the higher purpose sure;
Never can her heart receive thee
  Till thine own is rendered pure.

I but shone in truth above her;
  Psyche-like, she yearned to me,
And her soul, an Aphrodite,
  Rose above the ether sea.
Love. Love should and will inherit
  The divine Euphrosyne."

When at night, the gleaming heavens
  Throb through all their starry veins,
Oft I ponder on Orion,
  And I hear celestial strains
Passing through my soul, and flooding
  All its green immortal plains.

Then I pray for strength Promethean,
  Pray for power to endure;
Then I say, O soul, be steadfast!
  Make the lofty purpose sure;
And that love may be all-worthy,
  God of heaven, make me pure!

THE MYSTERY.

My mind is like a troubled sea
   O'er which the winds forever sweep;
Within its depths, eternally,
   My being's pulses throb and leap;
There germs of contemplation sleep,
   Like stars beyond the Milky Way,—
Like pearls within the gloomy deep,
   That never saw the light of day.

Oh, wondrous mind, how little known!
   Whence comes the thought that through my brain
Floats weirdlike as the pleasing tone
   That quickens a belovèd strain?
It may have graced some sweet refrain
   A thousand years ago, or more;
Some Norman Prince, some valiant Dane,
   May have imbibed it with their lore.

It may have strengthened Plato's soul,
   Its clarion echoes ringing through
His brain, the heaven-reaching goal
   Whence wisdom had its starry view;
It may have cheered the gifted few
   Whose minds were mints of royal song,
Who toiled where Shakespeare soared, and drew
   Down blessings from the grateful throng.

And on for ages yet to come,
   Through minds by heavenly impulse fired,
That thought may strike some scorner dumb,
   In all its regal guise attired;

Divinely blest, though uninspired,
  Some soul may change its swift career,
Bearing the great truth, long-desired,
  In triumph to the highest sphere.

Unbounded universe of Thought!
  Illimitable realms of mind!
Regions of Fancy, wonder-fraught!
  Imagination unconfined!
Temples of mystery! behind
  Whose veils the God-appointed plan
In perfect wisdom is enshrined,
  Beyond the pigmy reach of man:

I cannot—dare not—seek to know
  What finite vision, to the end,
Through years of strictest search below,
  Must ever fail to comprehend!
God! whose intents so far transcend
  Our poor discernment, let me see
Some portion of the truths that tend
  By slow gradations up to Thee:

That in the less imperfect years,
  When human frailty shall have died,
When the vexed riddle of the spheres,
  Interpreted and glorified,
Shall be as nothing to the tide
  Of light in which Thy hidden ways
Will be revealed: I may abide
  Thy meanest instrument of praise,
And from the broad calm ocean of Thy truth
And wisdom drinking, find eternal youth.

LOVE AND TRUTH.

Young Love sat in a rosy bower,
  Towards the close of a summer day;
At the evening's dusky hour,
  Truth bent her blessed steps that way;
    Over her face
    Beaming a grace
Never bestowed on child of clay.

Truth looked on with an ardent joy,
  Wondering Love could grow so tired;
Hovering o'er him she kissed the boy,
  When, with a sudden impulse fired,
    Exquisite pains
    Burning his veins,
Wildly he woke, as one inspired.

Eagerly Truth embraced the god,
  Filling his soul with a sense divine;
Rightly he knew the paths she trod,
  Springing from heaven's royal line;
    Far had he strayed
    From his guardian maid,
Perilling all for his rash design.

Still as they went, the tricksy youth
  Wandered afar from the maiden fair;
Many a plot he laid, in sooth,
  Wherein the maid could have no share
    Sowing his seeds,
    Bringing forth weeds,
Seldom a rose, and many a tare.

Save when the maiden was by his side,
  Love was erratic, and rarely true;
When she smiled on the graceful bride,
  Over the old world rose the new,
    Into life's skies
    Blending her dyes,
  Fairer than those of the rainbow's hue.

Sunny-eyed maidens, whom Love decoys,
  Mark well the arts of the wayward youth!
Sorrows he bringeth, disguised as joys,
  Rose-hued delights with cores of ruth;
    Learn to believe
    Love will deceive,
  Save when he comes with his guardian, Truth.

THE WREN.

Early each spring the little wren
    Came scolding to his nest of moss;
We knew him by his peevish cry,
    He always sung so very cross.
His quiet little mate would lay
Her eggs in peace, and think all day.

He was a sturdy little wren;
    And when he came in spring, we knew,
Or seemed to know, the flowers would grow
    To please him, where they always grew,
Among the rushes, cheerfully;
But not a rush so straight as he!

All summer long that little wren
    Would chatter like a saucy thing;
And in the bush attack the thrush
    That on the hawthorn perched to sing.
Like many noisy little men,
Lived, bragged, and fought that little wren.

There was a thoughtful maid, and I,
    We used to play along the shore,
Searching for shells, and culling flowers,
    As at the threshold of life's door,
Through which we had to pass, we stood,
Twin types of childish hardihood.

Year after year we gathered flowers,
    And grew apace, as children do;
And each returning spring we marked
    The little wrens, they never grew;
One over-quiet and sedate,
The other, a bird-reprobate.

But now the marsh is overflowed,
    The rushes rot beneath the sand;
No spring brings back the little wrens,
    No children loiter hand in hand;
The maiden rose-bud, pure and good,
Grown to the flower of womanhood.

GRANDPERE.

Old Grandpere sat in the corner,
   With his grandchild on his knee,
Looking up at his wrinkled visage,
   For his winters were ninety-three.

Fair Eleanor's locks were flaxen,
   The old man's once were gray,
But now, they were white as the snow-drift
   That lay on the bleak highway.

Her summers rolled on as golden
   As waves over sunny seas;
But Grandpere could perceive no summers,
   The winters alone were his.

He folded his arms around her,
   Like Winter embracing Spring;
And the angels looked down from heaven,
   And smiled on their slumbering.

But soon the angelic faces
   Were filled with seraphic light,
As they gazed on a beauteous spirit
   Passing up through the frosty night:

Till it stood serene before them,
   A youth most divinely fair;
And they saw that the new-born angel
   Was the spirit of old Grandpere.

ENGLAND'S HOPE AND ENGLAND'S HEIR.

  England's Hope and England's Heir!
   Head and crown of Britain's glory,
  Be thy future half so fair
   As her past is famed in story,
  Then wilt thou be great, indeed,
   Daring, where there's cause to dare;
  Greatest in the hour of need,
   England's Hope and England's Heir.

  By her past, in acts supreme,
   By her present grand endeavour,
  By her future, which the gleam
   Of our fond hopes brings us ever:
  We can trust that thou wilt be
   Worthy of a fame so rare,
  Worthy of thy destiny,
   England's Hope and England's Heir.

  Be thy spirit fraught with hers,
   Queen, whom we revere and honour;
  Be thine acts love's messengers,
   Brightly flashing back upon her;
  Be what most her trust would deem,
   Help the answer to her prayer,
  Realize her holiest dream,
   England's Hope and England's Heir.

  Welcome, Prince! the land is wide,
   Wider still the love we cherish;
  Love that thou shalt find, when tried,
   Is not born to droop and perish;

Welcome to our heart of hearts;
  You will find no falsehood there,
But the zeal that truth imparts,
  England's Hope and England's Heir.

Welcome to our woodland deeps,
  To our inland lakes, and rivers,
Where the rapid roars and sweeps,
  Where the brightest sunlight quivers.
Loyal souls can never fail;
  Serfdom crouches in its lair;
But our British hearts are hale,
  England's Hope and England's Heir.

ROSE.

When the evening broods quiescent
   Over mountain, vale and lea,
And the moon uplifts her crescent
   Far above the peaceful sea,
Little Rose, the fisher's daughter,
   Passes in her cedar skiff
O'er the dreamy waste of water,
   To the signal on the cliff.

Have a care, my merry maiden!
   Young Adonis though he be,
Many hearts are secret-laden
   That have trusted such as he.
Has he worth, and is he truthful?
   Thoughtless maiden rarely knows;
But, "He's handsome, brave and youthful,"
   Says the heart of little Rose.

Hark! the horn—its shrill vibrations
   Tremble through the maiden's breast,
As the sweet reverberations
   Dwindle to their whispered rest;
Sweeter far the honied sentence
   Sealing up her mind's repose;
Love as yet needs no repentance
   In the heart of little Rose.

Heaven shield thee, trusting mortal!
   Love has heaved its firstborn sigh;
But from the pellucid portal
   Of her calm, indignant eye,

Darts that make the strong man tremble
  Pierce his bosom ere he goes;
Rank and station may dissemble,
  There is truth in little Rose.

Take my hand, my fisher maiden,
  There's a grasp for thee and thine;
Constancy is love's bright Aiden,
  Self-denial is divine.
Take my hand upon this pláteau,
  Let me share thy mortal throes;
Come, dear Love! we'll build our château
  In the heart of little Rose.

THE DREAMER.

Spirit of Song! whose whispers
   Delight my pensive brain,
When will the perfect harmony
   Ring through my feeble strain?

When will the rills of melody
   Be widened to a stream?
When will the bright and gladsome Day
   Succeed this morning dream?

"Mortal," the spirit whispered,
   "If thou wouldst truly win
The race thou art pursuing,
   Heed well the voice within:

And it shall gently teach thee
   To read thy heart, and know
No human strain is perfect,
   However sweet it flow.

And if thou readest truly,
   As surely shalt thou find
That truths, like rills, though diverse,
   Are choicest in their kind.

The souls of Poet-Dreamers
   Touch heaven on their way;
With the light of Song to guide them
   It should be always Day."

NIGHT AND MORNING.

The winds are piping loud to-night,
   And the waves roll strong and high;
God pity the watchful mariner
   Who toils 'neath yonder sky!

I saw the vessel speed away,
   With a free, majestic sweep,
At evening as the sun went down
   To his palace in the deep.

An aged crone sat on the beach,
   And, pointing to the ship,
"She'll never return again," she said,
   With a scorn upon her lip.

The morning rose tempestuous,
   The winds blew to the shore,
There were corpses on the sands that morn,
   But the ship came nevermore!

WITHIN THINE EYES.

Within thine eyes two spirits dwell,
    The sweetest and the purest
That ever wove Love's mystic spell,
    Or plied his arts the surest:
        No smile of morn,
        Though heaven-born,
    Nor sunshine earthward straying,
        E'er charmed the sight
        With half the light
    That round thy lips is playing.

The stars may shine, the moon may smile,
    The earth in beauty languish,
Life's sorrows these can but beguile,
    But thou canst heal its anguish.
        Thy voice, like rills
        Of silver, trills
    Such sounds of liquid sweetness,
        Each accent rolls
        Along our souls,
    In lyrical completeness.

If Friendship lend thee such a grace,
    That men nor gods may slight it,
How blest the one who views thy face
    When Love comes down to light it!
        And, oh, if he
        Who holds in fee
    Thy beauty, truth, and reason,
        A traitor prove
        To thee and Love,
    We'll spurn him for his treason.

GERTRUDE.

Underneath the maple-tree
Gertrude worked her filigree,
    All the summer long;
To sweet airs her voice was wed,
As she plied her golden thread;
Echo stealing through the grove
Filched away the words of love,
And the birds, from tree to tree,
Bore the witching melody
    Through avenues of Song.

Underneath the maple-trees
Zephyrs chant her melodies,
    All the summer long;
Words and airs no longer wed,
Death has snapped the vocal thread
Echo sleeping in the grove
Dreams of liquid airs of love,
And the birds among the trees
Fill with sweetest symphonies
    Whole avenues of Song.

FLOWERS.

Thank God I love the Flowers!
   Mute voices of the Spring,
That gladden all her bowers
   With their varied blossoming;
They weave a charm around them
   On each summer dale and bough,
For a Fairy train has bound them
   In wreaths upon her brow.

Far up along the mountain,
   And in the valleys green,
In the field, and by the fountain,
   The smiling ones are seen;
Some looking up to heaven,
   With eyes of deepest blue;
Some stooping down at even
   To quaff the sparkling dew.

And from them all there speaketh
   A language sweet and pure,
Fitted for him who seeketh
   A God's nomenclature.
As tidal pulses thrill the seas,
   And moments build the hours,
Heaven breathes her unvoiced mysteries
   In sermons from the Flowers.

THE UNATTAINABLE.

I yearn for the Unattainable;
 For a glimpse of a brighter day,
  When hatred and strife,
  With their legions rife,
 Shall forever have passed away;
  When pain shall cease,
  And the dawn of peace
 Come down from heaven above,
 And man can meet his fellow-man
 In the spirit of Christian Love.

I yearn for the Unattainable;
 For a Voice that may long be still,
  To compel the mind,
  As heaven designed,
 To work the Eternal Will;
  When the brute that sleeps
  In the heart's still deeps
 Will be changed to Pity's dove,
 And man can meet his fellow-man
 In the spirit of Perfect Love.

YEARNINGS.

I long for diviner regions,—
  The spirit would reach its goal;
Though this world hath surpassing beauty,
  It warreth against the soul.

There's a cloud in the eastern heaven;
  Beyond it, a cold gray sky;
But I know that the sun's rare radiance
  Will brighten it by and by.

In the fane of my soul is glowing
  The joy of a hope to come,
That will touch with its Memnon finger
  The lips that are cold and dumb:

Till illumed by the smile of heaven,
  And blest with a purer life,
Will the gloom that o'ershades my spirit
  Depart like a vanquished strife.

INGRATITUDE.

Full on the wave the moonlight weeps,
    To quiet its weary breast;
Cruelly cold the mad wave leaps,
    With the moonshine on its crest;
Or with scowl, or growl, to the shore it creeps,
    And sinks to its selfish rest.

Full on yon man-brute smiles the wife,
    To gladden his turbid breast;
Savagely stern he seeks the life
    Where he erewhile sought for zest;
With a curse, or worse, he ends the strife,
    And sinks to his drunken rest.

Sea! has the moon no charms for thee
    That can touch thy cruel breast?
Man! cannot woman's charity
    Give ease to thy soul oppressed?
Thou shalt flee, O sea! the moon's witchery,
    Till man has his final rest!

TRUE LOVE.

Her love is like the hardy flower
  That blooms amid the Alpine snows;
Deep-rooted in an icy bower,
  No blast can chill its sweet repose;
  But fresh as is the tropic rose,
Drenched in mellowest sunny beams,
It has as sweet delicious dreams
  As any flower that grows.

And though an avalanche came down
  And robbed it of the light of day,
That which withstood the tempest's frown
  In grief would never pine away.
  Hope might withhold her feeblest ray,
Within her bosom's snowy tomb
Love still would wear its everbloom,
  The gayest of the gay.

AN EVENING THOUGHT.

Bird of the fanciful plumage,
   That foldest thy wings in the west,
Imbuing the shimmering ocean
   With the hues of thy delicate breast,
Passing away into Dreamland,
   To visions of heavenly rest!

Spirit! when thou art permitted
   To bask in the sunset of life;
Serene in thine eventide splendour,
   Thy countenance victory rife;
Leaving the world where thou'st triumphed
   Alike o'er its greatness and strife:

Thine be the destiny, spirit,
   To set like the sun in the west;
Folding thy wings of rare plumage,
   Conscious of infinite rest;
Heralded on to thy haven,
   The Fortunate Isles of the Blest.

A THOUGHT FOR SPRING.

I am happier for the Spring;
  For my heart is like a bird
That has many songs to sing,
  But whose voice is never heard
Till the happy year is caroling
  To the daisies on the sward.

I'd be happier for the Spring,
  Though my heart had grown so old
Like a crone 'twould sit and sing
  Its shrill runes of wintry cold;
For I'd know the year was caroling
  To the daisies on the wold.

THE SWALLOWS.

I asked the first stray swallow of the spring,
"Where hast thou been through all the winter drear?
Beneath what distant skies did'st fold thy wing,
    Since thou wast with us here,
When Autumn's withered leaves foretold the passing
        year?"

And it replied, " Whither has Fancy led
The plumy thoughts that circle through thy brain?
Like birds about some mountain's lofty head,
    Singing a sweet refrain:
There, without bound, I've been, and must return
        again."

SONG.—CLARA AND I.

We have a joke whenever we meet,
    Clara and I;
Prattle and laughter, and kisses sweet,
    Clara and I.
Were I but twenty, and not two score,
Clara and I would laugh still more,
With plenty of hopeful years in store
  For Clara and I, Clara and I;
With plenty of hopeful years in store
    For Clara and I.

We will be true as Damascus steel,
    Clara and I;
Sealing our truth with a honied seal,
    Clara and I.
Eyes so loving, and lips of rose,
Cheeks where the dainty ripe peach grows,
And mouth where the sly god smiles jocose
  At Clara and I, Clara and I;
And mouth where the sly god smiles jocose
    At Clara and I.

We have a kiss whenever we part,
    Clara and I;
Grasping of hand, and flutter of heart,
    Clara and I.
Were she but twenty, and not sixteen,
Over my love she'd reign the queen,

And no fair rival should come between
    My Clara and I, Clara and I;
And no fair rival should come between
    My Clara and I.

THE APRIL SNOW-STORM.—1858.

Spread lightly, virgin shower,
    Your winding-sheet of snow;
Winter has lost his power,
    But mock not at his woe.

Fall not so cold and bleak,
    Nor blow the breath of scorn;
Gently. Thy sire is weak;
    And thou, his latest-born.

Frail type of life thou art:
    At first, pure as the snow
We come—abide—depart;
    What more, th' Immortals know.

Fall gently, virgin shower,
    Though wild the west wind raves;
Watch through this midnight hour
    Above the new-made graves!

Spread gently, virgin shower,
    Your winding sheet of snow;
My heart has lost its power,
    But mock not at its woe.

Fall not so cold and bleak,
    Treat not her corse with scorn;
Gently. My heart is weak;
    She, too, was April-born.

Fall gently, virgin shower;
  The heart once strong and brave
Hath lost its wonted power;
  'Tis buried in her grave.

GOOD NIGHT.

We never say, "Good Night;"
For our eager lips are fleeter
Than the tongue, and a kiss is sweeter
   Than parting words,
   That cut like swords;
So we always kiss Good Night.

We never say "Good Night."
Words are precious, love, why lose 'em?
Fold them up in your maiden bosom;
   There let them rest,
   Like love unconfessed,
While we kiss a sweet Good Night.

There comes a last Good Night.
Human life—not love—is fleeting;
Heaven send many a birth-day greeting;
   Dim years roll on
   To life's gray-haired dawn,
Ere we kiss our last Good Night.

———

We've kissed our last Good Night!
Love's warm tendrils torn and bleeding,
Vain all human interceding!
   Oh, life! how dark!
   Its one vital spark
Was quenched with our last GOOD NIGHT!

HOPELESS.

I think through the long, long evenings,
    Such thoughts of intensest pain,
And I hope and watch for her coming,
    But I hope and watch in vain;
My life is a long, long journey
    Over a barren moor,
With nought but my own dark shadow
    Hastening on before.

I'm weary of all this watching,
    Aweary of life and thought;
For there's little hope in the distance,
    And for peace—I know it not!
Oh, why must we think and shudder,
    And shudder and think again?
When life's but a dance of shadows
    Haunting a barren plain!

Into the Silent Land.

INTO THE SILENT LAND.

I.

"Oh for a pen of light, a tongue of fire,
That every word might burn in living flame
Upon the age's brow, and leave one name
Engraven on the future! One desire
Fills every nook and cranny of my heart;
One hope—one sorrow—one belovèd aim!
She whose pure life was of my life a part,
As light is of the day, could she inspire
My unmelodious muse, or tune the lyre
To diapasons worthy of the theme,
How would her joy put on its robes of light,
And nestle in my bosom once again,
As when life, like an Oriental dream,
Fanned by Arabian airs, glode down the stream
To music whose remembrance is a pain.
The foot of time might trample on my strain,
But could not quench its essence. There was might,
And majesty, and greatness in the love
She blest me with—a blessing without stain,
And that was earthly; since her spirit-sight
Looked through the veil, and learned love's true delight,
Which sainted ministrants alone can prove
Who taste the waters of eternal love:
I pause to think how wonderful has grown
The love that was to me so wondrous here!
Chained as I am to this terrestrial sphere,
Groping my way through darkness, and alone,

Like a blind eaglet soaring towards the sun,
How would her full experience lift and cheer
The heart that never feels its duty done,
And with a girdle of pure light enzone
My flowery world of thought, and make it all her own."

Thus mused the Minstrel, for his heart was sad.
Death had bereaved him of his bride, while youth,
And looming years of future trust and truth,
Knit them together, till their souls were clad
With joy ineffable. Love's great High Priest
Sacrificed in their hearts to Him that doeth
All things well; and such rare, perpetual feast
Of love and truth no mortals ever had,
To keep their memories green, their lives serene and
 glad.

He sat again within the quiet room,
Where Death had snapped one golden thread of life,
And the pale hand of Sickness, sorrow-rife,
Robbed the plump cheek of childhood of its bloom;
Where she, another Philomena, moved
Like a fond Charity—the coming wife
Ordained to crown his being: And he loved.
The future rose before him, joy and gloom;
For where the sunlight shone, there waved the sable
 plume.

And yet he failed not, for the coming pain;
The coming bliss would counterbalance all.
The sight prophetic that perceived the pall,
Looked far beyond for the celestial gain.

They do not truly love who cannot yield
The mortal up at the Immortal's call,
Or fail to triumph for the soul that's sealed.
His mind was strung to one harmonious strain:
To give when God should ask, and not resign in vain.

Love was to him life's chiefest victory;
He knew no greater, and he sought no less.
Like a green isle surrounded by the sea
That gives it health and vigour, so was he
The centre of love's sphere of perfectness;
He breathed its heavenly atmosphere; the key
That opened every chamber in love's court
Was in his hand; love's mystery was his sport;
He knelt within love's fane and worshipped there—
But not alone, for one was by his side
Whose love refined his being, filled the air
Of life's irradiated sky with light,
As the sun floods the heavens with a tide
Of renovating freshness, as the night
Is mellowed by the ample moon.
And hoping for the recompense
That would be theirs in life's approaching noon,
They built on hope's high eminence
Their airy palaces, whose magnificence
Surpassed the dreams that fancy drew,
So fair the promised land that lay within their view.

And here they lived; just within reach of heaven.
They could put forth their hands and touch the skies
That brooded o'er the walls of chrysolite,
The airy minarets, and golden domes

Of their new home, by Love, the Maker, given,
Steeped in his brightest dyes.
All nature opened up her ponderous tomes,
Whereby they had new knowledge and new sight,
Learned greater truths, and saw the paths of light,
Mosaic-paven, which to Duty led.
And there were secrets written overhead,
In burning hieroglyphs of thought,
From which they gleaned such lessons as are taught
Only to those whom heaven, in graciousness,
Lifts in her arms with a divine caress.
Earth, like a joyous maiden whose pure soul
Is filled with sudden ecstacy, became
A fruitful Eden; and the golden bowl
That held their elixir of life was filled
To overflowing with the rarest draught
Ever by gods or men in rapture quaffed;
Till from the altar of their hearts love's flame
Passed through the veins of the world, and thrilled
The soul of the rejoicing universe,
Which became theirs, and like true neophytes
They drained the sweet nepenthe, and love's rites
Wiped from their hearts all trace of the primeval curse.

The happy months rolled on; each wedded day
A bridal; and each calm and holy eve
Strewed with rare blessings all the sunny way
Through which they passed, with so divine a joy
That in his brain would meditation weave
Love's roses into garlands of sweet song,
To deck the brow of his devoted wife.

In this their El Dorado, no alloy
Mixed with the coinage of their wedded life;
The workmen in the mint an honest throng.
No wonder, then, that with so fine a bliss
Informing every fibre of his brain,
His thoughts begat impressions such as this;
Linking their lives together with a chain
Of melody as rare as some divine refrain:

    Like dew to the thirsty flower,
      Like sweets to the hungry bee,
    Is love's divinest dower,
    Its tenderness and power,
      To thee, dear Wife! to thee.

    Like light to the darkened spirit,
      Like oil to the turbid sea,
    Like truthful words to merit,
    Are the blessings I inherit
      With thee, dear Wife! with thee.

    Afar in the distant ages,
      Soul-ransomed, and spirit-free,
    I'll read all being's pages,
    Unread by mortal sages,
      With thee, dear Wife! with thee.

  None but the happy heart could carol thus;
A feather stolen from Devotion's wing,
To keep as a memento of the time
When earth met heaven, in life's duteous
And prayerful journey towards the shadowy clime;

Ere they descended from their height sublime,
Where at Love's well-filled table, banqueting,
They sat, and watched the first glad year,
Earthlike, revolving round the sun
Of their true life. Within that sphere
Was the new Eden. One by one
The precious moments dropped like golden sands,
And formed the solid hours. No perilous strands
Delayed life's blissful current, as it sped
Through flowery realms with blue skies overhead,
To songs and laughter musically sweet,
As if all sorrow had forever fled;
And idylls, sung with cheerful tone,
Haunted the calm, enchanted zone
That hemmed them in,
Where, like a stately queen,
Sate Peace, beatified, serene,
The guardian, heaven-sent, of this their fair demesne:

LOVE'S ANNIVERSARY.

Like a bold, adventurous swain,
   Just a year ago to-day,
I launched my bark on a radiant main,
   And Hymen led the way :
"Breakers ahead!" he cried,
   As he sought to overwhelm
My daring craft in the shrieking tide,
But Love, like a pilot bold and tried,
   Sat, watchful, at the helm.

And we passed the treacherous shoals,
  Where many a hope lay dead,
And splendid wrecks were piled, like the ghouls
  Of joys forever fled.
Once safely over these,
  We sped by a fairy realm,
Across the bluest and calmest seas
That were ever kissed by a truant breeze,
  With Love still at the helm.

We sailed by sweet, odorous isles,
  Where the flowers and trees were one;
Through lakes that vied with the golden smiles
  Of heaven's unclouded sun:
Still speeds our merry bark,
  Threading life's peaceful realm,
And 'tis ever morn with our marriage-lark,
For the Pilot-Love of our safety-ark
  Stands, watchful, at the helm.

II.

A beautiful land is the Land of Dreams,
  Green hills and valleys, and deep lagoons,
Swift-rushing torrents and gentle streams,
  Glassing a myriad silver moons;
Mirror-like lakelets with lovely isles,
  And verdurous headlands looking down
On the Neread shapes, whose smiles
  Were worth the price of a peaceful crown.

We clutch at the silvery bars
Flung from the motionless stars,
   And climb far into space,
   Defying the race
Who ride in aërial cars.

We take up the harp of the mind,
  And finger its delicate strings;
    The notes, soft and light
    As a moonbeam's flight,
Departing on viewless wings.
Afar in some fanciful bower,
  Some region of exquisite calm,
Where the starlight falls in a gleaming shower,
    We sink to repose
    On our couch of rose,
Inhaling no mortal balm.
The worlds are no longer unknown,
  We pass through the uttermost sky,
    Our eyelids are kissed
    By a gentle mist,
    And we feel the tone
    Of a calmer zone,
As if heaven were wondrous nigh.

A fanciful land is the Land of Dreams,
  Where earth and heaven are clasping hands;
    No heaven—no earth,
    But one wide, new birth,
Where Beauty and Goodness, and human worth,
Make earth of heaven and heaven of earth;
And angels are walking on golden strands.

And the pearly gates of the universe
Of mind and fancy, opening
To the touch of the dainty finger-tips
Of elegant Peris with rose-bud lips,
Delicate, weird-like sounds are born
From the amber depths of odorous morn,
And spirits of beauty and light rehearse
  Such strains as the young immortals sing,
    When the souls of the blest
    Are borne to their rest,
On luminous pinions of light serene
To the fragrant bowers of evergreen;
O'er the rosy plains, where the dying hours
Are changed by a spell to celestial flowers,
Where the skies have a hue no name can express,
For the tone of their passionate loveliness
  Surpasseth all human imagining.

Such was their beautiful Dream of Life;
  Each stern reality softened down;
Earth seemed to have ended her age of Strife,
  And Harmony reigned, her olive crown
Resting on the Parian brow
  Of the fair victor, like the gleam
Of the silvery moon on waves that flow
  Thoughtfully down the summer stream.
Such was their earnest Dream of Life!
Was it some angel, with jealous eye,
Seeing such love beneath the sky
As never yet in world or star,
Or spheral height, that reached so far
'Twas never beheld by mortal sight,

Or elsewhere, save in highest heaven,
Was duly earned, or truly given,
That leagued with the usurper, Death,
To quench the light that shone so bright
That in all the earth there was not a breath
So foul as to change their day to night?

Alone! alone! Oh, word of fearful tone!
Well might the moon withhold her light,
The stars withdraw from human sight,
When Love was overthrown.
The Minstrel's heart how changed!
Love's principalities,
O'er which he reigned supreme,
Usurped by earth's realities;
The realm through which he ranged
Become a vanished dream!
And yet he sung, as sings
The dying swan that droops its wings
And drifts along the stream:

THE LIGHT IN THE WINDOW PANE.

A joy from my soul's departed,
  A bliss from my heart is flown,
As weary, weary-hearted,
  I wander alone—alone!
The night wind sadly sigheth
  A withering, wild refrain,
And my heart within me dieth
  For the light in the window pane.

INTO THE SILENT LAND.

The stars overhead are shining,
  As brightly as e'er they shone,
As heartless—sad—repining,
  I wander alone—alone!
A sudden flash comes streaming,
  And flickers adown the lane,
But no more for me is gleaming
  The light in the window pane.

The voices that pass are cheerful,
  Men laugh as the night winds moan;
They cannot tell how fearful
  'Tis to wander alone—alone!
For them, with each night's returning,
  Life singeth its tenderest strain,
Where the beacon of love is burning—
  The light in the window pane.

Oh, sorrow beyond all sorrows
  To which human life is prone:
Without thee, through all the morrows,
  To wander alone—alone!
Oh, dark, deserted dwelling!
  Where Hope like a lamb was slain,
No voice from thy lone walls welling,
  No light in thy window pane.

But memory, sainted angel!
  Rolls back the sepulchral stone,
And sings like a sweet evangel:
  " No—never, never alone!

True grief has its royal palace,
  Each loss is a greater gain;
And Sorrow ne'er filled a chalice
  That Joy did not wait to drain!"

"Man must be perfected
  By suffering," he said;
"And Death is but the stepping-stone, whereby
  We mount towards the gate
  Of heaven, soon or late.
Death is the penalty of life; we die,

Because we live; and life
  Is but a constant strife
With the immortal Impulse that within
  Our bodies seeks control—
  The time-abiding Soul,
That wrestles with us—yet we fain would win.

And what? the victory
  Would make us slaves; and we,
Who in our blindness struggle for the prize
  Of this illusive state
  Called Life, do but frustrate
The higher law—refusing to be wise."

Rightly he knew, indeed,
  Earth's brightest paths but lead
To the true wisdom of that perfect state,
  Where Knowledge, heaven-born,
  And Love's eternal morn,
Awaiteth those who would be truly great.

With what abiding trust
He rose from out the dust,
As Death's swift chariot passed him by the way;
No visionary dream
Was his—no trifling theme—
The Soul's great Mystery before him lay:

THE SOUL.

All my mind has sat in state,
  Pond'ring on the deathless Soul:
  What must be the Perfect Whole,
When the atom is so great!

God! I fall in spirit down,
  Low as Persian to the sun;
  All my senses, one by one,
In the stream of Thought must drown.

On the tide of mystery,
  Like a waif, I'm seaward borne;
  Ever looking for the morn
That will yet interpret Thee.

Opening my blinded eyes,
  That have strove to look within,
  'Whelmed in clouds of doubt and sin,
Sinking where I dared to rise:

Could I trace one Spirit's flight,
  Track it to its final goal,
  Know that 'Spirit' meant 'the Soul,'
I must perish in the light.

All in vain I search, and cry:
  "What, O Soul, and whence art thou?"
  Lower than the earth I bow,
Stricken with the grave reply:

"Wouldst thou ope what God has sealed—
  Sealed in mercy here below?
  What is best for man to know,
Shall most surely be revealed!"

Deep on deep of mystery!
  Ask the sage, he knows no more
  Of the soul's unspoken lore
Than the child upon his knee!

Cannot tell me whence the thought
  That is passing through my mind!
  Where the mystic soul is shrined,
Wherewith all my life is fraught?

Knows not how the brain conceives
  Images almost divine;
  Cannot work my mental mine,
Cannot bind my golden sheaves.

Is he wiser, then, than I,
  Seeing he can read the stars?
  I have rode in fancy's cars
Leagues beyond his farthest sky!

Some old Rabbi, dreaming o'er
  The sweet legends of his race,
  Ask him for some certain trace
Of the far, eternal shore.

No. The Talmud page is dark,
   Though it burn with quenchless fire;
   And the insight must pierce higher,
That would find the vital spark.

O, my Soul! be firm and wait,
   Hoping with the zealous few,
   Till the Shekinah of the True
Lead thee through the Golden Gate.

SONNETS,

WRITTEN IN THE ORILLIA WOODS.

August, 1859.

DEDICATED

TO

My Friends

AT

"ROCKRIDGE," ORILLIA, C. W.

SONNETS.

PROEM.

 ALICE, I need not tell you that the Art
That copies Nature, even at its best,
Is but the echo of a splendid tone,
Or like the answer of a little child
To the deep question of some frosted sage.
For Nature in her grand magnificence,
Compared to Art, must ever raise her head
Beyond the cognizance of human minds:
This is the spirit merely; that, the soul.
We watch her passing, like some gentle dream,
And catch sweet glimpses of her perfect face;
We see the flashing of her gorgeous robes,
And, if her mantle ever falls at all,
How few Elishas wear it sacredly,
As if it were a valued gift from heaven.
God has created; we but re-create,
According to the temper of our minds;
According to the grace He has bequeathed;
According to the uses we have made
Of His good-pleasure given unto us.
And so I love my art; chiefly, because
Through it I rev'rence Nature, and improve
The tone and tenor of the mind He gave.
God sends a Gift; we crown it with high Art,

And make it worthy the bestower, when
The talent is not hidden in the dust
Of pampered negligence and venial sin,
But put to studious use, that it may work
The end and aim for which it was bestowed.
All Good is God's; all Love and Truth are His;
We are His workers; and we dare not plead
But that He gave us largely of all these,
Demanding a discreet return, that when
The page of life is written to its close
It may receive the seal and autograph
Of His good pleasure—the right royal sign
And signet of approval, to the end
That we were worthy of the gift divine,
And through it praised the Great Artificer.

In my long rambles through Orillian woods;
Out on the ever-changing Couchiching;
By the rough margin of the Lake St. John;
Down the steep Severn, where the artist sun,
In dainty dalliance with the blushing stream,
Transcribes each tree, branch, leaf, and rock and flower,
Perfect in shape and colour, clear, distinct,
With all the panoramic change of sky—
Even as Youth's bright river, toying with
The fairy craft where Inexperience dreams,
And subtle Fancy builds its airy halls,
In blest imagination pictures most
Of bright or lovely that adorn life's banks,
With the blue vault of heaven over all;
On that serene and wizard afternoon,
As hunters chase the wild and timid deer

We chased the quiet of Medonte's shades
Through the green windings of the forest road,
Past Nature's venerable rank and file
Of primal woods—her Old Guard, sylvan-plumed—
The far-off Huron, like a silver thread,
The clue to some enchanted labyrinth,
Dimly perceived beyond the stretch of woods,
Th' approaches tinted by a purple haze,
And softened into beauty like the dream
Of some rapt seer's Apocalyptic mood;
And when at Rockridge we sat looking out
Upon the softened shadows of the night,
And the wild glory of the throbbing stars;
Where'er we bent our Eden-tinted way:
My brain was a weird wilderness of Thought:
My heart, love's sea of passion tossed and torn,
Calmed by the presence of the loving souls
By whom I was surrounded. All the while
They deemed me passing tame, and wondered when
My dreamy castle would come toppling down.
I was but driving back the aching past,
And mirroring the future. And these leaves
Of meditation are but perfumes from
The censer of my feelings; honied drops
Wrung from the busy hives of heart and brain;
Mere etchings of the artist; grains of sand
From the calm shores of that unsounded deep
Of speculation, where all thought is lost
Amid the realms of Nature and of God.

I.

My soul goes out to meet her, and my heart
Flings wide the portals of its love, and yearns
To have her enter its serene retreat.
A poor stray lamb, not wand'ring from the fold,
But all unstudied in the worldling's art,
Turning life's mintage into seeming gold,
Wherewith to purchase love and love's returns;
Unknowing that love's waters, though so sweet,
Lead to some bitter Marah. So my soul
Goes out to meet her, and it clasps her home,
And seeks to bear her upward to the goal
At which the righteous enter. From the dome
Of starriest Night two blest Immortals come,
To bear us spheral-ward to God's own mercy-seat.

II.

'Tis summer still, yet now and then a leaf
Falls from some stately tree. True type of life!
How emblamatic of the pangs that grief
Wrings from our blighted hopes, that one by one
Drop from us in our wrestle with the strife
And natural passions of our stately youth.
And thus we fall beneath life's summer sun.
Each step conducts us through an opening door
Into new halls of being, hand in hand
With grave Experience, until we command
The open, wide-spread autumn fields, and store
The full ripe grain of Wisdom and of Truth.
As on life's tott'ring precipice we stand,
Our sins like withered leaves are blown about the land.

III.

Oh, holy sabbath morn! thrice blessed day
Of solemn rest, true peace, and earnest prayer.
How many hearts that never knelt to pray
Are glad to breathe thy soul-sustaining air.
I sit within the quiet woods, and hear
The village church-bell's soft inviting sound,
And to the confines of the loftiest sphere
Imagination wings its airy round;
A myriad spirits have assembled there,
Whose prayers on earth a sweet acceptance found.
I go to worship in Thy House, O God!
With her, thy young creation bright and fair;
Help us to do Thy will, and not despair,
Though both our hearts should bend beneath Thy
    chastening rod.

IV.

The birds are singing merrily, and here
A squirrel claims the lordship of the woods,
And scolds me for intruding. At my feet
The tireless ants all silently proclaim
The dignity of labour. In my ear
The bee hums drowsily; from sweet to sweet
Careering, like a lover weak in aim.
I hear faint music in the solitudes;
A dreamlike melody that whispers peace
Imbues the calmy forest, and sweet rills
Of pensive feeling murmur through my brain,
Like ripplings of pure water down the hills
That slumber in the moonlight. Cease, oh, cease!
Some day my weary heart will coin these into pain.

V.

Blest Spirit of Calm that dwellest in these woods!
Thou art a part of that serene repose
That ofttimes lingers in the solitudes
Of my lone heart, when the tumultuous throes
Of some vast Grief have borne me to the earth.
For I have fought with Sorrow face to face;
Have tasted of the cup that brings to some
A frantic madness and delirious mirth,
But prayed and trusted for the light to come,
To break the gloom and darkness of the place.
Through the dim aisles the sunlight penetrates,
And nature's self rejoices; heaven's light
Comes down into my heart, and in its might
My soul stands up and knocks at God's own temple-
    gates.

VI.

Through every sense a sweet balm permeates,
As music strikes new tones from every nerve.
The soul of Feeling enters at the gates
Of Intellect, and Fancy comes to serve
With fitting homage the propitious guest.
Nature, erewhile so lonely and oppressed,
Stands like a stately Presence, and looks down
As from a throne of power. I have grown
Full twenty summers backwards, and my youth
Is surging in upon me till my hopes
Are as fresh-tinted as the checkered leaves
That the sun shines through. All the future opes
Its endless corridors, where time unweaves
The threads of Error from the golden warp of Truth.

VII.

Our life is like a forest, where the sun
Glints down upon us through the throbbing leaves;
The full light rarely finds us.   One by one,
Deep rooted in our souls, there springeth up
Dark groves of human passion, rich in gloom,
At first no bigger than an acorn-cup.
Hope threads the tangled labyrinth, but grieves
Till all our sins have rotted in their tomb,
And made the rich loam of each yearning heart
To bring forth fruits and flowers to new life.
We feel the dew from heaven, and there start
From some deep fountain little rills whose strife
Is drowned in music.   Thus in light and shade
We live, and move, and die, through all this earthly
    glade.

VIII.

Above where I am sitting, o'er these stones,
The ocean waves once heaved their mighty forms;
And vengeful tempests and appalling storms
Wrung from the stricken sea portentous moans,
That rent stupendous icebergs, whose huge heights
Crashed down in fragments through the startled nights.
Change, change, eternal change in all but God!
Mysterious nature! thrice mysterious state
Of body, soul, and spirit! Man is awed,
But triumphs in his littleness. A mote,
He specks the eye of the age and turns to dust,
And is the sport of centuries. We note
More surely nature's ever-changing fate;
Her fossil records tell how she performs her trust.

IX.

Another day of rest, and I sit here
Among the trees, green mounds, and leaves as sere
As my own blasted hopes. There was a time
When Love and perfect Happiness did chime
Like two sweet sounds upon this blessed day;
But one has flown forever, far away
From this poor Earth's unsatisfied desires
To love eternal, and the sacred fires
With which the other lighted up my mind
Have faded out and left no trace behind,
But dust and bitter ashes. Like a bark
Becalmed, I anchor through the midnight dark,
Still hoping for another dawn of Love.
Bring back my olive branch of Happiness, O dove!

X.

Poor snail, that toilest at my weary feet,
Thou, too, must have thy burden! Life is sweet,
If we would make it so. How vast a load
To carry all its days along the road
Of its serene existence! Christian-like,
It toils with patience, seeking sweet repose
Within itself when wearied with the throes
Of its life-struggle. The low sounds that strike
Upon the ear in wafts of melody,
Are cruel mockeries, O snail, of thee.
The cricket's chirp, the grasshopper's shrill tone,
The locust's jarring cry, all mock thy lone
And dumb-like presence. May this heart of mine,
When tried, put on a resignation such as thine.

XI.

Oh, that I were the spirit of these wilds!
I'd make the zephyrs dance for my delight,
And lead a life as happy as a child's.
Echo should tremble with unfeigned affright,
And mock its own weird answers. I would kiss
Eliza's cheek, and touch her lips with dew
Stol'n from the scented rose. And Carrie's laugh
Should be a portion of the silver rills'
Sweet music, breathed mellifluously through
The hearts of generations. She should quaff
The nectar of inspired song, and thrills
Of sweet remembrances of her should strew
The woodland air, as sand-grains strew the shore;
And these two hearts should be my joy for evermore.

XII.

The moon shone down on fair Eliza's face,
And made it beautiful. No fitter place
Could she have chosen for her gracious smile;
For as she sat there in the languid light,
Methought I'd found a soul as free from guile
As ever came from God. Oh, favored Night!
Oh, mild, impassioned moon and starry spheres!
To gaze upon her through the silent years
Without rebuke. But I have looked within,
And found the truest beauty; have laid bare
A spiritual excellence as rare
As ever mortal being hoped to win.
  Heart, mind, and soul, I analysed them all,
And saw where heaven kept divinest carnival.

XIII.

I've almost grown a portion of this place;
I seem familiar with each mossy stone;
Even the mimble chipmunk passes on,
 And looks, but never scolds me. Birds have flown
And almost touched my hand; and I can trace
 The wild bees to their hives. I've never known
So sweet a pause from labour. But the tone
Of a past sorrow, like a mournful rill
Threading the heart of some melodious hill,
Or the complainings of the whippoorwill,
 Passes through every thought, and hope, and aim.
It has its uses; for it cools the flame
 Of ardent love that burns my being up—
Love, life's celestial pearl, diffused through all its cup.

XIV.

There is no sadness here. Oh, that my heart
Were calm and peaceful as these dreamy groves!
That all my hopes and passions, and deep loves,
Could sit in such an atmosphere of peace,
Where no unholy impulses would start
Responsive to the throes that never cease
To keep my spirit in such wild unrest.
'Tis only in the struggling human breast
That the true sorrow lives. Our fruitful joys
Have stony kernels hidden in their core.
Life in a myriad phases passeth here,
And death as various—an equal poise;
Yet all is but a solemn change—no more;
And not a sound save joy pervades the atmosphere.

XV.

Last night I heard the plaintive whippoorwill,
And straightway Sorrow shot his swiftest dart.
I know not why, but it has chilled my heart
Like some dread thing of evil.   All night long
My nerves were shaken, and my pulse stood still,
And waited for a terror yet to come
To strike harsh discords through my life's sweet song.
Sleep came—an incubus that filled the sum
Of wretchedness with dreams so wild and chill
The sweat oozed from me like great drops of gall;
An evil spirit kept my mind in thrall,
And rolled my body up like a poor scroll
On which is written curses that the soul
Shrinks back from when it sees some hellish carnival.

XVI.

My footsteps press where, centuries ago,
The Red Men fought and conquered; lost and won.
Whole tribes and races, gone like last year's snow,
Have found the Eternal Hunting-Grounds, and run
The fiery gauntlet of their active days,
Till few are left to tell the mournful tale:
And these inspire us with such wild amaze
They seem like spectres passing down a vale
Steeped in uncertain moonlight, on their way
Towards some bourn where darkness blinds the day,
And night is wrapped in mystery profound.
We cannot lift the mantle of the past:
We seem to wander over hallowed ground:
We scan the trail of Thought, but all is overcast.

XVII.

There was a time—and that is all we know!
No record lives of their ensanguined deeds:
The past seems palsied with some giant blow,
And grows the more obscure on what it feeds.
A rotted fragment of a human leaf;
A few stray skulls; a heap of human bones!
These are the records—the traditions brief—
'Twere easier far to read the speechless stones.
The fierce Ojibwas, with tornado force,
Striking white terror to the hearts of braves!
The mighty Hurons, rolling on their course,
Compact and steady as the ocean waves!
The stately Chippewas, a warrior host!
Who were they?—Whence?—And why? no human tongue can boast!

XVIII.

I do not wonder that the Druids built
Their sacred altars in the sacred groves.
Fit place to worship God.   The native guilt
Of our poor weak humanity behoves
That we should set aside no little part
Of the devotion of the yearning heart
To rest and peace, as typical of that
Sweet tranquil rest to which the good aspire.
Calm thoughts are as the purifying fire
That burns the useless dross from life's mixed gold,
And lights the torch of mind.   While grasping at
The shadow for the substance, youth grows old,
And groves of palm spring up in every heart—
Temples to God, wherein we pray and sit apart.

XIX.

How my heart yearns towards my friends at home!
Poor suffering souls, whose lives are like the trees,
Bent, crushed, and broken in the storm of life!
A whirlwind of existence seems to roam
Through some poor hearts continually. These
Have neither rest nor pause; one day is rife
With tempest, and another dashed with gloom;
And the few rays of light that might illume
Their thorny path are drenched with tearful rain.
Yet these pure souls live not their lives in vain;
For they become as spiritual guides
And lights to others; rising with the tides
Of their full being into higher spheres,
Brighter and brighter still through all the coming
    years.

XX

I sat within the temple of her heart,
And watched the living Soul as it passed through,
Arrayed in pearly vestments, white and pure.
The calm, immortal Presence made me start.
It searched through all the chambers of her mind
With one mild glance of love, and smiled to view
The fastnesses of feeling, strong—secure,
And safe from all surprise. It sits enshrined
And offers incense in her heart, as on
An altar sacred unto God. The dawn
Of an imperishable love passed through
The lattice of my senses, and I, too,
Did offer incense in that solemn place—
A woman's heart made pure and sanctified by Grace.

XXI.

Intense young soul, that takest hearts by storm,
And chills them into sorrow with a look!
Some minds are open as a well-read book;
But here the leaves are still uncut—unscanned,
The volume clasped and sealed, and all the warm
And passionate exuberance of love
Held in submission to these threadbare flaws,
And creeds of weaknesses, poor human laws.
Stand up erect—nay kneel—for from above
God's light is streaming on thee. Fashion's daws
May fawn and flatter like a cringing pack
Of servile hounds beneath the keeper's hand,
But these are not thy peers; they drive thee back:
Urge on the car of Thought, and take a higher stand!

XXII.

Dark, dismal day—the first of many such!
The wind is sighing through the plaintive trees,
In fitful gusts of a half-frenzied woe;
Affrighted clouds the hand might almost touch,
Their black wings bend so mournfully and low,
Sweep through the skies like night-winds o'er the seas.
There is no chirp of bird through all the grove,
Save that of the young fledgeling rudely flung
From its warm nest; and like the clouds above
My soul is dark, and restless as the breeze
That leaps and dances over Couchiching.
Soon will the last duett be sweetly sung;
But through the years to come our hearts will ring
With memories, as dear as time and love can bring.

AU REVOIR.

That morn our hearts were like artesian wells,
Both deep and calm, and brimming with pure love.
And in each one, like to an April day,
Truth smiled and wept, while Courage wound his
    horn,
Dispatching echoes that are whispering still
Through all the vacant chambers of our souls;
While Sorrow sat with drooped and aimless wing,
Within the solitary fane of thought.
We wished some warlike Joshua were there
To make the sun stand still, or to put back
The dial to the brighter side of time.
A cloud hung over Couchiching; a cloud
Eclipsed the merry sunshine of our hearts.
We needed no philosopher to teach
That laughter is not always born of joy.
"All's for the best," the fair Eliza said;
And we derived new courage from her lips,
That spake the maxim of her trusting heart.
We even smiled, at some portentous sign
That signified—well, if it turn out true,
Then, I'll believe it. Heaven works in signs.
More parting words, more lingering farewells,
Pressure of hands, and thrilling touch of lips,
A waving of white handkerchiefs, and Love
Grew prayerful, and knelt down, and wept
His scattered rosary of human hearts.

Soon looking back, we saw where Ramah lay;
Cold, wan, and cheerless as the race it holds.
And as we neared the Lake the sun came forth,
As tardily as if the sluggard day
Had slept more soundly for the piping storm,
That, veering round, had flung its challenge out
In sullen menace to the western sky,
Now black with clouds. A flash, a muffled roll
Of elemental passion, broke the spell,
And down on Simcoe fell the sudden rain,
Veiling the gloomy landscape from our sight.
Throughout the changeful day, alternate cloud
And sunshine left their traces on our hearts,
Until the evening reared its dreamy piles
Of cloud-built châteaux steeped in gorgeous tints,
That from celestial censers are outpoured
When the grand miracle of sunset draws
Our souls, all yearning with a joy divine,
To share the fleeting glory, ere it goes
To glean new splendors for the ruby morn.
'Tis ever thus with true impassioned love :
Love's sun, like that of day, may set, and set,
It hath as bright a rising in the morn.
True love has no gray hairs; his golden locks
Can never whiten with the snows of time.
Sorrow lies drear on many a youthful heart,
Like snow upon the evergreens; but love
Can gather sweetest honey by the way,
E'en from the carcass of some prostrate grief.
We have been spoiled with blessings. Though the
    world

Holds nothing dearer than the hope that's fled,
God ever opens up new founts of bliss—
Spiritual Bethsaidas where the soul
Can wash the earth-stains from its fevered loins.
We carve our sorrows on the face of joy,
Reversing the true image; we are weak
Where strength is needed most, and most is given.

Thus musing, as they chatted in the train,
The whistle broke my reverie, as one
Might be awakened from a truthful dream.
The city gas-lights flashed into our eyes;
And we, half-shrinking from the glare and din,
Thought but of two more partings on the morn,
When Love should be enfettered, hand and foot,
For the long æon of a human year.

THE END.

Sangster's Canadian Poems.

THE "ST. LAWRENCE AND THE SAGUENAY."

OPINIONS OF THE PRESS.

MRS. SUSANNA MOODIE.

BELLEVILLE, July 28th, 1856.

SIR,—Accept my sincere thanks for the volume of beautiful Poems with which you have favored me. If the world receives them with as much pleasure as they have been read by me, your name will rank high among the gifted Sons of Song. If a native of Canada, she may well be proud of her Bard, who has sung in such lofty strains the natural beauties of his native land. Wishing you all the fame you so richly deserve, I subscribe myself, your sincere admirer.

To Mr. Charles Sangster. SUSANNA MOODIE.

REV. J. MACGEORGE.

Amongst the very few Bards which Canada has yet produced, Mr. Sangster occupies the very first rank, and he will even occupy a prominent position in the literary annals of our Province.

LONDON NATIONAL MAGAZINE.

Western Canada is enabled to boast, and does boast somewhat .oudly, of Charles Sangster, who has celebrated in Spenserian Stanzas the beauties and the sublimities of the St. Lawrence and the Saguenay. Well may the Canadians be proud of such contributions to their infant literature; well may they be forward to recognize his lively imagination, his bold masterly style, and the fulness of his imagery. * * * There is much of the spirit of Wordsworth in this writer, only the tone is reli-

OPINIONS OF THE PRESS.

gious instead of being philosophical. * * * * In some sort, and according to his degree, he may be regarded as the Wordsworth of Canada.

His whole soul seems steeped in love and poesy, and finds utterance in expression generally eloquent, bold and musical. He is thoroughly sentimental, teeming with ideas of the sublime and beautiful, and bears evident marks of enthusiastic poetical conception. Mr. Sangster is a poet of no mean order, and his volume is far the most respectable contribution of Poetry that has yet been made to the infant literature of Canada.—*Huron Signal.*

We hail the publication of these Poems, to which we readily invite attention. They are chiefly upon topics incidental to British America; betray considerable talent, and no slight poetic skill and taste, while to their good feeling and admirable tone we give our warmest testimony.—*Canadian (London) News.*

Mr. Sangster, in his description of the St. Lawrence and the Saguenay has vividly pourtrayed the Scenery through which they pass; his book is destined to create a great sensation, and should be in the hands of every tourist who visits, or may have visited, the beautiful scenery he so charmingly depicts.—*Toronto Colonist.*

These Poems are written in a bold masterly style, full of imagery, and displaying ability of no ordinary kind. Mr. Sangster is a Poet, in the true sense of the term, and leads his readers in burning language of inspiration from Nature up to Nature's God.—*Ottawa Times.*

This is a book that, as a Canadian, we are proud of. The subject upon which it treats is one well worthy the high talents of the Author. We are glad the volume has been published; it is a great addition to the literary products of the Province. To tourists it is indispensable. As they pass along on their tour of pleasure over these two rivers, it would be a treat to read his chaste and classic muse.—*Montreal Pilot.*

The material of "Pleasant Memories" is original and excellent. Mr. Sangster is something more than one of the mob of gentlemen who write with ease. We should be glad to hear from him again.—*New York Albion.*

OPINIONS OF THE PRESS.

The Poem entitled "The St. Lawrence and the Saguenay" is a master piece; and in fact the whole book breathes the spirit of a master mind. It is in every way creditable to Mr. Sangster, and shows unmistakably that he is a Poet of decided ability, of whom Canada, his native place, ought to be proud.—*Ottawa Monarchist.*

The description of the Thousand Isles is very fine, the Lyric to the Isles very musical and beautiful; there are many fine passages in the description of the Saguenay.—*Montreal Gazette.*

A writer who will yet make his mark in the literary world.—*Buffalo Republic.*

Purity pervades every line, and pure thoughts expressed in chaste and glowing words blend in the harmony of the measure. His Poetry breathes of that faith which penetrates the unseen.—*Utica Herald.*

The work is essentially Canadian; but its strongest claim is its own intrinsic merits. The spirit, style and sentiment are on the whole eminently Poetical.—*Newburg Index.*

What we most admire in Mr. Sangster is his warm and ardent love for the beautiful and the good, and his never-failing charity; that he possesses poetical talent in a high degree any one capable of judging with allow. His reverence of the God-like, his love of the beautiful, his adoration of the true, commend his first breathings in the world of authorship to every right-thinker.—*Kingston Commercial Advertiser.*

We hail this contribution to the scanty store of Canadian Literature, and we congratulate Kingston in having in its midst one possessed of poetical talent in so high a degree.—*Kingston News.*

These Poems as a whole are every way worthy the Genius of a true-born poet like Mr. Sangster, our Native Bard; the public may well afford to patronize the best the country has produced.—*Hamilton Spectator.*

Mr. Sangster is a Canadian Poet of no inconsiderable talent. The portions of the larger Poem, "The St. Lawrence and the Saguenay," which we have perused, give us a very favorable

OPINIONS OF THE PRESS.

opinion of the book. Mr. Sangster possesses a lively imagination, united to good descriptive powers, and is likely to make himself widely known as a genuine friend of the Muses.—*Toronto Globe.*

In "The St. Lawrence and the Saguenay," there breathes a spirit of description which might do credit to an author of greater fame.—*Chatham Advertiser.*

This volume of Poems is a credit to Canadian Literature.—*British Whig.*

A Canadian Poet, whose poems are far above mediocrity—whose songs are of Canada—her mountains, maidens, manners, morals, lakes, rivers, valleys, seasons, woods, forests, and aborigines, her faith and hope, merits encouragement. Will he get it?—*McKenzie's Message.*

Index of Titles

HESPERUS AND OTHER POEMS AND LYRICS

A Royal Welcome	59
A Thought for Spring	128
An Evening Thought	127
Au Revoir	184
Autumn	65
Brock	84
Colin	68
Crowned	29
Death of Wolfe	83
Dedicatory Poem	9
England's Hope and England's Heir	114
Eva	76
Flowers	122
Gertrude	121
Glimpses	100
Good Night	134
Grandpere	113
Her Star	104
Hesperus	11
Hopeless	135
Ingratitude	125
Into the Silent Land	139
Lost and Found	96
Love and Truth	109
Malcolm	61

Margery	70
Mariline	30
My Prayer	102
Night and Morning	119
Proem	159
Rose	116
Song — Clara and I	130
Song for Canada	86
Song — I'd be a Fairy King	89
Song — Love While You May	91
Sonnet I	162
Sonnet II	163
Sonnet III	164
Sonnet IV	165
Sonnet V	166
Sonnet VI	167
Sonnet VII	168
Sonnet VIII	169
Sonnet IX	170
Sonnet X	171
Sonnet XI	172
Sonnet XII	173
Sonnet XIII	174
Sonnet XIV	175
Sonnet XV	176
Sonnet XVI	177
Sonnet XVII	178
Sonnet XVIII	179
Sonnet XIX	189
Sonnet XX	181

Sonnet XXI I	182
Sonnet XXII	183
The April Snow-storm — 1858	132
The Comet — October, 1858	63
The Dreamer	118
The Falls of the Chaudière, Ottawa	53
The Happy Harvesters	40
The Mystery	107
The Plains of Abraham	80
The Poet's Recompense	77
The Rapid	94
The Snows	92
The Swallows	129
The Unattainable	123
The Wine of Song	78
The Wren	111
True Love	126
Within Thine Eyes	120
Yearnings	124
Young Again	99

Select Bibliography

In addition to the two volumes reprinted here Sangster published a third book and a number of poems in anthologies and literary periodicals:

Our Norland   Toronto, Copp Clark [1886? 1893?] 14 p.

'Taapookaa' and 'A Northern Rune' appear in E.H. Dewart's *Selections from Canadian Poets* (Montreal, John Lovell 1864). 'Taapookaa' also appears in *Songs of the Great Dominion*, edited by W.D. Lighthall (London, Walter Scott 1899).

'The Orphan Girl' and 'Bright Eyes,' in *The Literary Garland*, New Series, VIII, December 1850

'The Recluse,' in *The Literary Garland*, New Series, IX, January 1851

Baker, Ray Palmer   *A History of English-Canadian Literature to Confederation.* Cambridge, Harvard University Press 1920. pp. 159-65

Bourinot, Arthur Stanley   *Five Canadian Poets.* Montreal, Quality Press 1954. pp. 8-14

Brown, E.K.   *On Canadian Poetry.* Toronto, Ryerson 1943. pp. 29-33

Dewart, E.H.   'Charles Sangster,' in *The Canadian Magazine*, VII, May 1896. pp. 29-34

Hamilton, W.D.   *Charles Sangster.* New York, Twayne 1971. 163 p.

Klinck, Carl F.   *Literary History of Canada*, eds. Klinck et al. Toronto, University of Toronto Press 1965. pp. 147-8

Morgan, Henry J. *Sketches of Celebrated Canadians.* Quebec,
   Hunter Rose 1862. pp. 684-93
— *Bibliotheca Canadensis.* Ottawa, Desbarats 1867. pp. 335-7
Pacey, Desmond   *Ten Canadian Poets.* Toronto, Ryerson 1958.
   pp. 1-33

CPSIA information can be obtained
at www.ICGtesting.com
Printed in the USA
BVHW081515010821
613046BV00002B/12

9 780802 061690